WILLIAM R. MCDONALD AND ABIGAIL FOWLER
of Herkimer County, New York and Their Descendants

A supplemental addition to
A Revolutionary American Family:
The McDonalds of Somerset County, New Jersey,
affirming the relationship of William R. McDonald
to Maj. Richard McDonald of
Pluckemin and Bedminster, New Jersey

by Laurence Overmire

Indelible Mark Publishing
West Linn, OR

Enumerating the families of
Timothy Bliss and Margaret McDonald,
William McDonald and Joanna Axford &
Philo Fowler McDonald and Thirza Spencer

Featuring McDonald families of Macomb, Washtenaw and
Wayne Counties in Michigan; Wright County, Minnesota;
Travis County, Texas; Maricopa County, Arizona;
and San Diego County, California

And including interrelated families: Adair, Ala, Alter, Apes,
Barrett, Betts, Bliss, Brown, Cavanagh, Cavanaugh, Coggill,
Collins, Connet, Cooke, Correll, Deitering, Debler, Dickinson,
Diehl, Dowd, DuPont, Furtick, Garrett, Gerren, Gibson, Harger,
Harris, Hill, Hower, Jenney, Kutsche, Lancashire, Mackstaller,
McCarty, McCrory, McIntyre, Merry, Mikesell, Morgan, Moseley,
Oley, Parr, Schalkofski, Schroeder, Smith, Stuckey,
Summerrow, Vincent, Wallace, Wilcox, Wilder
and many more.

Indelible Mark Publishing 2021

Library of Congress Control Number: 2020951526

ISBN 978-1-7349408-0-0

Front cover photo: American militia at reenactment of the Battle of Bound Brook, Abraham Staats House in South Bound Brook, NJ *(photo by Jody Gibian-Miles, 2014)*

Back cover photo: Author Laurence Overmire kneels by the grave of Maj. Richard McDonald at the Old Somerville Cemetery in Somerville, NJ *(photo by Nancy McDonald, 2014)*

Book design and editing by Nancy McDonald

INDELIBLE MARK PUBLISHING, LLC
6498 Lowry Drive, # 4
West Linn, OR 97068
www.indeliblemarkpublishing.com

DEDICATION

For Michael John McDonald (1939-2020) whose keen desire
to know his McDonald forbears inspired us to learn more and more
about the McDonalds of Somerset County, New Jersey and their descendants.
His DNA helped prove the relationship of the families in this book.

CONTENTS

INTRODUCTION

One of the best things about publishing a genealogy book is that it encourages people in the extended family to start talking with one another about family history. Additional important details about the family origins begin to emerge. Soon other long lost branches of the tree discover that they, too, might be related and begin to share previously undisclosed information that has been handed down from their forebears.

Such is the case here. After *A Revolutionary American Family: The McDonalds of Somerset County, New Jersey* was released on May 29, 2015, on the 281st birthday of Revolutionary War veteran, Maj. Richard McDonald, a descendant of another as yet unconfirmed branch of the McDonald tree contacted this author with some striking new evidence of early McDonald family history. This descendant and his brother proceeded to send a mysterious genealogical blueprint that was handed down in their branch of the tree with some startling revelations about the McDonalds of Somerset County.

The authenticity of that blueprint has now been established to this author's satisfaction, the details of which will be presented here as we introduce the family of William R. McDonald and his wife, Abigail Fowler. William R. was the eldest son of Maj. Richard McDonald of Pluckemin, New Jersey, as well as the elder brother of the famous lawyer, Col. George McDonald, Esq.

Previously, there was very little evidence of what happened to William, son of Maj. Richard. The only approximate birth date we had for him was about 1765, according to R. G. Clarke's *Early New Netherlands Settlers*. We knew he was alive in 1820 as he was named as an executor in Maj. Richard's will. But curiously, William did not sign the will as did the other executors, Peter I. Stryker and Matthew Williamson.

A. V. D. Honeyman stated that William McDonald was alive in 1840 (*Somerset County Historical Quarterly*, Vol. 5, 72). Our research revealed that Honeyman was probably referring to a list dated Feb. 4, 1840, that included "William McDonald" as an elder at the Dutch Reformed Church in North Branch, Raritan, New Jersey. In light of the new revelations of the blueprint, it now appears that that "William McDonald" must have been William, son of the lawyer George McDonald, not William, son of Maj. Richard.

The blueprint is the ONLY document that has yet been found that states that William R. McDonald of Herkimer County, New York, was the son of Maj. Richard McDonald of Pluckemin. It represents a family oral tradition that offers some tantalizing clues about the origins of the McDonalds of Somerset County, and deepens our understanding of the mystery of the McDonalds and their Scottish ancestors.

In the pages that follow, we will carefully examine the blueprint for what it reveals about the McDonald heritage and we will trace the descendants of William R. and Abigail (Fowler) McDonald. They were pioneers who traveled

Somerset County, New Jersey
by David Benbennick

all across this country and established themselves in the north, south, east and west. There are heroic tales here and there are tragic tales – stories of triumph and defeat. This is, after all, a history of real people and real life.

All of us have a lot to learn about who they were and who we are because of them.

This book, however, represents only one small branch of the extensive McDonald family tree that took root in Somerset County, New Jersey. The rest of the history, the fascinating origins of this family and the progenitors who brought it into being, are discussed in their entirety in *A Revolutionary American Family: The McDonalds of Somerset County, New Jersey*. This book is a supplemental addition to that much larger work.

Now take a breath, sit back and relax. You are about to meet William R. and Abigail (Fowler) McDonald of Herkimer County, New York and their descendants.

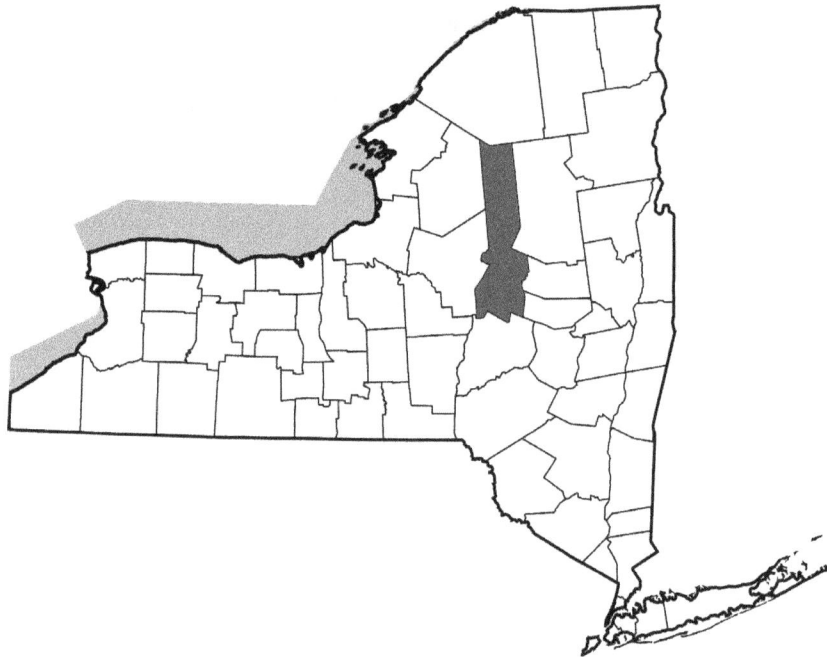

Herkimer County, New York
by David Benbennick

Chapter 1

WILLIAM R. AND ABIGAIL (FOWLER) MCDONALD
of Herkimer County, NY

Great Grandparents: William and Florance MacDonel
Grandparents: Col. William McDonald and Unknown First Wife
Parents: Maj. Richard McDonald and Margrietje Schamp
Siblings: Richard, Phebe, George, Sarah

WILLIAM R. MCDONALD (1761-1853)
+ Abigail Fowler (1767-1849)

1. Richard (I) McDonald (1788, died in infancy)
2. Rachel McDonald (1790-1804)
3. Margaret McDonald (1792-1838, m. Timothy Bliss)
4. William M. McDonald (1794-1856, m. Joanna Axford)
5. Abigail McDonald (1796-1854)
6. Richard (II) McDonald (1798-aft. 1840, m. Mathilda Brannard)
7. Philo Fowler McDonald (1800-1854, m. Thirza Spencer)
8. George McDonald (1802, died in infancy)
9. George Scham McDonald (1803-1815)
10. Benjamin McDonald (1806-aft. 1831, m. Margaret H. Apes)
11. Aaron McDonald (1808-1834, m. Rebecca Apes)

William R. McDonald was the eldest son of Maj. Richard McDonald of Pluckemin and Bedminster, New Jersey. We know of his existence because he was named as an executor of the will of Maj. Richard in 1820, but there are no other primary source records that mention him: no birth or baptism records, no census records, nothing.

Curiously, William did not sign the will of his father as his co-executors did, Peter I. Stryker and Matthew Williamson. Was he not available at the time, perhaps too far away?

The only evidence we have that tells us what happened to William is a mysterious genealogical blueprint, heretofore of unknown origins. After a thorough examination of the family history, we have now determined that the blueprint must have been compiled about 1912-1913 by William R. McDonald's grandson, John McDonald (1834-1913), working in cooperation with his son, Burt McDonald (1860-aft. 1930), both of whom were architects. Burt apparently then handed down the blueprint to his son, Kenneth Walthersdorf McDonald

(1893-1957), who in turn, handed it down to his daughter, Diane McDonald Shaul, and thence to Kenneth's grandchildren. Two of those grandchildren, Thomas Corey McDonald and Raymond Bart McDonald, contacted this author and provided a digital copy of the blueprint for examination.

THE MYSTERIOUS BLUEPRINT

The blueprint was not signed or dated. It begins thusly:

> The Genealogical Table of the McDonald family is made up from the records preserved in the family bibles of Wm R Mc Donald and John McDonald according to family tradition related to John McDonald by Wm R McDonald.[1]

The John McDonald in question above was the grandson of William R. McDonald. He is the man responsible, we now believe, for creating the blueprint. John's descendants, Thomas Corey McDonald and Raymond Bart McDonald, report, however, that the present whereabouts of these two bibles of William R. and John McDonald are unknown; they are probably no longer in existence. This is indeed unfortunate. We cannot be absolutely certain where the specific details contained in the blueprint are coming from, but, as it turns out, we have a very good idea.

Before giving any credence to the document, however, it was necessary to establish its authenticity.

The blueprint has a genealogical chart that shows the family tree of many of the descendants of William R. and Abigail (Fowler) McDonald. The dates, we presume, were compiled from the two bibles mentioned in the blueprint's opening statement. These dates are consistent with official records with very few errors, so the data is, for the most part, accurate.

But how do we know who made the blueprint? The writing is uniform and consistent on all parts of the document. Clearly, one person created it and probably in a short period of time. Otherwise, we would see variations in the handwriting. The last generation shown on the document is that of Kenneth Walthersdorf McDonald, John McDonald's grandson, who was born June 5, 1893. His marriage about 1926 and the name of his spouse, Georgia Isabel Dellinger, are NOT shown. The latest date shown on the blueprint is Mar. 15, 1912, the death date of John McDonald's brother, William (b. 1830).

The blueprint must have been completed sometime after Mar. 15, 1912. We note further that the death date for John McDonald, Sept. 3, 1913, was not recorded on the document. This suggests that the blueprint was completed while John was still alive.

But who was John McDonald? Did he, in fact, create the blueprint?

JOHN MCDONALD OF AUSTIN, TEXAS

John McDonald, born Oct. 18, 1834, was the grandson of William R. McDonald and the great grandson of Maj. Richard McDonald, at least according to the blueprint. John was an architect, contractor, builder and machinist who was a prominent figure in the local history of Austin, Texas. In fact, he was the mayor of the city of Austin from 1890-1895. He died, as we said before, on Sept. 3, 1913, a little over a year after the last date on the blueprint.

Mayor John's eldest son, Burton "Burt" McDonald (b. 1860), was also an architect and could have been involved with the production of the blueprint, perhaps in collaboration with his father. In fact, the granddaughter of Burt, Diane McDonald Shaul, reported that her mother, Georgia Isabel McDonald, told her that Burt made the blueprint.[2] But if Burt is the one who made it, why didn't he include the death date of his father, John, in 1913? Did he complete it before then? That appears to be the case. Both John and Burt were living in Phoenix, Arizona, in 1912, when John's brother, William, died.

It seems most likely, then, that Mayor John McDonald himself was responsible for seeing that the blueprint was completed. With his brother's death, John probably sensed his own end was near. He knew it was time to record the family history for posterity's sake. It was probably Burt who actually created the blueprint in his architect's office at his father's instigation. In fact, the handwriting on the blueprint is probably Burt's, but it seems pretty clear that Mayor John is the source of the information, perhaps dictating to Burt as they went, and consulting the family bibles at their disposal as stated in the blueprint.

The entire project must have been completed before John's death in 1913. Otherwise, Burt would have included his father's death date on the document. Soon after it was finished, Burt probably sent the blueprint to his ex-wife, Edna Walthersdorf McDonald, with instructions to give it to their only child, Kenneth Walthersdorf McDonald. Kenneth, in turn, eventually passed it down to his daughter, Diane McDonald Shaul.

Mayor John McDonald, we can also affirm, was a man worthy of respect, trusted by his fellow citizens. There is no reason to suspect that the information he presented in the blueprint was anything other than what he believed to be true. Author Lewis E. Daniell said of him in his *Types of Successful Men of Texas,* "few men have so strong a hold upon the respect, confidence and esteem of the community where their lot is cast as John McDonald has upon the good citizens of his adopted city Austin."

John McDonald was an accomplished man held in high regard, but the blueprint he left behind may be his most enduring legacy for it clearly shows that William R. McDonald was the son of Maj. Richard McDonald of Pluckemin.

But remember, it is the ONLY document that tells us that William R. McDonald was Maj. Richard's son. The family bibles have long since disappeared and there are no historical records that indicate the relationship of William R. to Maj. Richard.[3] William has not been found in any Bedminster or Somerset County records.

VERIFYING THE CLAIM

Now that we have established the authenticity of the blueprint, its creators John and Burt McDonald, and the approximate date of its creation, somehow we need to verify that William R. McDonald is indeed the son of Maj. Richard and really the only thing we have to work with is the blueprint itself.

The blueprint shows William R., son of Maj. Richard, was born Jan. 13, 1761 (probably in Bedminster, Somerset County, New Jersey). This is the only document that has a precise birth date for William. He must therefore be the eldest child of Maj. Richard and his first wife, Margrietje Schamp, whom Richard must have married about 1760.[4]

Interestingly, the blueprint does not show a wife for Maj. Richard, the mother of William R. McDonald. Her identity, then, was unknown to Mayor John McDonald and his descendants. Perhaps her name was not included in the William R. McDonald family bible and certainly not in the John McDonald family bible. This is a key point because, as it turns out, the surname Schamp helps to confirm the blueprint's legitimacy.

What the blueprint does show and what turns out to be of the utmost significance is that William R. McDonald had a son, George Scham McDonald, born Oct. 19, 1803, and died July 5, 1815. (The poor child only lived 11 years.) There is no other known document that shows that the boy ever lived at all. Only the family of William R. McDonald maintained his memory by recording his birth and death, presumably in their family bible. The name George Scham is revealing. William R. McDonald's maternal grandfather was Joost, aka George, Schamp. The name may have been pronounced "Scham" with a silent "p," hence the misspelling.

This strongly establishes that the information John McDonald entered into his blueprint was indeed accurate family history as it was handed down to him. John would have had no clue that George Scham McDonald was named after William R. McDonald's maternal grandfather, because he had no idea who William R. McDonald's mother was: Margrietje Schamp.

One more bit of evidence from the blueprint bears testament to its authenticity: the mention of the name Pluckemin, misspelled in the document as "Pluckinim."

> Richard McDonald's family during war near Pluckinim [sic] 20 miles from New York.[5]

Note that there is no indication here that John McDonald knew that Pluckemin was located in New Jersey. He and Burt were living in Phoenix, Arizona. They probably had no idea where Pluckemin was or how it was properly spelled. We now know Pluckemin, a village located within the larger Bedminster Township in New Jersey, was about 40 miles from New York City and about 28 miles from Perth Amboy across the river from the southwestern end of Staten Island, New York.

Though the mileage and the spelling may not have been entirely accurate, John knew that Maj. Richard McDonald lived near Pluckemin, key information that no doubt came from William R. McDonald, Richard's son, who was probably born there.

A third key piece of information in this branch of the tree further establishes that William R. McDonald was indeed the son of Maj. Richard. William R. McDonald's grandson, through his eldest surviving son, William M. McDonald (1794-1856),[6] was named Theodore Frelinghuysen McDonald. The Frelinghuysens, of course, were intimately connected to Maj. Richard McDonald, who served directly under Col. Frederick Frelinghuysen in the Somerset militia in the Revolutionary War. Col. Frederick, as a lawyer, was a mentor to Maj. Richard's son, Col. George McDonald, and was the father of Theodore Frelinghuysen (1787-1862), the namesake of William M. McDonald's son. These Frelinghuysens and McDonalds probably maintained their strong family connections for generations. Perhaps William M. knew Theodore (who was seven years older than he was) personally.

Theodore Frelinghuysen became Attorney General for the state of New Jersey in 1817, and in 1829, a U.S. Senator.

INVESTIGATING THE FAMILY TRADITION

Now that we've established that it was almost certainly Mayor John McDonald of Austin, Texas, who was responsible for creating the blueprint, we need to assess the accuracy of the family tradition that he and his son, Burt, set down.

First of all, we need to consider that Mayor John would have been 77 years old in 1912 when the blueprint was probably made. His own death was not far away in September of 1913. What was the state of his health at the time? And, more importantly, how sharp was his memory?

Physically, John's hand was probably not as steady as it once was, a good reason to think that it was his son, Burt, who actually wrote the blueprint, probably on John's instruction.

We all know how difficult it can be to remember details of events and stories over the passage of time. Most of us have trouble remembering what we had for lunch yesterday! It would not be at all surprising if Mayor John McDonald couldn't recall the exact details of the family tradition that he probably heard more than 60 years before. He may well have gotten a few things mixed up. Not only that, but John's grandfather, William R. McDonald, may have misremembered some details himself that were told to him by his father, Maj. Richard, when William R. was but a young man.

As we saw in *A Revolutionary American Family* (Book 2, Chap. 2),[7] there are several different traditions that have been handed down in the various branches of the McDonald family tree, all of which differ from one another and conflict in their assertions as to the family's origins. This tradition handed down by John McDonald represents yet one more version that needs to be examined.

As every genealogist knows (or as any child who has played "the telephone game" can tell you) most oral traditions usually become distorted in some way and embellished over time as stories are transmitted from one person to another. Sometimes fanciful details might be added and facts might be misinterpreted or misremembered, but usually every family tradition also contains kernels of truth. The difficulty is in sorting out fact from fiction.

This is not to say, however, that Mayor John McDonald deliberately changed or falsified the details of his family history to make his ancestors seem greater than they were. What he reported about his family must have been what he believed to be the truth to the best of his knowledge and recollection just before he died. Our task is to see what the historical record reveals. Is there any evidence to back up the claims made in the blueprint?

Let's take a look at the entire opening passage at the top of the blueprint and then break it down bit by bit.

> The Genealogical Table of the McDonald family is made up from the records preserved in the family bibles of Wm R Mc Donald and John McDonald according to family tradition related to John McDonald by Wm R McDonald. Richard McDonald and his brother who was chief of

one of the McDonald Clans left Scotland and joined the English army on account of a religious dispute among the members of the clan. They came to America with Gen Wolfe's army and took part in the capture of Quebec on Sept 13, 1759. Richard McDonald remained in America and later joined the army of the Revolution serving on Washington's Staff, also as his secretary, with rank of Major. Wm R McDonald served a short time in Revolutionary army but was given his discharge by Gen Washington because, being the eldest child in a large family Gen Washington thought that he ought to be at home to take care of the younger children while his father was away in the army.

Richard McDonald's family during war near Pluckinim [sic] 20 miles from New York. Wm R. settled in Herkimer Co, NY. and his son Philo Fowler was a pioneer in the dairy business in that county. Harriet McDonald, William McDonald and John McDonald were born in Herkimer Co N.Y. During 1812 Wm R McDonald lived in Amsterdam N.Y. Richard McDonald had a large family but the records are not available to place them in the list. Other children of Wm R McDonald had large families besides Philo Fowler McDonald especially Margaret McDonald who married Timothy Bliss and Wm McDonald but at present time a clear and complete record is not in the posession [sic] of this branch of the family. The place near which Richard McDonald lived during the Revolution may not be correctly spelled and he may have enlisted either from New York or from New Jersey.[8]

On first blush, some of the details presented here ring a bell from what we know of the research compiled in *A Revolutionary American Family,* but there are also some extraordinary claims here. Was Richard's brother a McDonald clan chief? Did Richard serve as secretary to Gen. George Washington? Was William R. McDonald a Revolutionary War veteran who was discharged by Washington himself?

Let's go through the two paragraphs point by point and see what we can make of it.

Richard McDonald and his brother who was chief of one of the McDonald clans left Scotland and joined the English army on account of a religious dispute among the members of the clan.[9]

First of all, the blueprint doesn't identify who Richard's brother is. Richard's known brothers were the infamous Bill McDonald, who was cashiered from the army, and his half-brother Samuel, the illegitimate son of Col. William McDonald and Ruth Leferty, who was tried and hanged for murder. Some have suggested that Col. William McDonald was Richard's brother. While it is true that there is no birth record for Col. William that tells us exactly when he was born, there is considerable evidence that he was indeed the father of Maj. Richard McDonald as affirmed by A. V. D. Honeyman, the editor of the *Somerset County Historical Quarterly.*[10] Honeyman was the first person to do extensive research on the McDonalds. He made it very clear that Maj. Richard McDonald was Col. William McDonald's son. There was no doubt about it.

Secondly, there is no evidence that any of our known McDonalds were clan chiefs. In fact, William MacDonel, the father of Col. William McDonald, was a yeoman, not a nobleman. Futhermore, the DNA of descendant Michael John McDonald, as explained in *A Revolutionary American Family,* shows no descent from Somerled, the ancient forebear of Clan Donald, whereas a clan chief would very likely be among Somerled's descendants.

The claim, then, that Richard McDonald's brother was a clan chief seems dubious at best. But what if some of the details were scrambled in the retelling of the story as handed down to John McDonald?

We recall from *A Revolutionary American Family* that there were indeed two brothers who were involved in a religious dispute and one of them was a clan chief. But those two brothers were Lord Neil Campbell and his brother, the chief of Clan Campbell, Archibald Campbell, 9th Earl of Argyll. The Presbyterian Covenanters, led by the Campbell Earls of Argyll, were being persecuted in Scotland in the 1680's during the "Killing Time." The 9th Earl, we recall, raised an army in 1685 as part of the Monmouth Rebellion to overthrow the Catholic James II. The rebellion came to a head near Bridgewater in Somerset in the southwest of England at the Battle of Sedgemoor on July 6, 1685. The rebels were defeated. The leaders of the rebellion, the Duke of Monmouth and Archibald Campbell, the 9th Earl of Argyll, were seized and executed. Other participants in the uprising were hanged, drawn and quartered in nearby Bedminster in Bristol. Isn't it curious that the place names Somerset, Bridgewater, Monmouth and Bedminster are all places in New Jersey associated with our McDonalds?

Upon the death of the 9th Earl, the chieftainship of the clan would have passed to his younger brother, Lord Neil Campbell. Fearing for his life, Lord Neil quickly bought some land in New Jersey and fled Scotland with a shipload of emigrants to found a settlement on the North Branch of the Raritan River, where the father of Col. William McDonald, William MacDonel, later apparently established his farm. (See *A Revolutionary American Family*, Book II.)

Now let's look at the next sentence:

> They came to America with Gen Wolfe's army and took part in the capture of Quebec on Sept 13, 1759.[11]

Clearly, the evidence shows our McDonalds were in America well before 1759. William MacDonel, the father of Col. William McDonald, died in Somerset County in 1746. As early as 1744, records show that Col. William McDonald had a mill in Pluckemin. In fact, the obituary of Mayor Richard McDonald (1803-1894), the son of Col. George, the lawyer, tells us definitively that the McDonald family came to America in 1685.[12]

As for taking part in the Battle of Quebec, we don't know. We do know that Col. William McDonald was a captain in the 1st New Jersey Regiment, aka The Jersey Blues, in 1759, but no records have been discovered that place him at Quebec. Maj. Richard was a captain as early as 1768, but we don't know with what military unit he served. We suspect he was also part of the 1st New Jersey Regiment prior to the Revolution.

In any case, the assertion that our McDonalds were involved somehow with the Battle of Quebec is certainly intriguing and might be true. Col. William was deeply involved in the French and Indian War and might well have had some connection to Quebec.

Moving on to the next sentence:

> Richard McDonald remained in America and later joined the army of the Revolution serving on Washington's Staff, also as his secretary, with rank of Major.[13]

Richard did indeed serve in the Revolution. He was promoted to major of the First Somerset Militia under the command of Col. Frederick Frelinghuysen on Feb. 28, 1777. Note however that Richard served in the New Jersey militia, not in Washington's Continental Army. There is no evidence whatsoever that Maj. Richard served on Washington's staff as his secretary.[14]

What the blueprint story does indicate, however, is that Maj. Richard knew George Washington personally. That certainly appears to be true. Maj. Richard would have helped accommodate Gen. Washington and his staff during the Pause at Pluckemin in January 1777 and during the Pluckemin Cantonment in the winter of 1778-1779.[15] A family tradition handed down among the descendants of Mayor Richard McDonald (1803-1894) says Maj. Richard was among those who showed Gen. Washington the lookout from where he could view the British troop movements, a vantage point now celebrated at Washington Rock State Park in Green Brook Township, Somerset County, New Jersey.[16]

The next sentence of the blueprint tells us about William R. McDonald, Maj. Richard's son:

> Wm R McDonald served a short time in Revolutionary army but was given his discharge by Gen Washington because, being the eldest child in a large family Gen Washington thought that he ought to be at home to take care of the younger children while his father was away in the army. Richard McDonald's family during the war near Pluckinim [sic] 20 miles from New York.[17]

There is an unidentified William McDonald who served in Capt. Andrew McMyers's company of the First Battalion (1st New Jersey Regiment), First Establishment. The regiment was organized in 1775 at Elizabethtown and Perth Amboy from Somerset County and other counties.[18] Was this man William R. McDonald? William R. would have only been about 14 years old at the time, so it seems unlikely. Then again, young boys did do service in the Revolution often as messengers, water carriers and drummers, though typically the soldiers were 18-24 years old.

Whether William McDonald of Capt. McMyers's company in 1775 was our William R. McDonald or not, and there is no way to prove it one way or the other, the lad certainly could have served in some capacity as the war continued. The records that have survived are incomplete, so there is no way of knowing for sure. It does seem very likely, however, given the patriotic fervor of his McDonald family, that William R. definitely wanted to join in the fight for independence as soon as he was able and probably did serve for at least a short time. His grandson, John, would not claim William was a Revolutionary War soldier if he did not know it to be true. That would have been a detail John and his immediate family would have known and remembered for certain.

The other part of the story seems a bit fanciful. Did Gen. Washington himself discharge the lad and tell him to go home? Then again, we remember that Gen. George Washington was known personally to the McDonald family. Maybe the story really does have some truth in it. Young William R. McDonald may have met the General in 1777 during the Pause at Pluckemin when he was about 16 or again in the winter of 1778-1779 when Gen. Knox was camped in the McDonald fields during the Pluckemin Cantonment. Was William R. in attendance at Pluckemin's Grand Alliance Ball in February 1779? As the 18-year-old son of one of the most prominent families of Pluckemin, it seems most likely he was. He might even have been in the army at that time. Might Gen. Washington have advised the young man then, in a moment of fatherly candor, that while Maj. Richard was needed in service of the army, it would be best for William to stay at home with his mother and help her take care of the children?

No doubt that's what William did. The mother in question, though, was not his birth mother, Margrietje Schamp. She had passed away in 1773. Not long after her death, Maj. Richard took a second wife, Catherine Rosbrugh McCrea, the widow of John McCrea, the first pastor of the Lamington Presbyterian Church. Catherine had brought children of her own to the marriage. So William probably had his hands full helping Catherine out as the man of the house.

And now let's look at the last part of the blueprint's oral tradition:

> Wm R. settled in Herkimer Co, NY. and his son Philo Fowler was a pioneer in the dairy business in that county. Harriet McDonald, William McDonald and John McDonald were born in Herkimer Co N.Y. During 1812 Wm R McDonald lived in Amsterdam N.Y. Richard McDonald had a large family but the records are not available to place them in the list. Other children of Wm R McDonald had large families besides Philo Fowler McDonald especially Margaret McDonald who married Timothy Bliss and Wm McDonald but at present time a clear and complete record is not in the posession [sic] of this branch of the family. The place near which Richard McDonald lived during the Revolution may not be correctly spelled and he may have enlisted either from New York or from New Jersey.[19]

There is no reason to dispute any of the above. Three children of Philo Fowler McDonald are mentioned – Harriet, William and John (the creator of the blueprint) – all born in Herkimer County.

Richard McDonald, son of William R. McDonald, who "had a large family," married Mathilda Brannard. Unfortunately, we have not been able to identify any of the children of Richard and Mathilda.

All in all, the blueprint contains quite of bit of intriguing and useful information of note to all the descendants of the McDonalds of Somerset County. It represents one more fascinating piece of family history and lore.

WHAT WE NOW KNOW ABOUT WILLIAM R. MCDONALD

Now thanks to the data we have gleaned from the blueprint, it is fairly certain that William R. McDonald was indeed the son of Maj. Richard McDonald of Pluckemin,[20] that he was born Jan. 18, 1761, and died May 21, 1853, aged 92. He married Abigail Fowler on Jan. 8, 1787. She was born Oct. 7, 1767, and died Sept. 13, 1849, aged 81.[21]

Early Connecticut Marriages confirms the marriage date for William and Abigail. They were married in Washington, Litchfield County, Connecticut.[22] He was living in New York City at the time. By 1787, then, less than a year after Richard's half-brother, Samuel, was executed for murder, William apparently had left Somerset County and moved to New York.[23]

A family bible in the possession of Barbara Lewis says Abigail was the daughter of Philo Fowler.[24] There were a lot of Fowlers in Litchfield County, descended most likely from Ambrose Fowler (1626-1704), one of the first settlers of Windsor, Connecticut. Ambrose was an Englishman from Derbyshire who appears in the records in Windsor as early as 1640.[25]

William R. McDonald was a farmer. He appears in the 1810 census in Amsterdam, Montgomery County, New York. This is consistent with the blueprint, which noted he was living in Amsterdam in 1812.

By 1820, William R. had moved to Norway, Herkimer County, New York, and by 1840, he was living in Ohio, Herkimer County. He was still there in Ohio in 1850 at 89 years old. His farm had a cash value of $1600 on Aug. 14 of that year.[26] William was living with his daughter, Abigail, who no doubt was taking care of him in his old age. William's wife, Abigail Fowler McDonald, had died the year before at the age of 81. She was buried in Brondstatter Cemetery in Cold Brook, Herkimer County, New York.[27]

Several of the existing records for William show him with the middle initial "R." The blueprint also records that middle initial for William. We don't know what it stood for, perhaps "Richard," after his father. In any case, that "R." must have been an important part of William's identity as it is included in so many records.

THE CHILDREN OF WILLIAM R. AND ABIGAIL (FOWLER) MCDONALD

William and Abigail had 11 children. Only three of them have known descendants today: Margaret who married Timothy Bliss, William M. who married Joanna Axford, and Philo Fowler who married Thirza Spencer. Their lines will be discussed in subsequent chapters.

As for the other children, Richard the eldest, no doubt named after William's father, was born May 28, 1788, and died less than two months later on July 18, 1788. The second child, Rachel, was born Jan. 18, 1790, and died Dec. 26, 1804, aged 14.[28]

Abigail, the fifth child, was born in New York on July 29, 1796, so William and Abigail (Fowler) and their family must have been living in New York at that time.[29] The daughter, Abigail, apparently took care of her father until his death in 1853. She died a year later at the age of 57.[30] Her burial place is unknown as is her father's.

The sixth child was again named Richard. According to the blueprint, he was born Aug. 31, 1798, married Mathilda Brannard on Dec. 8, 1817, and apparently had a lot of descendants.

> Richard McDonald had a large family but the records are not available to place them in the list.[31]

Unfortunately, none of those descendants or even the names of Richard's children have been identified. The 1820 census indicates that Richard was engaged in agriculture in Norway, Herkimer County, New York, and had a daughter, probably born between 1817 and 1820. The 1840 census shows he was in Danube, Herkimer County, and working in manufacture and trade. He apparently had two children at that time, a boy and a girl, both under five years old. The census also indicates Richard and his wife could not read and write, a perplexing revelation considering how Richard's McDonald forebears valued education. After the 1840 census, these McDonalds disappear from the records. It is interesting to note that Maj. Richard McDonald, in his will of 1820, bequeathed $25 to his grandsons named Richard, so this Richard, son of William R., must have received his share.

The blueprint and the 1810 federal census both show that William R. McDonald was in Amsterdam, Montgomery County, New York, at least from 1810-1812. Amsterdam is just northwest of Albany. The fact that William R.'s son, Richard, was in Herkimer County by 1820 is an indication that William R. must have moved west from Amsterdam to Herkimer between 1812 and 1820. It is no wonder, then, that William R. McDonald did not sign Maj. Richard's will as executor in 1820. He must have been living far away in New York. One wonders if he and his family were able to make it back to Somerville, New Jersey, for Maj. Richard's funeral. It would have been a very long and difficult journey of about 250 miles from Herkimer County.

The eighth child of William R. and Abigail (Fowler) McDonald was named George. He was born and died in 1802.[32]

The- ninth child was George Scham McDonald, according to the blueprint, but the middle name is actually Schamp. Named after his maternal grandfather, Joost "George" Schamp, he was born Oct. 19, 1803, and died July 5, 1815, aged 11.[33]

Benjamin McDonald, the tenth child, was born Mar. 10, 1806. On June 20, 1831, he married Margaret H. Apes.[34] Nothing more is known about this couple.

The last child, Aaron McDonald, was born Aug. 8, 1808. He married Rebecca Apes (probably a sister of Benjamin's wife, Margaret) on Jan. 2, 1832.[35] The blueprint says he died on Dec. 9, 1834, but the actual death date might have been Sept. 13, 1834.[36] He was only 26 years old. His probate records, dated Feb. 4, 1835 and Mar. 27, 1835, show he lived in West Brunswick, Herkimer County, and had no children. The value of his estate did not exceed $400. His wife, Rebecca, and brother, Benjamin, were given authority to dispose of his goods and chattels.[37] Aaron was buried in Brondstatter Cemetery, the same cemetery where his mother Abigail Fowler McDonald was buried. [38]

The Apes surname of Margaret and Rebecca (the wives of Benjamin and Aaron McDonald) is certainly intriguing. Apes was not a common name. There was a man named William Apess (1798-1839), who claimed his grandfather was a white man who married a Pequot Indian woman who was the granddaughter of Philip, King of the Pequot Tribe.[39] King Philip's Indian name was Metacomet. He was the son of Massasoit, who was an ally of the *Mayflower* pilgrims of Plymouth, Massachusetts. Hostilities between the English and the Native Americans gradually escalated into King Philip's War in 1675-1678.

The Apes surname is associated with the Pequots, according to author Barry O'Conell. They were located in early times in Connecticut in places like New London, Colchester, Stonington and Groton.[40] Benjamin and Aaron's mother's Fowler family was also associated with Connecticut, particularly the Litchfield County area.

It could well be then, that the Apes women whom Benjamin and Aaron McDonald married were of Native American ancestry, at least in part.

It is indeed sad and unfortunate that the lines of Benjamin and Aaron have been lost. Without the genealogical blueprint, we would never have known they even existed. The lesson for all of us who are now living is clear: if we don't write our family stories down, they might very easily disappear forevermore behind the curtains of history.

Thankfully, we have been able to find evidence and information for three of William R. and Abigail (Fowler) McDonald's children: Margaret McDonald Bliss, William M. McDonald, and Philo Fowler McDonald. Their stories and their descendants will be revealed in the following chapters.

Chapter 2

TIMOTHY AND MARGARET (MCDONALD) BLISS
and Their Descendants

Great Great Grandparents: William and Florance MacDonel
Great Grandparents: Col. William McDonald and Unknown First Wife
Grandparents: Maj. Richard McDonald and Margrietje Schamp
Parents: William R. McDonald and Abigail Fowler

MARGARET MCDONALD (1792-1838)
+ Timothy Bliss (1783-1862)

1. Aaron Bliss (1814-1883, m. Almeda Vincent)
2. William Bliss (1816-1884)
3. Timothy Bliss Jr. (1818-1844)
4. Margaret Bliss (1820-1865, m. Henry Moseley)

Margaret McDonald, the third child of William R. and Abigail (Fowler) McDonald, was born in New York on June 15, 1792. She was probably named after her father's mother, Margrietje, and his aunt, Margaret McDonald McKissack.

On Jan. 30, 1812, Margaret married Timothy Bliss.[41] Timothy was born in Brimfield, Hampden County, Massachusetts, on Nov. 4, 1783, the son of Thomas and Sarah (King) Bliss.[42]

Timothy Bliss was a farmer and stock dealer in Brimfield.[43] Margaret died in Brimfield on June 6, 1838, at the age of 45, and was buried in the cemetery there.[44] They had four children together: Aaron, William, Timothy Jr. and Margaret. Timothy Jr. lived only 25 years. Born Nov. 5, 1818, he died Aug. 2, 1844, in Brimfield and was buried in Brimfield Cemetery.[45]

Timothy, the elder, took a second wife, Susan W.[46] He died in Brimfield at the age of 79 on New Year's Eve, Dec. 31, 1862, in the midst of the Civil War, and was buried in Brimfield Cemetery.[47]

AARON BLISS (1814-1883) AND FAMILY
(Margaret McDonald Bliss, William R. McDonald, Maj. Richard, Col. William, William MacDonel)

Aaron Bliss, the eldest child of Timothy and Margaret (McDonald) Bliss, was born Jan. 20, 1814, in Brimfield, Hampden County, Massachusetts.[48] He married Almeda Vincent on Independence Day, July 4, 1837, in

Cuyahoga County, Ohio.[49] Almeda was born Apr. 16, 1814, in Cold Brook, Herkimer County, New York, the daughter of Dr. Justus H. and Lucinda (Overton) Vincent.[50]

At the time he married, Aaron was operating a woolen mill in Chagrin Falls, Cuyahoga County, Ohio.[51] By 1860, he had moved back to Brimfield, Massachusetts, to engage in farming. In 1870, he was living in Chicago, Cook County, Illinois, and working as a dealer in furnaces. By 1880, he had moved to Hyde Park, Cook County, Illinois, and was living with his daughter Marion Brown and her family.[52] He died in 1883 at the age of 68. His wife, Almeda, had died a few years previously in 1879 at the age of 64.[53]

Aaron and Almeda (Vincent) Bliss had six children:
1. Martha A. (1838-1872, m. Samuel Fowler Dickinson)
2. Harriet M. (1840-aft. 1880)
3. Marion M. (1842-1918, m. Calvin Walter Brown)
4. Champion (1843-1845)
5. Albert A. (1847-1854)
6. Orville Justus (1849-1875, m. Ellen Hope Rankin)

Champion and Albert did not survive to adulthood. Harriet, the second child, was born Feb. 5, 1840. A passport application dated 1872 described her as being 5' 2" tall and having dark hair and black eyes.[54] In 1880, at the age of 40, she was living in her sister Marion Brown's household in Hyde Park, Illinois, but that is the last we hear of her.

MARTHA A. BLISS DICKINSON (1838-1872) AND FAMILY
(Aaron Bliss, Margaret McDonald Bliss, William R. McDonald, Maj. Richard, Col. William,
  William MacDonel)

Martha A. Bliss, the eldest child of Aaron and Almeda (Vincent) Bliss, was born Apr. 12, 1838, in Chagrin Falls, Cuyahoga County, Ohio.

On Mar. 19, 1870, in Cook County, Illinois, she married Rev. Samuel Fowler Dickinson,[55] a Congregational minister, who was born July 25, 1839, in Heath, Franklin County, Massachusetts, the son of Aaron and Sarah (Miller) Dickinson.[56] It may be that the Rev. Dickinson was named after Samuel Fowler Dickinson (1775-1838), a prominent lawyer of Amherst, Massachusetts, who was also the grandfather of the poet, Emily Dickinson (1830-1886).

Martha died when she was only 34 years old on June 9, 1872.[57] She had given birth to a daughter, Mattie B. Dickinson, who was born on May 30, 1872, in Chicago.[58]

Rev. Dickinson married a second wife, Ella Amelia Massey, on Aug. 25, 1875, in Chicago. She was born on July 20, 1849,[59] and gave birth to three children:
1. Ray Massey (1878-1948, m. Harriet Belle Crissey)
2. Emma Miller (1880-1968, m. Oliver Perry Avery)[60]
3. Esther H. (1884-1969, m. William H. Clithero, Francis Henry McElfresh)[61]

Rev. Samuel Fowler Dickinson died on Aug. 7, 1897, aged 58. His second wife, Ella Massey Dickinson, died on June 11, 1916, aged 66. Both were buried in Evergreen Cemetery, Colorado Springs, El Paso County, Colorado.[62]

Mattie B. Dickinson, the daughter of Rev. Samuel and Martha (Bliss) Dickinson, was alive as late as 1885, and living with her parents in Newton, Jasper County, Iowa, but thereafter she disappears from the records.[63]

MARION M. BLISS BROWN (1842-1918) AND FAMILY
(Aaron Bliss, Margaret McDonald Bliss, William R. McDonald, Maj. Richard, Col. William,
 William MacDonel)

Marion M. Bliss, the third child of Aaron and Almeda (Vincent) Bliss, was born Apr. 27, 1842, in Chagrin Falls, Cuyahoga County, Ohio. She married Calvin Walter Brown, the son of Calvin Bishop and Aurelia A. (Cutler) Brown, on Apr. 19, 1863, in Brimfield, Hampden County, Massachusetts.[64] Calvin Walter Brown was born July 6, 1841, in Brimfield.[65]

Calvin was listed as a capitalist in the 1880 census, at which time they were living in Hyde Park, Cook County, Illinois. By 1910, they were living in Los Angeles County, California, where Calvin was engaged as a broker in the real estate business.

Marion Bliss Brown died on Feb. 26, 1918, at the age of 75. Not long after, on Oct. 3, 1918, her husband, Calvin, joined her in death. He was 77.[66]

Calvin Walter and Marion (Bliss) Brown had three children:
1. Herbert Cutler (1865-1947, m. Zoe E. Lowe, Katherine M. McNeff, Eloise V. Harding)
2. Frances Vincent (1872-1954, m. Edwin Forest Hill Sr.)
3. Walter Marion (1880-1934, m. Alma Haydon, Kathryn Unknown)

HERBERT CUTLER BROWN (1865-1947) AND FAMILY
(Marion Bliss Brown, Aaron Bliss, Margaret McDonald Bliss, William R. McDonald, Maj. Richard,
 Col. William, William MacDonel)

Herbert Cutler Brown, the eldest child of Calvin Walter and Marion M. (Bliss) Brown, was born July 31, 1865, in Illinois.[67] An attorney in Los Angeles County, California, he married Zoe Elsie Lowe on Valentine's Day, Feb. 14, 1895.[68] Zoe was born in Pennsylvania on Sept. 6, 1874,[69] the daughter of the famous aeronaut, scientist and inventor, Prof. Thaddeus Sobieski Constantino Lowe and his wife, Leontine Augustine Gaschon. During the Civil War, Prof. Lowe was appointed Chief Aeronaut of the Union Army Balloon Corps by President Abraham Lincoln. He was involved in spying operations via balloon flights over Confederate positions. He also invented and built the Mount Lowe Railway System in the San Gabriel foothills of California. The Lowe Army Basefield at Ft. Rucker, Alabama, is named after him.[70]

Herbert and Zoe (Lowe) Brown had two children:
1. Zoe Herberta (1897-1989, m. Unknown McEachern)

2.   Cutler Lowe (1903-1987, m. Lois P. Unknown, Iris K. Armes or Nelson)

Herbert and Zoe's marriage ended in divorce sometime before 1909.

On June 21, 1909, Herbert married Katherine Mary McNeff, the daughter of Canadian-born parents, John and Beatrice (Fitzgerald) McNeff. Katherine was born in Wisconsin on Apr. 1, 1882.[71] They had a son, Thomas J. Brown, born in Los Angeles County on Jan. 19, 1922.[72] This marriage, too, ended in divorce. Katherine died in Seattle, King County, Washington, on Apr. 30, 1944, aged 62.[73]

About 1925, Herbert married a third time, to Eloise Virginia Harding.[74]

Herbert died in Los Angeles on Jan. 31, 1947, at the age of 81.[75]

ZOE HERBERTA BROWN MCEACHERN (1897-1989) AND FAMILY
(Herbert Cutler Brown, Marion Bliss Brown, Aaron Bliss, Margaret McDonald Bliss, William R. McDonald, Maj. Richard, Col. William, William MacDonel)

Zoe Herberta Brown, the eldest of two children born to Herbert Cutler Brown and his first wife, Zoe Elsie Lowe, came into this world on Feb. 12, 1897.[76] She married a Mr. McEachern, lived a long life and passed away in Alameda County, California, on Aug. 15, 1989, at the age of 92.[77]

CUTLER LOWE BROWN (1903-1987) AND FAMILY
(Herbert Cutler Brown, Marion Bliss Brown, Aaron Bliss, Margaret McDonald Bliss, William R. McDonald, Maj. Richard, Col. William, William MacDonel)

Cutler Lowe Brown, the second child of Herbert Cutler Brown and his first wife, Zoe Elsie Lowe, was born in California on July 18, 1903.[78] He completed four years of high school. In 1940, he and his wife, Lois P., were working for a music store in Los Angeles – he as a radio technician, she as a secretary. Lois, whose maiden name is unknown, was born on Jan. 20, 1914, in North Dakota.[79]

In 1957, Cutler was the honored guest at the dedication of Lowe Army Basefield at Ft. Rucker, Alabama, named for Cutler's famous grandfather, Thaddeus S. C. Lowe.[80]

On June 24, 1971, Cutler's wife, Lois, died in Santa Barbara, California, at the age of 57.[81]

Apparently, Cutler married a second time to Iris K. Armes (or Nelson) on Sept. 26, 1972, in San Luis Obispo, California.[82]

Cutler died on Oct. 9, 1987, in Ventura, California, at the age of 84.[83] He had no known children.

FRANCES VINCENT BROWN HILL (1872-1954) AND FAMILY

(Marion Bliss Brown, Aaron Bliss, Margaret McDonald Bliss, William R. McDonald, Maj. Richard, Col. William, William MacDonel)

Frances Vincent "Fanny" Brown, the second child of Calvin Walter and Marion M. (Bliss) Brown, was born Jan. 9, 1872, in Chicago, Cook County, Illinois. She married Edwin Forest Hill (b. Oct. 9, 1870, Chicago), the son of Robert and Sarah Ann (Woodcock) Hill.[84]

Frances attended four years of college. Her husband, Edwin, was a merchant for a general store. They had two children: Marion Hope and Edwin Forest Jr.[85]

Frances and Edwin Sr. must have spent some time in Asia in 1938. Their daughter, Marion Barrett, and her family, were living in China at the time. Perhaps Frances and Edwin visited them there. In any case, on Mar. 31, 1938, Frances and Edwin sailed from Yokohama, Japan, on the *Hikawa Maru,* arriving in Seattle on Apr. 12, 1938. They were living in Oakland, CA, at the time.[86]

Frances was 82 years old when she died on Sept. 11, 1954, in Santa Clara County, California. Her husband, Edwin, died a few years later, also in Santa Clara County, on May 1, 1960. He was 89.[87]

MARION HOPE HILL BARRETT (1895-1968) AND FAMILY

(Frances Brown Hill, Marion Bliss Brown, Aaron Bliss, Margaret McDonald Bliss, William R. McDonald, Maj. Richard, Col. William, William MacDonel)

Marion Hope Hill, the eldest of two children of Edwin Forest Sr. and Frances Vincent (Brown) Hill, was born Dec. 2, 1895, in Chicago, Cook County, Illinois. She attended college for four years and about 1918 married Henry Lester Barrett, who was born in New York City on Nov. 3, 1892.[88]

Henry (aka Harry) Barrett attended Oregon State College in Corvallis, Benton County, Oregon from 1908-1909 and later transferred to the Physicians and Surgeons College in Los Angeles where he obtained his medical degree. He joined the military and in July 1917, received a commission at the Presidio in San Francisco.[89] He was a veteran of World War I.

In 1920, after his marriage to Marion Hill, Henry was a lieutenant with the 12th Infantry of the U.S. Army at Camp Meade in Anne Arundel, Maryland.[90] From 1922-1925, he was stationed with the Eighth Army in the Hawaiian Islands.

In 1930, the family was living in Corvallis, Oregon. Henry was a captain in the U.S. Army at that time.

From 1935-1938, Henry was stationed at Tienstin (Tianjin), China, with the United States Army 15th Infantry Regiment. He had his family there with him.[91]

On Mar. 2, 1938, Marion and her four children boarded the USAT *U.S. Grant* in Chinwangtao, China, and sailed to Tacoma, Pierce County, Washington, arriving on Mar. 23, 1938. Their permanent home at that time was in Fort Lewis, a military facility southwest of Tacoma.

In 1940, the Barretts were living in Eugene, Lane County, Oregon.

Henry eventually rose to the rank of colonel. For the first 25 years of his career, he was with the Army, but in 1941, he was transferred to the Air Force. During World War II, Henry was sent overseas to the China-Burma-India Theater where he served as Deputy Chief of Staff of Managements and Control under General Stratemeyer of the Far Eastern Air Command.[92]

After the war, he became an assistant professor of military science and air tactics at Oregon State College in Corvallis for Air Force ROTC units. He received a second ROTC assignment at the University of Oregon and a third at Stanford University in the summer of 1949.

Col. Barrett resigned from active duty on Nov. 30, 1952. Upon retirement, he moved to Los Altos, Santa Clara County, California, and to Riverside County, California,[93] where his wife, Marion, died on Feb. 14, 1968, at the age of 72.[94]

Henry took a second wife, Gabrielle M. "Gay" Vanperre Quoidbach, the widow of Valentin Pierre Quoidbach, both of whom were Belgian immigrants. Henry and Gay were married on Oct. 28, 1970, in San Francisco.[95]

Col. Henry L. Barrett's final years were spent in Longview, Cowlitz County, Washington. He was active in the Longview Rotary Club, the Longview Country Club and St. Rose Catholic Church. He died on Oct. 9, 1974, at the age of 81.[96] He and his first wife, Marion Hill Barrett, were buried in Perris Valley Cemetery, Perris, Riverside County, California.[97]

Col. Henry and Marion (Hill) Barrett had four children:
1. Marion Frances (1921-1983, m. Oswald Kennerly Furtick Sr.)
2. Barbara Ann (1922-1983, m. Lt. Col. Earl Edward DeMun)
3. Harriet Elizabeth (1925-2003, m. James Martin Brown)
4. Henry Lester Jr. (1932-1992)

Henry Lester Barrett, Jr., the youngest child of Henry and Marion, was born Jan. 2, 1932, at Fort Leavenworth, Kansas. He trained in the Marine Corps Signal Battalion and died in San Diego on Mar. 29, 1992, at the age of 60.[98]

MARION FRANCES BARRETT FURTICK (1921-1983) AND FAMILY
(Marion Hill Barrett, Frances Brown Hill, Marion Bliss Brown, Aaron Bliss, Margaret McDonald Bliss, William R. McDonald, Maj. Richard, Col. William, William MacDonel)

Marion Frances Barrett, the eldest child of Col. Henry Lester and Marion Hope (Hill) Barrett, was born at Treasure Island in San Francisco on Feb. 2, 1921. She married Oswald Kennerly Furtick, the son of Robert Maury and Lester Mae (Kennerly) Furtick.[99]

Born Dec. 4, 1917,[100] Oswald was a graduate of the Agricultural College of Clemson University.[101] He and Marion made their home in Springfield, Orangeburg County, South Carolina. In fact, Oswald was the mayor of Springfield in 1972, when the city hosted the fourth annual Governor's Frog Jumping Contest as part of a national tournament honoring Mark Twain's famous story, "The Celebrated Jumping Frog of Calaveras County." Springfield's contest had about 6,000 visitors and 150 competing frogs.[102]

Oswald and Marion (Barrett) Furtick had seven children:
1. Edward (m. Kathy Unknown)
2. John Walter Sr. (m. Glenda Unknown)
3. Oswald Kennerly Jr. (m. Mary Unknown)
4. Robert H.
5. Marion Frances "Missey" (m. Frank Oley)
6. JoAnne (m. Paul Cousins)
7. Barbara Ann (m. Unknown Cramer, Carroll Holloway, Unknown Strickland)[103]

Marion died on Oct. 4, 1983, in Springfield at the age of 62. Her widowed husband, Oswald, remarried to Mattie Davis Smith, the widow of Richard Able Smith and the daughter of Arthur Wells and Lou Ella (Unknown) Davis. Mattie was born in Norway, Orangeburg County, South Carolina, on Feb. 11, 1935.[104]

Oswald died on Aug. 17, 1990, in Columbia, Richland County, South Carolina, at the age of 72. His second wife, Mattie, passed on Aug. 22, 2005, aged 70. Oswald and both of his wives were buried in Springfield Cemetery in Springfield, South Carolina.[105]

BARBARA ANN BARRETT DEMUN (1922-1983)
(Marion Hill Barrett, Frances Brown Hill, Marion Bliss Brown, Aaron Bliss, Margaret McDonald Bliss, William R. McDonald, Maj. Richard, Col. William, William MacDonel)

Barbara Ann Barrett, the second child of Col. Henry Lester and Marion Hope (Hill) Barrett, was born in San Francisco on July 2, 1922. While her father was stationed in Tienstin (Tianjin), China, from 1935-1938, Barbara attended the French Convent there. She also attended the University of Oregon and was a member of Delta Gamma sorority. About 1947, she married Capt. Earl Edward DeMun, the son of Ray W. and Ethel (Thomas) DeMun of Wayland, Steuben County, New York. Earl was born Feb. 17, 1916, in Bath, Steuben County, New York. He was a veteran of World War II having served with the 9th Air Force in England.[106]

Earl eventually rose to the rank of lieutenant colonel in the United States Air Force and served in the Korean and Vietnam wars as well.

Barbara Ann died on Apr. 5, 1983, in Riverside County, California.[107] She was only 60 years old.

Earl passed away on Apr. 2, 1996, in the VA Hospital in Asheville, Buncombe County, North Carolina. He was a member of St. Stephen Catholic Church. He and Barbara Ann are buried in the Riverside National Cemetery in Riverside, California.[108]

HARRIET ELIZABETH BARRETT BROWN (1925-2003) AND FAMILY

(Marion Hill Barrett, Frances Brown Hill, Marion Bliss Brown, Aaron Bliss, Margaret McDonald Bliss,
 William R. McDonald, Maj. Richard, Col. William, William MacDonel)

Harriet Elizabeth Barrett, the third child of Col. Henry Lester and Marion Hope (Hill) Barrett, was born in El Paso County, Texas, on May 3, 1925.[109] She also appears in some records with the middle name Lester.

During World War II, on D-Day, June 6, 1944, Harriet was admitted to the Cadet Nursing Corps.[110] She married James Martin Brown (b. Nov. 12, 1922), the son of Frank Wesley and Christine (Ferguson) Brown, on Feb. 4, 1956, in Santa Clara County, California.[111] They had six children and lived in Tulare County, California.[112]

James Martin Brown died on Aug. 13, 1996, in Porterville in Tulare County at the age of 73. Harriet also died in Porterville on Nov. 24, 2003, at the age of 78.[113]

EDWIN FOREST HILL JR. (c. 1901-1982) AND FAMILY

(Frances Brown Hill, Marion Bliss Brown, Aaron Bliss, Margaret McDonald Bliss, William R. McDonald,
 Maj. Richard, Col. William, William MacDonel)

Edwin Forest Hill Jr., the second child of Edwin Forest Sr. and Frances Vincent (Brown) Hill, was born Aug. 18 or 19, 1900, or Aug. 19, 1901, in California.[114] He completed four years of college and married Ada Applegate Cameron, the daughter of Louis H. and Azalene "Lena" (Brown) Applegate, on Independence Day, July 4, 1923, in Berkeley, Alameda County, California.[115]

Edwin Jr. was working as a salesman in Chicago in 1930 and as an insurance broker in Oakland, California, in 1940. He died in Contra Costa County, California, on July 29, 1982, at the age of 81.[116]

Edwin Jr. and Ada had a son, Harrison Bliss Hill, born in San Francisco County, on Mar. 25, 1928.[117] He was a PFC in the U.S. Marine Corps. His wife, Joan Margaret Talbot, was born Aug. 31, 1930, and died July 3, 2012, aged 81. She was buried in the Rock Island National Cemetery in Rock Island, Rock Island County, Illinois.[118]

WALTER MARION BROWN (1882-1934) AND FAMILY

(Marion Bliss Brown, Aaron Bliss, Margaret McDonald Bliss, William R. McDonald, Maj. Richard,
 Col. William, William MacDonel)

Walter Marion Brown, the third child of Calvin Walter and Marion M. (Bliss) Brown, was born Feb. 11, 1880, in Chicago, Cook County, Illinois.[119] He married Alma Haydon, the daughter of Sanford Taylor and Jeanette (Green) Haydon, in Obion County, Tennessee, on Oct. 26, 1907.[120] Alma was born in "The Volunteer State" on Feb. 28, 1884.[121]

In 1910, Walter and Alma (Haydon) were living with his parents in Los Angeles, California. He was working as a real estate agent at that time. When he registered for the draft in 1917, he was of medium height and build with brown eyes and brown hair working as an auto dealer and repairman.

Walter and Alma had a daughter, Janette (Janet), born in California about 1915. The marriage ended in divorce.

When Walter died on Jan. 20, 1934, at the age of 53, he was married to a woman named Kathryn.[122]

Alma Haydon Brown, meanwhile, was raising her daughter, Janette, and working as a saleslady in Los Angeles in 1940.[123] Alma passed away on Jan. 19, 1977, in San Diego County. She was 92 years old.

ORVILLE JUSTUS BLISS, ESQ. (1849-1875)
(Aaron Bliss, Margaret McDonald Bliss, William R. McDonald, Maj. Richard, Col. William, William MacDonel)

Orville Justus Bliss, Esq., was called "one of the most talented young men in Chicago."[124] The youngest of six children of Aaron and Almeda (Vincent) Bliss, he was born in Cuyahoga County, Ohio, on May 17, 1849.[125] He attended Yale College and was its class orator in 1871.

In 1872, Orville toured Europe, Asia and the Middle East. He wrote some "brilliant letters" of his experiences in the Holy Land and other environs, which were published in the *Inter-Ocean*, a Chicago newspaper, and gained quite an enthusiastic following from its readership.

When he returned to America, he began an earnest study of the law in the office of Messrs. Isham & Lincoln. He was admitted to practice in the Missouri courts and was in the process of gaining admittance in Chicago as well.

On Mar. 9, 1875, he married Ellen Hope Rankin (1851-1944), daughter of William and Ellen Hope (Stevens) Rankin of Newark, New Jersey. The young lawyer and his new bride had commenced a trip through the southern United States when Orville took ill in Jacksonville, Duval County, Florida. He died there – exactly one month after he married – on Apr. 9, 1875. He was only 25 years old.[126]

The *Inter-Ocean* published its tragic story about Orville's death on Apr. 13, 1875:

> Before leaving Chicago he had engaged with us to write letters of travel for the Inter-Ocean during his absence, and at about the time when we looked for his first correspondence, we received the sad news of his death. Thus was a life, unusually full of promise, crushed, in the very morning of its brilliancy and usefulness.[127]

WILLIAM BLISS (1816-1907) AND FAMILY
(Margaret McDonald Bliss, William R. McDonald, Maj. Richard, Col. William, William MacDonel)

William Bliss, the second child of Timothy and Margaret (McDonald) Bliss, was born Oct. 27, 1816, in Brimfield, Hampden County, Massachusetts. He was no doubt named after his maternal grandfather, William R. McDonald. Raised on his father's farm, William received a solid "common school" education. In 1837, when he was 21, he moved to Chagrin Falls, Cuyahoga County, Ohio, and worked in his brother Aaron's woolen mill as a wool buyer for many years.[128]

On Sept. 8, 1841, in Chagrin Falls, he married Fannie M. Vincent, the daughter of Dr. Justus H. and Lucinda (Overton) Vincent. Born July 18, 1824, in Herkimer County, New York, she was the younger sister of William's brother Aaron's wife, Almeda Vincent.[129]

William traveled extensively throughout Indiana and returned to Brimfield, Massachusetts, for a time.[130] Then in 1857, he moved to Wolcottville, Noble County, Indiana, while continuing the manufacture of woolen goods at nearby Rome City under the firm name of William Bliss & Co.

About two years later, he purchased 210 acres of land and moved to what became Brimfield, Noble County, Indiana. William laid out the village himself and named it after his hometown in Massachusetts.[131]

William was a Republican. He and his wife were charter members of the Congregational Church at Chagrin Falls, but became Methodists when they lived in Brimfield, Indiana.[132] Fannie died in Brimfield at the age of 64 on Feb. 28, 1889. William lived quite a bit longer. He passed on Mar. 31, 1907, at the age of 90.[133] Both were buried in Orange Cemetery in Rome City, Noble County, Indiana.[134]

William and Fannie (Vincent) Bliss had four children:
1. Frank T. (1844-1915)
2. Charles W. (1846-1927, m. Hannah C. Clock)
3. Emily M. (1849-1921, m. Loren Madison)
4. Mary L. (1856-1916, m. William A. McCarty)

FRANK T. BLISS (1844-1915)
(William Bliss, Margaret McDonald Bliss, William R. McDonald, Maj. Richard, Col. William, William MacDonel)

Frank T. Bliss, the eldest child of William and Fannie M. (Vincent) Bliss, was born in Ohio on Sept. 22, 1844.[135] He moved to Chicago by 1870.[136]

A member of the Board of Trade and president of the grain commission firm of Frank T. Bliss & Co., Frank never married. He died in Chicago on Mar. 22, 1915, aged 70 years old.[137]

CHARLES W. BLISS (1846-1927) AND FAMILY
(William Bliss, Margaret McDonald Bliss, William R. McDonald, Maj. Richard, Col. William, William MacDonel)

Charles W. Bliss, the second child of William and Fannie M. (Vincent) Bliss, was born Jan. 31, 1846, in Brimfield, Hampden County, Massachusetts. He moved to Noble County, Indiana, with his parents when he was 14 years of age.

Charles began his young adult life as a farmer and continued in that occupation for many years. He married Hannah Cornelia "Nellie" Clock, the daughter of Methodist minister Rev. Jacob Willkie and Sarah Abigail (Groves) Clock, on Nov. 29, 1871, in Rome City, Noble County, Indiana.[138]

Charles was a Republican and a member of the Methodist Episcopal Church. He served as a precinct committeeman for Orange Township in his later years.

Nellie Bliss died on July 9, 1914, "after an extended illness resulting from paralysis." She was 68. Charles died at his home in Brimfield, Noble County, in May 1927. He was 81. Both were buried in Orange Cemetery in Rome City.

Charles and Nellie had one child, Fannie Bliss, born on Jan. 6, 1879, in Brimfield, Indiana. She died at the age of 60 on Mar. 11, 1939, in Kendallville, Noble County, Indiana. She never married and had lived alone since the death of her father in 1927. She was buried in Orange Cemetery.[139]

EMILY M. BLISS MADISON (1849-1921)
(William Bliss, Margaret McDonald Bliss, William R. McDonald, Maj. Richard, Col. William,
  William MacDonel)

Emily M. Bliss, the third child of William and Fannie M. (Vincent) Bliss, was born in Chagrin Falls, Cuyahoga County, Ohio, on June 16, 1849.[140] About 1913, when she was about 64 years old, she married Loren Madison of East Jordan, Charlevoix County, Michigan. They lived there for a few years until he died about 1918.

On Dec. 1, 1921, Emily, too, succumbed to death at the age of 72, passing away in the home of her brother, Charles, in Brimfield, Noble County, Indiana. Her funeral was held at the Brimfield Methodist Episcopal Church where she had been a member. She was laid to rest in Orange Cemetery, Rome City, Noble County, Indiana.[141]

MARY L. BLISS MCCARTY (1856-1916) AND FAMILY
(William Bliss, Margaret McDonald Bliss, William R. McDonald, Maj. Richard, Col. William,
  William MacDonel)

Mary L. Bliss, the fourth child of William and Fannie M. (Vincent) Bliss, was born in Ohio on Feb. 10, 1856.[142] She was a "graduate of music and a fine musician."[143] She married William A. McCarty (b. Apr. 1861) about 1883[144] and had three children:
1. Charles W. (1885-1888)
2. Frank Bliss (1887-1970, m. Hattie E. Nasshahn)
3. Agnes B. (1893-1936)

William A. McCarty was working as a grocer in 1900, a railroad electrician in 1920, and as a cook in 1930 for a railroad signal department.

Mary L. McCarty died on Nov. 27, 1916, at the age of 60. Her husband died in 1952 at age 90. Both were buried in Orange Cemetery in Rome City, Noble County, Indiana.[145] Their first child, Charles W., lived only 2 years and 8 months (July 1885-Mar. 22, 1888).[146] He, too, was buried in Orange Cemetery.

FRANK BLISS MCCARTY (1887-1970) AND FAMILY

(Mary Bliss McCarty, William Bliss, Margaret McDonald Bliss, William R. McDonald, Maj. Richard,
 Col. William, William MacDonel)

Frank Bliss McCarty, the second of three children of William A. and Mary L. (Bliss) McCarty, was born Mar. 23, 1887, in Brimfield, Noble County, Indiana.[147] About 1908, he married Hattie Elizabeth Nasshahn, who was born June 5, 1890 or 1891, in Lake County, Indiana.[148] Frank had attended one year of high school and Hattie had an eighth-grade education.[149] She was the operator of a beauty shop in 1930.

Frank was of medium height, slender with gray eyes and light hair and working as a farmer when he registered for the draft in 1917.[150] From 1930-1940, he was working as a telegraph operator for a railroad. Apparently, he spent most of his life in Orange Twp. in Noble County, Indiana. He died in Sept. 1970, aged 83.[151] Hattie died in 1978, aged 88. Both were buried in Orange Cemetery in Rome City.[152]

Frank and Hattie McCarty had two children: Francis Timothy and Mary Elizabeth. They also adopted a son, Buddie McCarty, who appears in the 1940 census born about 1917.

FRANCIS TIMOTHY MCCARTY (1887-1970) AND FAMILY

(Frank Bliss McCarty, Mary Bliss McCarty, William Bliss, Margaret McDonald Bliss, William R. McDonald,
 Maj. Richard, Col. William, William MacDonel)

Francis Timothy McCarty, the eldest son of Frank Bliss and Hattie (Nasshahn) McCarty, was born in Brimfield, Noble County, Indiana, on July 3, 1909. He married Evelyn R. Kepford, the daughter of Amos and Amanda (Friend) Kepford, on July 23, 1939, in Noble County.[153] Both Francis and Evelyn were college educated.

Francis was a repairman in a radio shop in 1930 and a supervisor in maintenance for a radio factory in 1940, at which time they were living in Kokomo, Howard County, Indiana.

Evelyn died at the age of 73 in 1982. Francis died in Fort Wayne, Allen County, Indiana, on Nov. 22, 1990. He was 81. Both were buried in Orange Cemetery in Rome City.[154] Francis's obituary noted that he was an industrialist and manufacturer. He and his wife were survived by a daughter, two grandchildren and two great-granchildren.[155]

MARY ELIZABETH MCCARTY ADAIR (1911-1995) AND FAMILY

(Frank Bliss McCarty, Mary Bliss McCarty, William Bliss, Margaret McDonald Bliss, William R. McDonald,
 Maj. Richard, Col. William, William MacDonel)

Mary Elizabeth McCarty, the second child of Frank Bliss and Hattie (Nasshahn) McCarty, was born in Brimfield, Noble County, Indiana, on Nov. 21, 1911. She received a high school education and married Max Adair, the son of Hobert and Mamie (Boner) Adair, on July 17, 1947, in Merrillville, Lake County, Indiana. Max was born in Wolf Lake, Noble County, Indiana, Oct. 2, 1919. He graduated from Albion High School, served his country in World War II, and was a member of American Legion Post 86 in Kendallville.[156]

Max served as Noble County recorder for 8 years and as an Orange Twp. precinct committeeman for many years. He was employed by Azar's Commissary for 10 years and worked for the Indiana State Toll Road until he retired in 1984.

Max and Mary Elizabeth were both members of the Brimfield United Methodist Church. Mary also served as its youth director for many years.

Mary Elizabeth was deputy recorder for the Noble County recorder's office, a bookkeeper for the Noble County treasurer's office and worked as a clerk for the State Highway Department's district office in Fort Wayne. She was also active with the Noble County Republican Women's Club.[157]

Max passed away on May 3, 1994, in Kendalville, Noble County, Indiana, at the age of 74.[158] Mary Elizabeth died a little over a year later, also in Kendalville, on July 19, 1995, at the age of 83. Both were buried in Orange Cemetery in Rome City, Noble County, Indiana.[159]

Max and Mary Elizabeth (McCarty) Adair had one daughter, Marcia, who married Jack Garrett. Jack and Marcia (McCarty) Garrett live in Brimfield and had four children: Douglas R., Tamara, Bryan and James.[160]

DOUGLAS R. GARRETT (1968-1999) AND FAMILY
(Marcia Adair Garrett, Mary McCarty Adair, Frank Bliss McCarty, Mary Bliss McCarty, William Bliss, Margaret McDonald Bliss, William R. McDonald, Maj. Richard, Col. William, William MacDonel)

Douglas R. Garrett, the son of Jack and Marcia (Adair) Garrett, was born on May 17, 1968, in Orange County, California. A U.S. Army veteran, he married Beth Travis on Apr. 14, 1990, in Kendalville, Noble County, Indiana. He was a production worker for Monaco Coach in Wakarusa, Elkhart County, Indiana.[161]

Douglas was a member of Brimfield United Methodist Church and an avid bowler. He was killed in a single-car accident near Goshen, Indiana, on Nov. 18, 1999. He was only 31 years old. He was buried in Orange Cemetery in Rome City, survived by his wife, Beth, and two children: Kaitlin and Logan.[162]

MARGARET BLISS MOSELEY (1820-1865) AND FAMILY
(Margaret McDonald Bliss, William R. McDonald, Maj. Richard, Col. William, William MacDonel)

Margaret Bliss, the fourth child of Timothy and Margaret (McDonald) Bliss, was born in 1820, probably in Brimfield, Hampden County, Massachusetts. She married Henry E. Moseley, who was born in Westfield, Hampden County, Massachusetts, on July 16, 1816.[163]

Henry and Margaret must have moved to Lake County, Ohio, sometime in the early 1840's. Two children died young there and were buried in Evergreen Cemetery in Painesville, Lake County:1) Henry Bliss Moseley, aged 7 months (Sept 1842-Apr. 9, 1843) and 2) Fidelia A. Moseley, aged 2 years (1844-Mar. 24, 1846).[164]

By 1860, the family had moved to Thompson, Geauga County, Ohio. Henry was a farmer. Thompson is located about 25 miles northeast of Russell, Geauga County, where Margaret's uncle, Philo Fowler McDonald, had settled in the 1840's.

Margaret died on June 17, 1865. She was 44 years old. Thirteen months later, almost to the day, her son, Aaron Freddie Moseley, died at the age of 9, on Jul 18, 1866. Henry E. Moseley lived to be 63. He died on May 24, 1880. All three were buried in Evergreen Cemetery.[165]

Besides the three children who died young, Henry and Margaret (Bliss) Moseley had five other children who survived to adulthood:
4. Edward Austin (1847-1906, m. Margaret E. Unknown)
5. Emma M. (1849-1930)
6. Timothy F. (1851-1925, m. Nettie L. Belknap)
7. Henry Elmer (1860-1930, m. Caroline M. Rice, Jane R. Freeman)
8. Alvin Bliss (c. 1861-1893, m. Charlotte L. Hinsdale)

At some point before 1880, all of these children moved to Grand Rapids, Kent County, Michigan, where the family established themselves in the wholesale produce business.

EDWARD AUSTIN MOSELEY (1847-1906) AND FAMILY
(Margaret Bliss Moseley, Margaret McDonald Bliss, William R. McDonald, Maj. Richard, Col. William, William MacDonel)

Edward Austin Moseley, the third child of Henry E. and Margaret (Bliss) Moseley, was born in Ohio on Feb. 21, 1847.[166] He married in 1872 when he was 25 years old. His wife, Margaret E., was born about 1852, but her surname is unknown.[167]

Edward and Margaret had two children born about 15 years apart:
1. Edward Louis (1875-bef. 1940, m. Margaret Remington)
2. Marguerite (c. 1890-aft. 1909)

Sometime before 1880, Edward and his brothers, Timothy and Alvin, moved to Grand Rapids, Kent County, Michigan, and formed the Moseley Brothers Company, a wholesale produce business.

Edward died at the age of 57 on Aug. 28, 1906, in Grand Rapids. He was buried in Oakhill Cemetery there. His wife, Margaret, was alive as late as 1930. She was living with her son, Edward Louis and his family in Piedmont, Alameda County, California, but her death date is unknown.

Marguerite Moseley, their only daughter, was living with her mother in Grand Rapids as late as 1908. In 1909, she was living alone in Grand Rapids and that is the last we know of her.[168]

EDWARD LOUIS MOSELEY (1875-bef. 1940) AND FAMILY
(Edward Austin Moseley, Margaret Bliss Moseley, Margaret McDonald Bliss, William R. McDonald, Maj. Richard, Col. William, William MacDonel)

Edward Louis Moseley was born Aug. 11, 1875, in Michigan. He attended the University of Michigan and was a member of the Delta Kappa Epsilon fraternity.[169] About 1901, he married Margaret R. "Madge" Remington, who was born in Michigan April 1, 1881, the daughter of Charles R. and Carrie B. Remington of Grand Rapids.[170] She was a high school graduate.

Their first child, a daughter named Dorothy Margaret, was born May 27, 1902, probably in Grand Rapids, as that is where Edward was living that year.[171]

In 1903, Edward was working in Battle Creek, Michigan, as general manager for Price Cereal Food.[172] By about 1908, he had relocated to Oakland, Alameda County, California. His second child, Margaret Elizabeth Moseley, was born there about that time. A third child, Jane, was born about 1911, and a fourth, Edna L. on Aug. 11, 1915, in Alameda County.

California voting records for 1916 show Edward and Madge were registered Republicans living on Adams St. in Oakland.[173]

In 1918, when Edward registered for the draft in World War I, he was a self-employed merchandise broker working in San Francisco and living in Piedmont, Alameda County, California. The records describe him as tall, of medium build, with blue eyes and dark hair.[174]

The 1920 census shows Edward's mother, Margaret, had come to live with the family in Piedmont.

By 1930, Edward was the proprietor of a wholesale grocery operation. Edward died sometime between 1930 and 1940. His wife, Madge, moved to Oakland and became an apartment manager.[175] She died in Alameda County on Oct. 24, 1953, at the age of 72.[176]

DOROTHY MARGARET MOSELEY COLLINS FANNING (1902-1994) AND FAMILY
(Edward Louis Moseley, Edward A., Margaret Bliss Moseley, Margaret McDonald Bliss, William R. McDonald, Maj. Richard, Col. William, William MacDonel)

Dorothy Margaret Moseley was born in Michigan on May 27, 1902, the eldest child of Edward Louis and Margaret R. (Remington) Moseley. On Sept. 19, 1922, she married Walter Edward Collins, an oil company salesman from Bakersfield, California.[177] They had a son, Walter Edward Collins Jr., born in 1925 in Alameda County.[178]

Dorothy's first marriage ended in divorce. She then married James Earle Fanning on Jan. 20, 1933, in Piedmont, Alameda County, California.[179] He was a college graduate working in business in San Francisco.[180]

James died in Alameda County on Aug. 30, 1968, at the age of 66. Dorothy lived quite a bit longer. She passed at the age of 91 on Feb. 28, 1994, in Alameda County.[181] Social Security records show her last residence was in Rockville, Montgomery County, Maryland.

DR. WALTER EDWARD COLLINS JR. (1925-2006)

(Dorothy Moseley Collins Fanning, Edward Louis Moseley, Edward A., Margaret Bliss Moseley, Margaret
  McDonald Bliss, William R. McDonald, Maj. Richard, Col. William, William MacDonel)

Walter Edward Collins Jr., the son of Walter Edward and Dorothy (Moseley) Collins, was born on Mar. 28, 1925, in Alameda County, California.[182] He was a doctor living in Anaheim, Orange County, California.[183] He died on July 8, 2006, at the age of 81.

MARGARET ELIZABETH MOSELEY DIEHL (c. 1908-unknown) AND FAMILY

(Edward Louis Moseley, Edward A., Margaret Bliss Moseley, Margaret McDonald Bliss, William R.
  McDonald, Maj. Richard, Col. William, William MacDonel)

Margaret Elizabeth Moseley was born in California about 1908, the second child of Edward Louis and Margaret R. (Remington) Moseley. She married Russell Erwin Diehl, the son of Harry P. and Virginia (Callebotta) Diehl, on Dec. 24, 1937, in Piedmont, Alameda County, California.[184] He was born in California on Oct. 27, 1903,[185] and was previously married to Thelma Joyce Hubbard.[186]

Russell and Margaret (Moseley) Diehl had a son, Russell Erwin Diehl Jr., born on Jan. 4, 1939, in Sutter, Sacramento County, California.[187] Russell Jr. now lives in Lake Oswego, Clackamas County, Oregon, and works as a real estate specialist for The Hasson Company.[188]

Margaret Mosely Diehl probably died sometime before 1964.

On July 6, 1964, Russell Sr. married his third wife, Ruth Richardson, in Alameda County, California.[189]

Russell Sr. died on June 17, 1968, in Contra Costa County, California, at the age of 64.[190]

JANE MOSELEY BROWN (c. 1911-unknown) AND FAMILY

(Edward Louis Moseley, Edward A., Margaret Bliss Moseley, Margaret McDonald Bliss, William R.
  McDonald, Maj. Richard, Col. William, William MacDonel)

Jane Moseley was born in California about 1911, the third child of Edward Louis and Margaret R. (Remington) Moseley. She attended a year of college and married Donald Falk Brown on Sept. 6, 1933, in Piedmont, Alameda County, California. He had a high school education and was working as a distributor for fire prevention equipment in 1940 in Oakland. They had a daughter, Donna, born about 1938. That is all that is known at present.

EDNA L. MOSELEY (1915-1995)

(Edward Louis Moseley, Edward A., Margaret Bliss Moseley, Margaret McDonald Bliss, William R.
  McDonald, Maj. Richard, Col. William, William MacDonel)

Edna L. Moseley was born Aug. 11, 1915, in Alameda County, California, the youngest of four daughters born to Edward Louis and Margaret R. (Remington) Moseley.[191] She attended the University of California at

Berkeley and was a member of Pi Beta Phi.[192] In 1951, she took a trip from San Francisco to Honolulu, Hawaii.[193] Her last residence was in Oakland, California. She died on Dec. 20, 1995, at the age of 80.[194]

———⟨////⟩———

EMMA M. MOSELEY (1849-1930)
(Margaret Bliss Moseley, Margaret McDonald Bliss, William R. McDonald, Maj. Richard, Col. William, William MacDonel)

Emma M. Moseley, the fourth child of Henry E. and Margaret (Bliss) Moseley, was born Sept. 8, 1849, in Thompson, Geauga County, Ohio.[195] In 1870, she was living in Painesville, Lake County, Ohio, as a "scholar" at the Lake Erie Female Seminary, a private educational institution for women.[196] By 1900, she was living in Grand Rapids, Kent County, Michigan, and working as a watercolor artist.

Emma never married. She died in Grand Rapids on Mar. 5, 1930, at the age of 80 and was buried in Oakhill Cemetery with other members of her family.[197]

TIMOTHY F. MOSELEY (1851-1925) AND FAMILY
(Margaret Bliss Moseley, Margaret McDonald Bliss, William R. McDonald, Maj. Richard, Col. William, William MacDonel)

Timothy F. Moseley, the fifth child of Henry E. and Margaret (Bliss) Moseley, was born Dec. 4, 1851, in Thompson, Geauga County, Ohio.[198]

Sometime before 1878, Timothy moved to Grand Rapids, Kent County, Michigan. He married Nettie L. Belknap there on Oct. 2, 1878.[199] She was born in Grand Rapids on Nov. 10, 1856, the daughter of James and Elsie (Sanborn) Belknap.[200]

Timothy and his brothers, Edward Austin and Alvin Bliss Moseley formed the Moseley Brothers Company, a wholesale produce business in Grand Rapids.

Timothy's wife, Nettie, died at the age of 56 on June 12, 1913, in Grand Rapids. Timothy himself died on Oct. 17, 1925, in Grand Rapids, at the age of 73. They were buried in Oakhill Cemetery.[201]

Timothy and Nettie (Belknap) Moseley had one child, Helen E. Moseley.

HELEN E. MOSELEY (1883-1928)
(Timothy F. Moseley, Margaret Bliss Moseley, Margaret McDonald Bliss, William R. McDonald, Maj. Richard, Col. William, William MacDonel)

Helen E. Moseley, the only child of Timothy F. and Nettie (Belknap) Moseley, was born in Michigan on Sept. 21, 1883.[202] She was an artist and probably lived with her parents most of her life.[203]

In 1926, Helen must have visited France as she appears on passenger records sailing on the SS *De Grasse* leaving Le Havre, France, on Apr. 28, 1926, and arriving in the port of New York on May 7, 1926.[204] She died almost two years later on Apr. 22, 1928, aged 44, and was buried in Oakhill Cemetery in Grand Rapids, Michigan.[205]

HENRY ELMER MOSELEY (1860-1930) AND FAMILY
(Margaret Bliss Moseley, Margaret McDonald Bliss, William R. McDonald, Maj. Richard, Col. William, William MacDonel)

Henry Elmer Moseley, the seventh child of Henry E. and Margaret (Bliss) Moseley, was born Oct. 24, 1860, in Thompson, Geauga County, Ohio.[206] Better known as Elmer, he graduated from the University of Michigan[207] and married Caroline Minena Rice, the daughter of Harvey A. and Carrie J. (Fallas) Rice on Apr. 10, 1890, in Grand Rapids, Kent County, Michigan.[208] Caroline was born June 1865, according to the 1900 census.

While his three brothers – Edward, Timothy and Alvin – were the operators of Moseley Brothers, Elmer established his own produce company under the name H. E. Moseley & Co. His wife, Caroline, died of stomach cancer on Feb. 24, 1912, at the age of 46.[209]

Elmer married his second wife, Jane R. Freeman, the daughter of Thomas S. and Helen (Randall) Freeman, on Mar. 29, 1913, in Grand Rapids.[210] She was born July 1868.[211]

By 1930, Elmer and Jane had moved to Tucson, Pima County, Arizona. He died there of pulmonary tuberculosis on Nov. 9, 1930, at the age of 70. [212]

Jane Freeman Moseley lived quite a bit longer. She died on Feb. 12, 1960, at the age of 91. All three Moseleys – Elmer, Caroline (Rice) and Jane (Freeman) – are buried in Oakhill Cemetery in Grand Rapids, Kent County, Michigan.[213] They had no issue.

ALVIN BLISS MOSELEY (1862-1893) AND FAMILY
(Margaret Bliss Moseley, Margaret McDonald Bliss, William R. McDonald, Maj. Richard, Col. William, William MacDonel)

Alvin Bliss Moseley, the eighth child of Henry E. and Margaret (Bliss) Moseley, was born Aug. 4, 1862.[214] He was a salesman in partnership with his elder siblings, Edward and Timothy, as part of Moseley Bros. in Grand Rapids, Michigan. He was "well known in that city" and "a leader among the young people of Park Congregational Church."[215]

On Nov. 1, 1892, at St. Mark's Episcopal Church in Evanston, Cook County, Illinois, Alvin married Charlotte Louisa Hinsdale, the daughter of Henry Walbridge and Eliza Jane (Chatfield) Hinsdale.[216] A little over a year later, Alvin was dead. He passed away in San Antonio, Bexar County, Texas, on Dec. 22, 1893, three days before Christmas. He was only about 32 years of age.

Alvin's only child, a daughter, Alice Bliss Moseley, came into the world after his death – on June 20, 1894.[217]

Charlotte and her daughter went to live with her mother, Eliza Jane Hinsdale (1834-1916), in Evanston.[218] Charlotte died there on Feb. 6, 1919,[219] and was buried in Graceland Cemetery in Chicago.[220] She was only 53.

ALICE BLISS MOSELEY WILDER (1894-1978) AND FAMILY
(Alvin B. Moseley, Margaret Bliss Moseley, Margaret McDonald Bliss, William R. McDonald, Maj. Richard, Col. William, William MacDonel)

Alice Bliss Moseley, the only child of Alvin Bliss and Charlotte Louisa (Hinsdale) Moseley, was born on June 20, 1894, almost six months after her father's premature death.

Alice was raised in her grandmother Eliza Jane Hinsdale's house in Evanston. She completed three years of high school and married Emory Hurlbut Wilder, the son of John Emery and Laura Gertrude (Hurlbut) Wilder, on Feb. 21, 1920, in Winnetka, Cook County, Illinois.[221]

Emory was born on Mar. 24, 1889, in Oak Park, Cook County, Illinois.[222] He was a graduate of Princeton University in New Jersey.[223] He had been employed in the Wilder Tanning Factory as an assistant treasurer. He was of medium height and build with gray eyes and brown hair.[224] The 1930 census says he was a veteran of World War I.

Emory and Alice lived in New Trier, Cook County, Illinois, in 1930, and in Barrington, Cook County, in 1940. Emory was treasurer of an electrical manufacturing company in 1940. He was working for Canal Construction Co. when he registered for the draft in 1942.[225]

Emory died on Jan. 7, 1952, at the age of 62.[226] Alice died in June 1978 when she was 83.

Emory and Alice (Moseley) Wilder had two known children:
1. Deborah (1925-2000, m. Capt. Henry E. Cooke Jr.)
2. Phoebe Alice (1926-1998)

DEBORAH WILDER COOKE (1925-2000) AND FAMILY
(Alice Moseley Wilder, Alvin B., Margaret Bliss Moseley, Margaret McDonald Bliss, William R. McDonald, Maj. Richard, Col. William, William MacDonel)

Deborah Wilder, the eldest child of Emory Hurlbut and Alice Bliss (Moseley) Wilder, was born in Illinois on Jan. 6, 1925.[227] In 1946, she married World War II veteran, Capt. Henry E. "Hank" Cooke Jr., the son of Henry Eleutheros and Martha Weare (Hubbard) Cooke.[228]

Born in Geneva, Lake County, Illinois, on Jan. 7, 1921, Henry Jr. graduated from Lake Forest Academy in 1940. Before the war, he worked as a salesman for General American Transportation Corps.

He enlisted in the Army in 1942. After completing Officer Candidate School, he was stationed at Pearl Harbor in 1944. He fought in the Philippines and at Okinawa. A battery commander, promoted to captain, he was awarded the Bronze Star for helping to defend a unit of about 30 men under attack by the Japanese.[229]

After the war, Henry returned to his job and built a home in Barrington Hills, Lake County, Illinois. He and Deborah had two children: Martha "Muffy" and John.

In 1948, Henry went to work as a salesman for T. C. Industries Inc. in Crystal Lake, a job he held until his retirement as a vice president in 1993.[230]

Henry was very active in his community. He volunteered as a marshal for the volunteer police department and served as president of the Barrington Countryside Fire Protection District. He was also a Barrington Township trustee.

Deborah Wilder Cooke died on Aug. 6, 2000. She was 75.[231] Henry passed away on Mar. 29, 2004, in Barrington. He was 83. He was buried in the St. James Episcopal Church Cemetery in West Dundee, Kane County, Illinois.[232]

PHOEBE ALICE WILDER (1926-1998)

(Alice Moseley Wilder, Alvin B., Margaret Bliss Moseley, Margaret McDonald Bliss, William R. McDonald, Maj. Richard, Col. William, William MacDonel)

Phoebe Alice Wilder, the second child of Emory Hurlbut and Alice Bliss (Moseley) Wilder, was born Oct. 4, 1926, in Illinois. She died on Dec. 27, 1998, at the age of 72. Her last residence was in Chicago. Apparently, she never married.[233]

Chapter 3

WILLIAM M. AND JOANNA (AXFORD) MCDONALD
and Their Descendants

Great Great Grandparents: William and Florance MacDonel
Great Grandparents: Col. William McDonald and Unknown First Wife
Grandparents: Maj. Richard McDonald and Margrietje Schamp
Parents: William R. McDonald and Abigail Fowler

WILLIAM M. MCDONALD (1794-1856)
+ Joanna Axford (1799-1856)

1. Unknown Son (abt. 1818-aft. 1820)
2. Philo McDonald (1820-1899, m. Unknown McChestney, Lucinda Smith)
3. Theodore Frelinghuysen McDonald (1821-1914, m. Elizabeth Ann Jones)
4. Margaret A. McDonald (1823-1858, m. Hiram M. Jenney)
5. Benjamin Fowler McDonald (1825-1878, m. Marie Duncan, Phoebe Burt)
6. Ann Elizabeth McDonald (c. 1829-1849)

William M. McDonald, the fourth child of William R. and Abigail (Fowler) McDonald, was born on Mar. 16, 1794, probably in New York.[234] The middle initial "M" is questionable. There are only a few official documents that show William McDonald and none of them has a middle initial for him. The blueprint of Mayor John McDonald of Austin, Texas, and William C. Armstrong's *The Axfords of Oxford, New Jersey*, compiled in part from Axford family records, also show no middle initial for William.[235] William's gravestone, however, appears to read: W. M. McDonald.[236] For that reason, we are including the middle initial "M" for William. For purposes of convenience in the compiling of this book, that middle initial "M" will also help to differentiate him from all the other William McDonalds.

On Jan. 17, 1818, he married Joanna Axford in Sussex County, New Jersey.[237] Joanna was the daughter of Samuel Axford I (1760-1836) and Margaret McDonald (1762-1818).[238]

Joanna was born on May 23, 1799, in Oxford Township, Warren County, New Jersey.[239] Oxford, according to some sources, was named after Joanna's ancestor, John Axford, one of the town's earliest settlers.[240]

Very little is known of William M. and Joanna. The 1820 federal census for Norway, Herkimer County, New York, shows them living next to William's father, William R. McDonald. Both men were working in agriculture. In other words, they were farming. That census also shows that William M. and his wife had 2 young males under 10 years old living with them.[241] One of them had to be Philo, who was an infant at the time. The identity of the other son is unknown. He was probably William and Joanna's first child, born about late 1818 or early 1819. He must have died young as he doesn't appear in any other known records.

Joanna gave birth to two more children in New York: Theodore Frelinghuysen McDonald was born in Little Falls in Herkimer County, New York, in 1821, and Margaret A. McDonald was born in 1823.[242]

The family must have moved to Macomb County, Michigan by about 1825 when another son, Benjamin Fowler McDonald, was born. The last child, Ann Elizabeth McDonald, was born about 1829, probably in Macomb County, as well.

The 1850 census shows William was making his living as a farmer in Macomb, Macomb County. He and Joanna were in their fifties. Their sons, Theodore and Benjamin, were living with them and probably helping them out on the farm.

William and Joanna both died a few years later. They share a gravestone in Clinton Grove Cemetery, Clinton Township, Macomb County, Michigan. The inscriptions are hard to read, but it looks like William died in 1856 or 1858, when he was about 62 or 64. Joanna died in 1856 at the age of 56. Their daughter, Ann Elizabeth (Anna) McDonald, is also on the gravestone. She died in 1849, only about 20 years old.[243]

PHILO MCDONALD (1820-1899) AND FAMILY
(William M. McDonald, William R., Maj. Richard, Col. William, William MacDonel)

Philo McDonald, the eldest known child[244] of William M. and Joanna (Axford) McDonald, was born, according to a descendant, on Jan. 20, 1820, in Herkimer County, New York.[245] The 1850 census of Macomb, Macomb County, Michigan, confirms this, in part, showing Philo born about 1820 in New York. He was married to Lucinda at the time.

Furthermore, *The Axfords of Oxford, New Jersey* identifies Philo as the eldest child of William M. and Joanna, but it does not have a birth date for him and says only "Philo McDonald married Miss McChestney."[246] Who was Miss McChestney? She must have been a first wife who died young.

The fact that Philo was in Macomb, Michigan, in 1850, does indeed suggest that he is the correct Philo, son of William and Joanna, who were both buried in Macomb County. Philo was a farmer. He had two children at the time: Isabel and Lewis.

Lucinda, wife of Philo in 1850, had the maiden name Smith, according to Michigan marriage records.[247] Lucinda, the census shows, was born in New York about 1820.

The Philo McDonald family has not been located in the 1860 census. It could be that they were in Arkansas at the time as two of Philo's daughters, Frances and Kate, were born in Arkansas according to census records. Indeed there are land office records dated May 1, 1860, showing Philo McDonald of Randolph County, Arkansas, and certifying the purchase of land in Batesville, Randolph County, Arkansas.[248]

In 1870, the McDonalds were living in Oakland, Avon County, Michigan. Isabel and Lewis were no longer in the household. There were three other children present: Anna, Frances and Kate.

The 1880 census of Rich, Lapeer County, Michigan, shows Philo, Lucinda and daughter Katie living together. Philo was still working as a farmer.

Michigan Deaths and Burials Index says that Chilo [sic] McDonald, born about 1821, died Jan. 3, 1899, in Columbian [sic], Lapeer, Michigan, at age 78. The record, as transcribed, shows his parents as Samuel [sic] McDonald and Jane Axford. This must be the correct record even though the transcription appears to be in error on several points. The correct name of the town is Columbiaville.[249]

All in all, there is good reason to believe that Philo McDonald of Macomb and Lapeer counties is the same person as Philo McDonald, son of William M. and Joanna McDonald, that he was born about 1820 in New York, that he married Lucinda (Smith) and died in 1899, but if anyone has further documentation from family bibles or other sources, it would be most helpful if they could share it, so that the entire extended family could have more confidence in the accuracy of this lineage.

Little is known of three of Philo's children. Isabel (b. abt. 1843, MI) and Lewis (b. abt. 1845, MI) disappear after 1850. Anna (b. abt 1852, MI) disappears after 1870. The other two children, Frances and Kate, will be discussed below.

FRANCES MCDONALD GILBERT (c. 1861-bef. 1920) AND FAMILY
(Philo McDonald, William M., William R., Maj. Richard, Col. William, William MacDonel)

Frances McDonald, the fourth child of Philo and Lucinda McDonald, was born about 1861, probably in Arkansas. She married Charles S. Gilbert, the son of Sidney A. and Mary J. Gilbert, on Nov. 1, 1882, in Lapeer, Lapeer County, Michigan.[250] Gilbert was a farmer born in Michigan about 1863. They were living in Wells, Tuscola County, Michigan, in 1900, next door to Frances's sister, Katie McDonald McIntyre.[251]

By 1920, Charles was a widower with no occupation living in Caro, Tuscola County, Michigan. Nothing more is known of them.

KATE MCDONALD MCINTYRE WOODARD WAGNER CLARK (1863-1943) AND FAMILY
(Philo McDonald, William M., William R., Maj. Richard, Col. William, William MacDonel)

Kate (Katie) McDonald, the fifth child of Philo and Lucinda McDonald, was born Oct. 20, 1863, in Randolph County, Arkansas, according to the research and family files of descendant Deanna McIntyre Hester. Kate married Samuel David McIntyre, son of John Benjamin and Phebe Jane (Lawrence) McIntyre, on Apr. 21, 1881, in Rich, Lapeer County, Michigan.[252]

Samuel and Katie (McDonald) McIntyre had seven sons:
1. James McDonald (1881-1955, m. Martha Therese Bannucher Bullock)
2. Marion Orman (1883-1962, m. Esther C. Deming, Rhoda Jane Johnson)
3. Walter Edward (1885-1942, m. Laura M. Wobus)

4. Paul David (1887-1956, m. Ida Lupeke)
5. Earl (c. 1889-1889, died in infancy)
6. William (1891-1891, died in infancy, twin of Wallace)
7. Wallace (1891-1891, died in infancy, twin of William)

The last three children all died in infancy. Earl was born about 1889 and died Oct. 15,1889. The twins, William and Wallace, were born May 10, 1891. Wallace died Aug. 13, 1891, and William died Sep. 11, 1891, in Rich, Lapeer County, Michigan.[253]

Samuel and Katie divorced in 1900.[254] At which time, Katie was running the farm with her sons James, Walter and Paul and living next door to her sister, Frances McDonald Gilbert.[255]

Katie would marry three more times: first, to Loran Woodard, the son of Chauncey and Harriet (Farr) Woodard, on Nov. 7, 1904, in Caro, Tuscola County, Michigan; second, to Jacob S. Wagner, the son of Jacob and Catherine (Steller) Wagner on Oct. 19, 1926, in Flint, Genesee County, Michigan; and third, to Arthur D. Clark, the son of Robert and Laura (Pamperion) Clark, on Apr. 16, 1936, also in Flint.[256] There were no more children from any of these marriages.

The 1940 census shows Katie and her husband, Arthur Clark, living in Burton, Genessee County, Michigan. She had a 7th grade education and he had a 5th grade education. It wasn't uncommon in those days for people to have little schooling.

Katie died on Oct. 11, 1943, in Flint, Genessee County, Michigan, at the age of 79.[257]

JAMES MCDONALD MCINTYRE (1881-1955) AND FAMILY
(Kate McDonald McIntyre, Philo McDonald, William M., William R., Maj. Richard, Col. William, William MacDonel)

James McDonald McIntyre, the eldest child of Samuel David and Kate (McDonald) McIntyre, was born Dec. 29, 1881, in Rich, Lapeer County, Michigan.[258] James was living in his mother's household and working as a farm laborer in Wells, Tuscola County, Michigan, in 1900.

When he registered for the draft in World War I in 1918, and again in the 1920 census, he was working in a cafeteria in San Diego, San Diego County, California. He was tall and slender with black eyes and black hair.[259] The 1930 census indicates he was not a military veteran.

About 1921, when he was about 40 years old, James married Martha Therese Bannucher Bullock, the daughter of German immigrants, Peter and Amelia Bannucher. Martha was born in New York on Aug. 24, 1884.[260] She had several children including a daughter, Pearl Bullock, from a previous marriage to Charles R. Bullock.

In 1930, James, Martha, Pearl, and James's mother-in-law, Amelia Bannucher, were living in San Diego. James owned a house valued at $3000. He was a farmer and rancher.[261]

In 1940, James and Martha were still living in San Diego, but James was working independently as a tool sharpener. The census for that year also shows that he had completed one yea*r of high school and Martha had completed the eighth grade.

James McDonald McIntyre died in San Diego on June 3, 1955, at the age of 73.[262] His wife, Martha, passed on Aug. 27, 1965, aged 80. She was buried in Mount Hope Cemetery in San Diego.[263]

MARION ORMAN MCINTYRE (1883-1962) AND FAMILY
(Kate McDonald McIntyre, Philo McDonald, William M., William R., Maj. Richard, Col. William, William MacDonel)

Marion Orman McIntyre, the second child of Samuel David and Kate (McDonald) McIntyre, was born in Rich Township, Lapeer County, Michigan, on Aug. 13, 1883.[264]

He enlisted in the army in New York City on July 12, 1904, as a private in Co. F of the 6th Infantry Regiment.[265] He was stationed at Fort Abraham Lincoln in North Dakota. In 1905 and 1907 he was commended as a 1st Class Marksman. He served in the Philippines from Mar. 27, 1905 to Oct. 10, 1906 and was discharged from the service on July 11, 1907. His commanding officer wrote that Marion's service was "honest & faithful."[266]

On June 30, 1915, in Silverwood, Lapeer County, Michigan, he married Esther C. Deming, born 1894.[267] She died months later on Sept. 1, 1915, only 21 years of age.

Marion married again on his 34th birthday, Aug. 13, 1917, to Rhoda Jane Johnson, the daughter of English immigrants, John and Anna (Valentine) Johnson.[268] Rhoda was born in Lancashire, England, on June 6, 1896.[269] She was about 13 years younger than Marion. They both had 8th grade educations.

In 1918, Marion registered for the World War I draft and signed his middle name "Orman."[270] Working as a farmer at the time, he was 5'9" tall, slender, with brown eyes and brown hair. Photographs reveal he and his wife certainly made a handsome couple.

In 1920, Marion was working as a cook in a restaurant in Caro, Tuscola County, Michigan. By 1930, Marion was working in an automobile factory as a machinist in Burton, Genesee County, Michigan. His 1942 draft record states he was working for Chevrolet Motor Co. in Flint.[271]

Marion and Rhoda (Johnson) McIntyre had three children:
1. David Johnson (1918-1978, m. Robbie L. Pike)
2. Frances Annie (1920-1988, m. Robert A. Gerren)
3. Loy Earl (1928-2000, m. Loretha Elizabeth Fuller)

Marion died on May 8, 1962, in Flint.[272] He was 78. Rhoda passed on Apr. 21, 1970, in Colorado Springs, El Paso County, Colorado. She was 73. Both are buried in Rich Township Cemetery, Lapeer County, Michigan.[273]

DAVID JOHNSON MCINTYRE (1918-1978) AND FAMILY
(Marion O. McIntyre, Kate McDonald McIntyre, Philo McDonald, William M., William R., Maj. Richard, Col. William, William MacDonel)

David Johnson McIntyre, the eldest child of Marion Orman and Rhoda Jane (Johnson) McIntyre, was born Apr. 17, 1918, in Lapeer County, Michigan.[274] He was a U.S. Army World War II veteran.[275]

On Aug. 2, 1941, in Palm Beach County, Florida, he married Robbie Lucille Pike, the daughter of Edward Roy and Leona (Wooten) Pike. Robbie was born Nov. 3, 1912, in Weiner, Poinsett County, Arkansas.[276]

David and Robbie (Pike) McIntyre had three children:
1. Robbie Jo (Dec. 8, 1944-Dec. 9, 1944)
2. Bryan David (m. Rebecca Lane Deloy; child: Katherine Lee)
3. Allison Lucille (m. David Wallace; child: Heather)[277]

David's first marriage ended in divorce. He married, secondly, Mary McInroe, the daughter of Leo and Madge (Daniels) McInroe. They had two children:
1. Ellen Maureen (m. Allen Moates)
2. Paul David (m. Michelle Unknown)[278]

David Johnson McIntyre died on Sept. 26, 1978, in Sacramento County, California.[279] He was 60 years old.

FRANCES ANNIE MCINTYRE GERREN (1920-1988)
(Marion O. McIntyre, Kate McDonald McIntyre, Philo McDonald, William M., William R., Maj. Richard, Col. William, William MacDonel)

Frances Annie McIntyre, the second child of Marion Orman and Rhoda Jane (Johnson) McIntyre, was born Apr. 13, 1920, in Mayville, Tuscola County, Michigan.[280] She attended college and was working as an assistant in a doctor's office in 1940 in Burton, Genesee County, Michigan.

In 1941, she married Robert A. "Bob" Gerren, the son of Bert A. and Hazel Beatrice (Hicks) Gerren, on June 21, 1941, in Flint, Genesee County, Michigan.[281] Robert was born in Clare, Michigan, on Nov. 6, 1919.[282]

Robert enlisted for service in World War II on May 29, 1942. An Army Air Corps veteran, he flew B-24 bombers with the 464th Bomb Group, 777th Squadron, which was part of the Fifteenth Air Force in Italy from 1944 until the end of the war.

> The group was awarded two Distinguished Unit Citations for its strategic missions. The first was for leading the 55th Wing to hit an oil refinery and marshalling yard at Vienna on 8 July 1944, the second for hitting an oil refinery at Pardubice on 24 August 1944. The group also flew a number of tactical missions to support the ground troops. During the advance on Rome the group was one of ten B-24 groups that took part in a 17 May 1944 attack on the harbours at Piombion, San Stefano and Porto Ferraio on Elba as part of the campaign to prevent supplies from reaching the German front line. In August 1944 the group supported Operation Dragoon,

the invasion of the south of France. In March 1945 it attacked targets in the Balkans to support the advancing Russians, and in April 1945 it attacked German supply lines in the north of Italy to support the final attacks of the US Fifth and British Eighth Armies into the Po Valley.[283]

Robert A. Gerren was a true war hero who earned a Distinguished Flying Cross, two Purple Hearts, two Air Medals, a Good Conduct Medal and campaign medals for the Germany, American, and European-African-Middle Eastern theaters.[284] He was discharged Nov. 5, 1945.[285]

After the war, Robert worked as a general contractor for over 50 years.

Frances died on July 14, 1988, in Colorado Springs, El Paso County, Colorado, at the age of 68. Robert lived a quite a while longer. He died in Colorado Springs on May 31, 2009, at the age of 89.[286] He requested that there be no memorial services, "just happy memories."[287]

Robert and Frances (McIntyre) Gerren raised one son: Richard A. Gerren. Richard works as a research associate in the Aero-Bioserve Space Techs Department at the University of Colorado at Boulder.[288] Richard's wife, Dr. Donna S. Gerren, obtained her Ph.D. in Aerospace Engineering from the University of Kansas in 1995. She is a senior instructor in the Department of Aerospace Engineering Sciences at the University of Colorado, Boulder.[289]

SGT. LOY EARL MCINTYRE (1928-2000) AND FAMILY
(Marion O. McIntyre, Kate McDonald McIntyre, Philo McDonald, William M., William R., Maj. Richard, Col. William, William MacDonel)

Sgt. Loy Earl McIntyre, the third child of Marion Orman and Rhoda Jane (Johnson) McIntyre, was born June 20, 1928, in Burton, Genesee County, Michigan.[290]

Loy graduated from Lapeer High School in 1946. He served as a radioman in the U.S. Air Force in North Africa and Greece.[291]

On June 13, 1953, he married Loretha Elizabeth "Retha" Fuller at the West Vienna Methodist Church in Clio, Genesee County, Michigan.[292] They had several children together.

Sgt. McIntyre, or "Mac" as he was affectionately known, was a City of Flint Firefighter until he retired in 1981. He and Loretha lived in North Carolina for a while, then they moved to Frederic, Michigan, and finally to Shelby, Oceana County, Michigan, where Mac died on Feb. 8, 2000, at the age of 71.[293] He was buried in West Vienna Cemetery, Clio, Genesee County, Michigan.[294]

WALTER EDWARD MCINTYRE (1885-1942) AND FAMILY

(Kate McDonald McIntyre, Philo McDonald, William M., William R., Maj. Richard, Col. William,
  William MacDonel)

Walter Edward McIntyre, the third of seven sons of Samuel David and Kate (McDonald) McIntyre, was born on Apr. 13, 1885, in Lapeer Co., Michigan.[295] A handsome man, he stood 5'11" tall with blue eyes and brown hair. He married Laura M. Wobus (b. 1882) on Sept. 8, 1913, in Genesee County, Michigan.[296]

Walter was working as an axle assembler for Mott Co. when he registered for the draft in 1918.[297] In 1942, when he registered again for the draft, he was working for Buick Motor Division.

His wife, Laura, passed away on Aug. 30, 1938, in Flint, Genesee County, Michigan. She was 56. Walter followed her on May 13, 1942, also in Flint. He was 56.[298]

Walter and Laura had four children: Catherine Alga, Carl F., Neva Barbara and Clara Belle. Catherine Alga and Carl F. were fraternal twins born on Dec. 20, 1914. Catherine did not live to be one year old. She died on Nov. 18, 1915, in Flint.[299] Carl F. also was short-lived. He died on Apr. 12, 1923, at the age of 8.[300]

NEVA BARBARA MCINTYRE MIKESELL (1916-1961) AND FAMILY

(Walter E. McIntyre, Kate McDonald McIntyre, Philo McDonald, William M., William R., Maj. Richard,
  Col. William, William MacDonel)

Neva Barbara McIntyre, the third child of Walter Edward and Laura M. (Wobus) McIntyre, was born on Nov. 26, 1916, in Flint, Genesee County, Michigan. In 1940, she was living and working as an assistant matron at the American Legion Billet, a children's home in Otter Lake, Lapeer County, Michigan.

On Mar. 23, 1942, in Flint, Neva married Frederick Mikesell, the son of James and Estella (Ohman) Mikesell. He was born about 1914 in Streator, Illinois.[301] They had two children, but the marriage ended in divorce in 1944.[302]

Neva died on Oct. 17, 1961, in Pontiac, Oakland County, Michigan. She was only 44 years old.[303]

CLARA BELLE MCINTYRE SCHALKOFSKI DEITERING (1922-2001)

(Walter E. McIntyre, Kate McDonald McIntyre, Philo McDonald, William M., William R., Maj. Richard,
  Col. William, William MacDonel)

Clara Belle McIntyre, the fourth child of Walter Edward and Laura M. (Wobus) McIntyre, was born July 16, 1922, in Flint, Genesee County, Michigan.[304]

On Dec. 1, 1941, six days before the bombing of Pearl Harbor, she married Reinhold A. Schalkofski (1915-1973). The marriage ended in divorce in 1948.[305]

Clara Belle married a second time to Arnold Peter Deitering, the son of Andrew and Mary (Brandhoff) Deitering, on Oct. 10, 1949, in Flint.[306] Arnold was born Oct. 7, 1913, in Chesaning, Saginaw County, Michigan.

He died at the age of 80 on June 10, 1994, and was buried in Evergreen Cemetery, Grand Blanc, Genesee County, Michigan.[307]

Clara Belle passed away on Sept. 15, 2001, at the age of 79. Her last residence was in Burton, Genesee County, Michigan.[308] She, too, was buried in the Evergreen Cemetery in Grand Blanc.[309]

SGT. PAUL DAVID MCINTYRE (1887-1956)
(Kate McDonald McIntyre, Philo McDonald, William M., William R., Maj. Richard, Col. William, William MacDonel)

Paul David McIntyre, the fourth of seven sons of Samuel David and Kate (McDonald) McIntyre, was born June 24, 1887, in Mayville, Tuscola County, Michigan.[310] The 1940 census shows he completed the fifth grade.

He was living in Detroit, Wayne County, Michigan, and working as a machinist for Bowers Roller Bearing Co. when he registered for the draft. He was of medium height and build with brown eyes and dark brown hair.[311]

Paul served his country in World War I. He was a sergeant in the U.S. Army in the Mechanical Repair Shop Unit #329 Corps.[312]

On June 29, 1919, when he was about 32, Paul married Ida Lupeke (b. abt. 1890), the daughter of William and Bertha (Zuidler) Lupeke.[313] She completed the eighth grade. They did not have children.

Paul was a mechanic and tool grinder who worked in automobile manufacturing. In 1942, he was working for Chrysler Corporation.[314]

Paul died on June 2, 1956, in Los Angeles County, Californa, aged 68. He was buried in Oakdale Memorial Park, Glendora, Los Angeles County, California.[315] We don't know what happened to Ida for sure, but she may be the Ida McIntyre who was born Dec. 3, 1889, in Michigan, and died Aug. 4, 1977, in San Diego.[316]

<hr/>

THEODORE FRELINGHUYSEN MCDONALD (1821-1914) AND FAMILY
(William M. McDonald, William R., Maj. Richard, Col. William, William MacDonel)

Theodore Frelinghuysen McDonald, the second child of William M. and Joanna (Axford) McDonald, was born on July 30, 1821, either in Little Falls, Herkimer County, New York, or in Trenton, Mercer County, New Jersey.[317]

He was no doubt named after Theodore Frelinghuysen (1787-1862), the Attorney General of New Jersey in 1817, who was the son of Col. Frederick Frelinghuysen, the commanding officer of William M. McDonald's grandfather, Maj. Richard McDonald, during the Revolutionary War. That William M. McDonald would name his son after Theodore Frelinghuysen is telling. The Frelinghuysens and McDonalds must have maintained strong family connections over the years.

Col. Frederick Frelinghuysen, in his capacity as a lawyer, we recall from *A Revolutionary American Family,* served as a mentor to Col. George McDonald, William M. McDonald's famous uncle.

It would not be at all surprising if somehow William M. McDonald knew Theodore Frelinghuysen, who was seven years older, personally. In 1829, Frelinghuysen became a U.S. Senator. He is remembered in history as leading the opposition, along with Congressman Davy Crockett, to Andrew Jackson's Indian Removal Act of 1830. Theodore was prescient in his characterization of the legislation saying, "Let us beware how, by oppressive encroachments upon the sacred privileges of our Indian neighbors, we minister to the agonies of future remorse."[318] The Removal Act led to the forced expulsion of many Indian tribes to the West, including the Cherokee, the Seminole, the Chickasaw, the Creek and the Chocktaw as part of what would become known as "The Trail of Tears."

Theodore Frelinghuysen McDonald had a lot to live up to, thanks to his famous namesake. Unfortunately, we know very little about his life. One thing we can infer is that he valued education, as did his forefathers, evidenced by the fact that his children and their descendants were well educated.

In 1850, Theodore and his younger brother, Benjamin, were farming with his parents in Macomb, Macomb County, Michigan. Probably about a year or two later, he married Elizabeth Ann Jones, born Sept. 9, 1833, the daughter of James and Elizabeth Ann (Funnell) Jones.[319]

Theodore and Elizabeth (Jones) McDonald had four children:
1. James Henry (1853-1934, m. Martha Ireton, Martha Wells McLellan, Christine Jewell)
2. Anna Elizabeth (1854-1940, m. Dr. Edward Branford Gibson)
3. Deborah A. (1856-1940)
4. Flora (1859-1927, m. Dr. David Pierce)

Before the Civil War, in 1860, the family was living in Ray, Macomb County. Theodore was still farming. After the Civil War, by 1870, he had become a grocer in Ann Arbor, Washtenaw County, Michigan.

Theodore's wife, Elizabeth, died on Feb. 27, 1896, in Ann Arbor. She was 62. Theodore lived quite a while longer. He died, also in Ann Arbor, at the age of 92 on Jan. 12, 1914, of cancer of the esophagus. Both were buried in Meade Cemetery in Ann Arbor.[320]

JAMES HENRY MCDONALD (1853-1934) AND FAMILY
(Theodore F. McDonald, William M., William R., Maj. Richard, Col. William, William MacDonel)

James Henry McDonald, the eldest child of Theodore Frelinghuysen and Elizabeth Ann (Jones) McDonald, was born Feb. 14, 1853, in Macomb, Macomb County, Michigan. He was 5' 8" tall with blue eyes, a lawyer by profession.[321]

On July 8, 1889, in Detroit, Wayne County, Michigan, he married Martha Ireton, the daughter of Joseph and Elizabeth Ireton.[322] She was born in Detroit on June 18, 1858.[323]

On April 10, 1890, James and Martha's first child, William, died in infancy and was buried in Roseland Park Cemetery, in Berkley, Oakland County, Michigan.[324]

A little over a year later, Martha died in childbirth on July 14, 1891, in Detroit. She was only 33 years old. She, too, was laid to rest in Roseland Park Cemetery.[325] Her infant daughter, Martha Ireton McDonald, however, that same day took the first breath of life and survived.

James married again on Sept. 12, 1894, in Detroit, to Martha Wells McLellan, the daughter of Andrew and Mary A. (Hallock) McLellan.[326] She gave birth to three daughters:
1. Mary M. (1896-aft. 1945, m. Wilmer C. Harris)
2. Elizabeth Anne (1896-1978, m. Clark Drake Smith)
3. Margaret Axford (1899-aft. 1960, m. MacGregor Armstrong Parr)[327]

Martha McLellan McDonald, James's wife, did not live long either. She passed away on Aug. 19, 1900, in Detroit, at the age of 26.[328] She was buried in Roseland Park Cemetery.[329]

James took a third wife on May 18, 1904, in Detroit. She was Christine Jewell, born Oct. 18, 1876, in Detroit, the daughter of William Franklin and Margaret Gilmore (Brownlee) Jewell.[330]

James and Christine had no children together, but they did do some family traveling. Shortly after the marriage of their eldest daughter, Martha Ireton McDonald, they took their three youngest daughters, Mary, Elizabeth and Margaret, on a trip to Canada, sailing on the S.S. *Trinidad* from Quebec on July 25, 1913, arriving at the Port of New York on July 31, 1913.[331]

On Nov. 30, 1920, James and Christine applied for passports with plans to visit France, Italy and Great Britain for recreational and educational purposes.[332] It is not clear when they made the trip, but perhaps it was in 1924 when records show they sailed on the S.S. *Ausonia* from Liverpool on Feb. 9, arriving in New York on Feb. 19.[333]

James and Christine also sailed back and forth to San Juan, Puerto Rico, in 1926 and 1929.[334]

James Henry McDonald died on Jan. 14, 1934, at the age of 80. He was laid to rest with his first two wives in Roseland Park Cemetery in Berkley.[335] Christine (Jewell) McDonald died ten years later on Sept. 8, 1944, but her burial location is unknown.[336]

MARTHA IRETON MCDONALD LANCASHIRE (1891-1952) AND FAMILY
(James H. McDonald, Theodore F., William M., William R., Maj. Richard, Col. William, William MacDonel)

Martha Ireton McDonald, the eldest child of James Henry McDonald by his first wife, Martha Ireton, was born July 14, 1891, in Detroit, Wayne County, Michigan.[337]

On June 10, 1913, in Detroit, she married Herbert Winterton Lancashire, born May 17, 1888, in Detroit, the son of Lawrence and Josephine (Connor) Lancashire.[338] Herbert was tall and slender with gray eyes and light brown hair. He was an automobile dealer in Toledo, Lucas County, Ohio, when he registered for the draft in 1917. He remained in that business at least until 1930.[339]

In 1942, Herbert was working for Buckeye Brewing Co. in Toledo.[340]

Martha Ireton McDonald Lancashire died on Aug. 1, 1952, in Polk County, Florida. She was 61.[341] Herbert died in Toledo on July 14, 1972, at the age of 84.[342]

Herbert and Martha Ireton (McDonald) Lancashire had six children:
1. Martha (1914-1996, m. Robert L. DuPont)
2. Josephine McDonald (1916-2010, m. Henry M. Kutsche)
3. Elizabeth Meredith (1917-2009, m. Jay Clarence Stuckey Sr.)
4. Lawrence Henry (1918-1997, m. Florence L. Tallman)
5. Mary Margaret (1919-2002, m. George F. Alter)
6. Lucy W. (1926-2003, m. Unknown Smith)

MARTHA LANCASHIRE DUPONT (1914-1996) AND FAMILY
(Martha McDonald Lancashire, James H. McDonald, Theodore F., William M., William R., Maj. Richard, Col. William, William MacDonel)

Martha Lancashire, the eldest child of Herbert Winterton and Martha Ireton (McDonald) Lancashire, was born June 1, 1914, in Toledo, Lucas County, Ohio.[343] Martha attended two years of college. She married Robert L. DuPont, the son of William James DuPont, an automobile dealer, and his wife, Jennie Alice Mewhort.[344]

Robert L. DuPont was born in Ohio on Dec. 6, 1910.[345] He was an automobile salesman in 1930 and a tobacco salesman in 1940. He attended one year of college.[346]

Robert died on July 19, 1986, in DeKalb County, Georgia, at the age of 75.[347] Martha passed away at the age of 82 on Oct. 12, 1996, in Atlanta, DeKalb County, Georgia.[348]

Robert and Martha (Lancashire) DuPont had three children:
1. Robert L. Jr. (b. 1936)
2. Herbert Lancashire (b. 1938, m. Margaret Wright)
3. Dianne (b. 1946, m. Alan I. Sacks)[349]

DR. ROBERT L. DUPONT JR. (1936-Living) AND FAMILY
(Martha Lancashire Dupont, Martha McDonald Lancashire, James H. McDonald, Theodore F., William M., William R., Maj. Richard, Col. William, William MacDonel)

Robert L. DuPont Jr., the eldest child of Robert L. Sr. and Martha (Lancashire) DuPont, was born in Toledo, Lucas County, Ohio, on Mar. 25, 1936. He graduated from Emory University in 1958 and received his M.D. from Harvard Medical School in 1963.[350]

In the late 1960's and early 1970's, Robert was working with heroin addicts and methadone treatments in Washington, D.C. His work was so impressive that it got the attention of President Nixon's White House Deputy Assistant for Domestic Affairs, Bud Krogh, who appointed him Director of the Narcotics Treatment Administration from 1970-1973.[351]

Eventually, Robert became a national leader in the formation of our country's marijuana policy, drug policy and treatment. From 1973-1978, he was the first Director of the National Institute on Drug Abuse. During those same years, President Nixon appointed him the second White House Drug Czar.[352] Over the course of his career, Robert also served under Presidents Gerald Ford and Jimmy Carter.

Since 1980, Dr. DuPont has been Clinical Professor at the Georgetown University School of Medicine. He maintains a psychiatric practice for the treatment of addiction and anxiety disorders.[353] He also served as president for the Institute for Behavior and Health, Inc., in Rockville, Maryland.[354]

He has come to believe that marijuana is the most dangerous drug. "Early marijuana use is particularly dangerous," he says. "Research has shown that adults age 18 and older who first started using marijuana use at age 14 or younger were most likely to have abused or been dependent on illicit drugs in the past year."[355]

In an interview for PBS Frontline in 2000, Robert summed up his views on the effectiveness of our national drug policies:

> So to me, the game has always been reducing the levels of use. That is the objective... And so when I look at a drug policy, I ask, "Does it reduce use, or does it not reduce use?" That's the most important question. . . . And what's happened over this 30 years is that politicians have come and gone. Drug czars have come and gone... But the enduring problem we have is that we have a society that prides itself on diversity, prides itself on privacy, prides itself on individuals making decisions for themselves, and we are confronted with a drug problem that tends to be tremendously magnified in exactly that kind of environment. And the question is, how do we then create, for the first time in world history, a social response that respects the fundamental values of the society, and also is realistic about the nature of the drug problem?... I think the drug war is being won – not as well as it might be, and it's sure not a slam-dunk. But if you just look at the levels of use in the society, they have come down since 1985. And that's something people need to feel good about.

Dr. DuPont is the author of several books including *The Selfish Brain: Learning from Addiction* (1997), *Drug Testing in Treatment Settings* (2005), and *Drug Testing in Correctional Settings* (2005). In 1998, he collaborated with his two daughters, Elizabeth DuPont Spencer, MSW, and Caroline M. DuPont, M.D., to write *The Anxiety Cure: An Eight-Step Program for Getting Well.*

Dr. DuPont has also made frequent appearances on television as a health commentator for ABC's "Good Morning America."[356]

DR. HERBERT LANCASHIRE DUPONT (1938-Living) AND FAMILY

(Martha Lancashire Dupont, Martha McDonald Lancashire, James H. McDonald, Theodore F., William M., William R., Maj. Richard, Col. William, William MacDonel)

Herbert Lancashire "Burt" DuPont, the second child of Robert L. Sr. and Martha (Lancashire) DuPont, was born in Toledo, Lucas County, Ohio, on Nov. 12, 1938. He graduated from Ohio Wesleyan University in Delaware, Ohio, in 1961, and received his medical degree from Emory University in Atlanta in 1965. From 1965-1967, he was a resident at the University Minnesota Medical Center in Minneapolis. He married Margaret Wright on June 9, 1963.[357]

A Republican politically and a member of the Methodist Church, Herbert served his country as a lieutenant commander for the United States Navy from 1967-1969.[358]

Herbert has had a long and distinguished career as a medical educator and researcher, specializing in infectious diseases. From 1967-1969, he worked as an officer in the epidemic intelligence service for the Centers for Disease Control and Prevention in Atlanta, Georgia. From 1973-1978, he was professor and director of the Infectious Diseases Program & Clinical Microbiology at the University of Texas (UT) at Houston. Since 2000, he has served as UT's director of the Center for Infectious Diseases, School of Public Health.[359] He has also been an adjunct professor of the Internal Medicine Service at Baylor St. Luke's Medical Center as well as a clinical professor at Baylor College of Medicine in Houston.[360]

Herbert is the author of various medical books and was associate editor of *American Journal Epidemiology* from 1978-1981 and the *Journal of Infectious Diseases* from 1983-1988.[361]

JOSEPHINE MCDONALD LANCASHIRE KUTSCHE (1916-2010) AND FAMILY

(Martha McDonald Lancashire, James H. McDonald, Theodore F., William M., William R., Maj. Richard, Col. William, William MacDonel)

Josephine McDonald "Jo" Lancashire, the second child of Herbert Winterton and Martha Ireton (McDonald) Lancashire, was born on Jan. 8, 1916, in Toledo, Lucas County, Ohio.[362] She grew up in Maumee, Lucas County, near the Maumee River. When her family's boat exploded at the Toledo Yacht Club about 1926, Josephine heroically saved her youngest sister, Lucy, from drowning by pulling her out of the water.[363]

Josephine attended Hollins College and the University of Toledo. She met Henry Mattimoe Kutsche in a chemistry lab and the combination proved compatible. They were married in 1938 at St. Paul's Episcopal Church in Maumee, a union which endured for 53 years.[364]

Henry Kutsche was born in Toledo on Jan. 31, 1915. He graduated from the University of Toledo and served in the U.S. Army in World War II. He worked as a salesman for Dayton Rubber Manufacturing Co. in Dayton, Ohio, for a while. He also worked for AP Parts and was a partner in the Waller-Kutsche Insurance Agency for 12 years. In 1975, at the age of 60, he retired from the Ohio Department of Health. He was a member of the American Legion and Swanton Lodge 555 F&AM.[365]

Henry and his family lived in Swanton, Ohio, for 30 years.

Josephine McDonald Lancashire Kutsche became a cytotechnologist, i.e. someone who microscopically examines cells to determine if they are cancerous or have other abnormalities. She worked at Flower Hospital in Sylvania and also as a property manager.

Josephine was a loving and caring mother, whose baked cookies were the delight of her children and grandchildren. She enjoyed making quilts and afghans and loved researching the family history and genealogy.

Henry died on Mar. 31, 1991, at the age of 76. Josephine passed on Sept. 26, 2010, at Hospice of Northwest Ohio in Perrysburg, Wood County, Ohio. She was 94. She donated her body to the University of Toledo Medical Center.

Henry and Josephine (Lancashire) Kutsche had three children:
1. Henry M. "Hank" Jr. (m. Carol O'Meara)
2. Mary Louise (m. Charles Hurst)
3. James M. "Jamie" (m. Carol Unknown)

At the time of Josephine's passing in 2010, they also had eight grandchildren, seventeen great grandchildren and one great great grandchild.[366]

ELIZABETH MEREDITH LANCASHIRE STUCKEY (1917-2009) AND FAMILY
(Martha McDonald Lancashire, James H. McDonald, Theodore F., William M., William R., Maj. Richard, Col. William, William MacDonel)

Elizabeth Meredith "Bede" Lancashire, the third child of Herbert Winterton and Martha Ireton (McDonald) Lancashire, was born Feb. 5, 1917, in Toledo, Lucas County, Ohio.[367] She attended the University of Arizona in Tucson, joining the Alpha Chi Omega sorority and excelling in swimming as a member of the U. of A. Aquatic Mermaids. She met her husband Jay Clarence Stuckey at the University. Born on Sept. 24, 1916, in Jay County, Indiana, he was the son of Clarence and Grace (Pape) Stuckey. Jay and Elizabeth were married in 1939.[368]

Jay was the founder of Stuckey Insurance in Phoenix, which opened its doors in 1939, providing liability insurance particularly for the architect and for the engineering industry. The company eventually passed to Jay's son, Larry.[369]

Jay was the secretary-treasurer of the Valley Investment Company in 1951.[370]

Elizabeth, known as "Bede" to her family and friends, made her home in Phoenix and became very active in the community. She was involved with the Phoenix Little Theatre, the Trinity Cathedral Altar Guild and the Arizona Historical Society.

Jay and Elizabeth especially loved traveling. They converted a bus into a motor home and spent their summers exploring America, eventually visiting all 50 states. They also toured much of Canada and Mexico.

Most of all, Elizabeth enjoyed her family. She and Jay had four children: Jay Clarence Jr., Elizabeth, Larry and Grace.[371] Their son, Larry, is now president of Stuckey Insurance.

Jay Stuckey Sr. passed on Nov. 26, 2000, at the age of 84. Elizabeth lived to be 92. She passed on Apr. 7, 2009. Both were laid to rest in Greenwood Memory Lawn Cemetery in Phoenix. Maricopa County, Arizona.[372]

JAY CLARENCE STUCKEY JR. (1941-Living)
(Elizabeth Lancashire Stuckey, Martha McDonald Lancashire, James H. McDonald, Theodore F., William M., William R., Maj. Richard, Col. William, William MacDonel)

Jay Clarence Stuckey Jr. , the eldest child of Jay Clarence Sr. and Elizabeth Meredith (Lancashire) Stuckey, was born in 1941. He attended the James E. Rogers College of Law at the University of Arizona in Tucson. He was admitted to practice law in Arizona in 1964.[373] On Aug. 27, 1966, he married Mary Sue Samples (b. 1946).[374] Jay and his partner, Hamilton E. McRae III, formed the law firm Stuckey & McRae.[375]

LT. LAWRENCE HENRY LANCASHIRE (1918-1997) AND FAMILY
(Martha McDonald Lancashire, James H. McDonald, Theodore F., William M., William R., Maj. Richard, Col. William, William MacDonel)

Lawrence Henry "Larry" Lancashire, the fourth child of Herbert Winterton and Martha Ireton (McDonald) Lancashire, was born Apr. 20, 1918, in Toledo, Lucas County, Ohio.[376] He attended two years of college and about 1939 married Florence Lorraine Tallman, who was born on May 12, 1919, in Pontiac, Livingston County, Illinois. Lorraine was a high school graduate. Larry was working as an insurance salesman in 1940 before the war.

On Feb. 26, 1941, he enlisted for service in the army.[377] He became a 2nd lieutenant in the U.S. Army Air Corps assigned to the 8th Air Force, 93rd Bomb Group, 409th Bomb Squadron. Lawrence was the co-pilot of a B-24 Liberator or "Honky Tonk Gal," as dubbed by aviators.

On Aug. 1, 1943, Larry took off on a mission known as Operation Tidal Wave to bomb the oil refineries at Ploesti, Romania. To avoid radar detection, the bombers flew in low and released time-delayed bombs. Larry's plane must have encountered difficulties. They crash-landed the aircraft and must have felt lucky to have survived, but Larry and his fellow crew members were promptly captured as Prisoners of War.[378] Apparently they were sent to a German POW camp and later released.[379] One of the crew, Bombardier 1st Lt William H. Little, died of his wounds at a Romanian hospital.[380]

After the war, Larry decided to try his fortunes in the wilds of Alaska. He and his wife, Lorraine, and their three daughters, Martha, Lorraine and Abby, became homesteaders in Kenai. Life on the Alaskan frontier was not easy. Larry operated a cocktail lounge called Larry's Club in Kenai and the Maverick Saloon in Soldotna.

Lorraine, who had been a former model for Montgomery Ward, became very active in the community. She started and owned a travel agency and was the first mail route carrier in North Kenai. She also joined the Kenai

Art Guild, the Veterans of Foreign Wars, the Elks Club and served on the board of directors of the Kenai Community Library.

In 1954, a writer knocked on the cabin door, conducted an interview "about the city folks turned homesteaders" and featured Larry's family in an issue of *Better Homes & Gardens* (Feb. 1955).[381]

Lorraine, also known as "Rusty," helped in the effort to gain Alaska's statehood and was an alternate to the Constitutional Convention in 1955.[382] She must have been very proud when Alaska became the 49th state on Jan. 3, 1959.

Larry and Lorraine were married for 58 years. He died the day after Christmas, Dec. 26, 1997, at Soldotna, Kenai Peninsula, Alaska. He was 79 years old.[383] Lorraine passed away in Soldotna on Apr. 11, 2000, at the age of 80. They are survived by their daughters and their husbands: Martha and Donald Merry, Lorraine and David Mackstaller, and Abby and Harry Ala.[384]

MARY MARGARET LANCASHIRE ALTER (1919-2002) AND FAMILY
(Martha McDonald Lancashire, James H. McDonald, Theodore F., William M., William R., Maj. Richard, Col. William, William MacDonel)

Mary Margaret "Ta" Lancashire, the fifth child of Herbert Winterton and Martha Ireton (McDonald) Lancashire, was born in Ohio on July 9, 1919.[385] About 1947, she married George Frederick Alter, the son of Francis William and Edna Mariah (Hegley) Alter.[386]

George Frederick Alter was born on July 28, 1916.[387] He completed four years of college and was working as an accountant for a glass manufacturer in Toledo in 1940. He was a U.S. Army veteran of World War II, having enlisted on Aug. 5, 1941.[388] As an interesting side note, George Alter's first cousin was Karl Joseph Alter (1885-1977), Bishop of Toledo (1931-1950) and Archbishop of Cincinnati (1950-1969). Archbishop Alter High School in Dayton, Ohio, was named after him. Nancy McDonald, the wife of the author of this book, graduated from that school in 1972. Little did she know that her McDonald family was connected to Archbishop Alter.

Mary Margaret Lancashire Alter was president of Church Women United of Toledo.[389] Later she and George moved to St. Petersburg, Pinellas County, Florida. George died there in March 1984 at the age of 67. She died much later on Nov. 10, 2002, at the age of 83.[390]

George and Mary Margaret (Lancashire) Alter had five children:
1. George Frederick Jr. (m. Barbara Jeanne Lamale)
2. Charlie (m. Terry Teufel)
3. Connie (m. Bill Ramsey)
4. Katherine (m. Foster Lott)
5. Bill (m. Debbie Unknown)[391]

GEORGE FREDERICK "JEFF" ALTER JR. (1953-2015) AND FAMILY

(Mary Margaret Lancashire Alter, Martha McDonald Lancashire, James H. McDonald, Theodore F., William M., William R., Maj. Richard, Col. William, William MacDonel)

George Frederick "Jeff" Alter Jr. was born July 15, 1953, in Toledo, Lucas County, Ohio, the eldest child of George Frederick and Mary Margaret (Lancashire) Alter. Jeff, as he was best known, graduated from Bowsher High School in 1971 and went on to study at Ohio University in Athens, Athens County, Ohio. He moved to Boulder, Colorado, for a while, then returned to Toledo. He married Barbara Jeanne Lamale, who was born on Aug. 12, 1955.[392] They had two dogs, Corky and Ringo, that they dearly loved.

Jeff owned a house painting and remodeling business. Always the life of a party, Jeff really enjoyed his time on this Earth – fishing, hunting, cooking, live music (especially the Grateful Dead) and sports. His favorite teams were the Detroit Tigers, the Detroit Lions and the Ohio State Buckeyes.[393]

Barbara passed away on Sept. 20, 2003, in Toledo.[394] She was only 48. Jeff passed away much too soon as well on Feb. 19, 2015. He was 61. He will be sorely missed "by all his family and friends who dearly loved him."[395]

LUCY W. LANCASHIRE SMITH (1926-2003) AND FAMILY

(Martha McDonald Lancashire, James H. McDonald, Theodore F., William M., William R., Maj. Richard, Col. William, William MacDonel)

Lucy W. Lancashire, the youngest of six children of Herbert Winterton and Martha Ireton (McDonald) Lancashire, was born on Nov. 7, 1926, in Toledo, Lucas County, Ohio. When she was a very young child, her older sister, Josephine, saved her life from the dangerous waters of the Maumee River when the family boat exploded at the Toledo Yacht Club.[396]

Lucy attended four years of college. She died on Mar. 13, 2003, in Maumee, Lucas County, Ohio, at the age of 76. Her husband, Mr. Smith, whose first name is unknown, passed before she did.[397]

MARY M. MCDONALD HARRIS (1896-aft. 1945) AND FAMILY

(James H. McDonald, Theodore F., William M., William R., Maj. Richard, Col. William, William MacDonel)

Mary M. McDonald, the first child of James Henry McDonald by his second wife, Martha Wells McLellan, was born June 22, 1896, in Detroit, Wayne County, Michigan.[398] She was well-educated, attending four years of college.

On Dec. 27, 1919, in Detroit, she married Wilmer Carlyle Harris, the son of William Folwell and Isabel (Martin) Harris.[399] Born in Ovid, Michigan, on Oct. 6, 1881,[400] William was highly educated, completing eight years of higher education.[401] He was a professor of history who taught at various colleges, including Ohio University in Athens, Athens County, Ohio, in 1930. He stood 5'11" tall with grayish blue eyes and dark hair and was a veteran of World War I.[402]

Wilmer and Mary (McDonald) Harris had three children:
1. Elizabeth McDonald (1921-2007, m. Unknown Coggill)

2. Joseph Folwell (1926-2014, m. Hilda Unknown)
3. Charlotte (b. abt. 1928)

In 1942, Wilmer and Mary were farming in Pataskala, Licking County, Ohio.[403] By 1945, the family had moved to Pinellas County, Florida, where Wilmer was once again engaged in teaching.[404] Thereafter, Wilmer, Mary and daughter Charlotte disappear from the records.

ELIZABETH MCDONALD HARRIS COGGILL (1921-2007)
(Mary McDonald Harris, James H. McDonald, Theodore F., William M., William R., Maj. Richard, Col. William, William MacDonel)

Elizabeth McDonald Harris, the first child of Wilmer Carlyle and Mary M. (McDonald) Harris, was born Mar. 26, 1921, in Indianapolis, Marion County, Indiana. She completed four years of high school and married a Mr. Coggill. She died on Feb. 19, 2007, aged 85. Her last residence was Orono, Penobscot County, Maine.[405]

JOSEPH FOLWELL HARRIS (1926-2014) AND FAMILY
(Mary McDonald Harris, James H. McDonald, Theodore F., William M., William R., Maj. Richard, Col. William, William MacDonel)

Joseph Folwell "Joe" Harris, the second child of Wilmer Carlyle and Mary M. (McDonald) Harris, was born on Feb. 12, 1926, in Athens, Athens County, Ohio. Joe served his country in the Merchant Marines during World War II and in the U.S. Army during the Korean War. He was initially employed by the Taylor Forge and Pipe Works and later established his own businesses.

Joe and his wife, Hilda, had three sons: David, Jaime and Joseph Jr.

Joe passed away on Mar. 15, 2004, at the age of 88. His obituary said that he was a man who had led a very adventurous life and enjoyed sharing his many stories.[406] He was buried in Grand View Memorial Park in Pasadena, Harris County, Texas.[407]

ELIZABETH ANNE MCDONALD SMITH (C. 1897-1978) AND FAMILY
(James H. McDonald, Theodore F., William M., William R., Maj. Richard, Col. William, William MacDonel)

Elizabeth Anne McDonald, the second child of James Henry McDonald by his second wife, Martha Wells McLellan, was born Dec. 9, 1896 or 1897, in Detroit, Wayne County, Michigan.[408] Elizabeth attended the University of Michigan at Ann Arbor as did her husband, Clark Drake Smith,[409] who was born Jan. 22, 1895, in Detroit, the son of Luther and Clara (Jeffrey) Smith.[410] They were married Feb. 10, 1923, in Detroit.[411]

When Clark registered for the draft in 1917, he indicated that he had already enlisted in the Medical Reserve Corps. The 1930 census notes that he was a World War I veteran. He was of medium build with gray eyes and light brown hair. In 1917, he was working as the manager of a printing plant, by 1920 he was the manager of an auto factory. In 1930, he was an automobile salesman and in 1940 he was an accountant in private practice.

The 1920 census is interesting in that it shows there was a Clarence Eoff living in Clark's household. He was listed as a son of Clara Smith, and therefore a brother of Clark's. He may have been adopted. Readers of *A Revolutionary American Family* will recall that Jacob Eoff owned the first tavern in Pluckemin, Somerset County, New Jersey, and was well known to the McDonalds. It may be that Clarence was a descendant of Jacob.

Clark and Elizabeth Anne (McDonald) Smith had four children:
1. Christine McDonald (b. Mar. 11, 1924)
2. Sarah S. (b. abt. 1926)
3. Arthur M. (b. abt. 1929)
4. Elizabeth A. (b. abt. 1930)

Clark died on Apr. 1, 1977, in Detroit at the age of 82. Elizabeth died on June 23, 1978, in Detroit. She was 81.

MARGARET AXFORD MCDONALD PARR (1899-aft. 1960) AND FAMILY

(James H. McDonald, Theodore F., William M., William R., Maj. Richard, Col. William, William MacDonel)

Margaret Axford McDonald, the third child of James Henry McDonald by his second wife, Martha Wells McLellan, was born Jan. 4, 1899, in Detroit.[412] She attended the University of Michigan at Ann Arbor.[413] On July 7, 1923, she married MacGregor Armstrong Parr, the son of Irish immigrants, Georges and Mary Ann (Armstrong) Parr.[414]

MacGregor was born in Royal Oak, Oakland County, Michigan, on June 25, 1890.[415] In 1917, when he registered for the draft, he indicated that he had served as a private for nine months at Michigan Agriculture College, which later became Michigan State University. He was tall and slender with blue eyes and light hair. He was working as an adding machine inspector at that time.[416] In 1930, he was working for an oil company. In 1940, he was owner and manager of a food products manufacturing business and in 1942, he was involved in U.S. Army Ordnance.[417] He was the president of an electro-plating company at the time of his death.

Margaret was working as a supervisor of the food products business in 1940. Census records also tell us that MacGregor and Margaret were living in Shorewood, Milwaukee County, Wisconsin in 1930, and in Houston, Harris County, Texas, in 1940.

MacGregor died of lung cancer on Oct. 25, 1960, in Houston, at the age of 70.[418] He was buried in San Jacinto Memorial Park in Houston, Harris County, Texas.[419] Margaret survived him, but a record of her death has not been found.

MacGregor and Margaret (McDonald) Parr had two children, both born in Michigan:
1. James McDonald (b. abt. 1924)
2. MacGregor Armstrong II (b. July 31, 1925, m. Dorothy Lee Harmon)

MacGregor II had a son, MacGregor Armstrong III, born Jan. 6, 1953, in Houston, and died Oct. 18, 1992, aged 39.[420]

ANNA ELIZABETH MCDONALD GIBSON (1854-1940) AND FAMILY
(Theodore F. McDonald, William M., William R., Maj. Richard, Col. William, William MacDonel)

Anna Elizabeth McDonald, the second child of Theodore Frelinghuysen and Elizabeth Ann (Jones) McDonald, was born on Aug. 12, 1854, in Macomb County, Michigan.[421] She graduated from the University of Michigan at Ann Arbor in 1877 and became a teacher.[422] On Independence Day, July 4, 1887, she married Dr. Edward Branford Gibson, the son of Thomas and Ellen (Branford) Gibson. The father, Thomas Gibson, was born in Ireland in 1810 and emigrated to America in 1837.[423]

Born in Toronto, Ontario, Canada, on Dec. 12, 1845, Edward was a leading physician in Washtenaw County, Michigan, as well as a farmer and dairyman. He graduated from the University of Michigan's medical school in 1887, the same year he married Anna McDonald. Politically, Edward was a Republican. He was a member of the Methodist Episcopal Church, as well as the Royal Arch Masons, Washtenaw Chapter. He also served as Justice of the Peace.[424]

The good doctor's productive life ended on June 29, 1923, in Ann Arbor, Washtenaw County, Michigan, at the age of 77.[425] His wife, Anna Elizabeth, died on Apr. 14, 1940 in Detroit. She was 85. Both are buried in Forest Hill Cemetery, Ann Arbor.[426]

Dr. Edward Branford and Anna Elizabeth (McDonald) Gibson had six children:
1. Theodore Thomas (1888-1991, m. Helen Mar Kidd)
2. Helen Elizabeth (1889-1992, m. Unknown LaCroix, Edge Taylor Cope III)
3. Deborah McDonald (1891-1971)
4. Florence E. (1893-1965, m. Lloyd George Dowd Sr.)
5. Edward Branford Jr. (1895-1918)
6. Ann E. (1897-1946)

THEODORE THOMAS GIBSON (1888-1991) AND FAMILY
(Anna McDonald Gibson, Theodore F. McDonald, William M., William R., Maj. Richard, Col. William, William MacDonel)

Theodore Thomas Gibson, the eldest child of Dr. Edward Branford and Anna Elizabeth (McDonald) Gibson, was born on Mar. 26, 1888, in Detroit, Wayne County, Michigan, named no doubt after his maternal grandfather, Theodore Frelinghuysen McDonald.[427] Of medium height and build with gray eyes and brown hair, the handsome Theodore was working as a chemist for the Hooker Chemical Company in Niagara Falls, New York, when he registered for the draft in 1917. He had married Helen Mar Kidd, the daughter of Joseph and Ella (Hall) Kidd on Aug. 11, 1914, in Pontiac, Oakland County, Michigan.[428] They had two sons: James E. (b. abt. 1916) and Theodore Thomas Jr. (b. 1917).

In 1920, the family was living in University City, St. Louis County, Missouri, and by 1930, they had moved back to Pontiac, Michigan. Theodore had become a salesman in radio at that time and Helen was working as a saleslady in dry goods. In 1942, when he registered for the draft, Theodore and Helen were living in

Weathersfield, Hartford County, Connecticut. He was employed by G. D. Searle Co. of Skokie, Illinois, a pharmaceutical business founded in 1888.[429]

Helen Mar Kidd Gibson passed away on Apr. 6, 1987, in Los Angeles County, California. She was 96. Theodore lived even longer. He died at the incredible age of 103 on Oct. 3, 1991, in Los Angeles County.[430] He currently holds the record for being the longest-living descendant of Revolutionary War veteran Maj. Richard McDonald of Somerset County, New Jersey.

Theodore and Helen now rest peacefully in Davisburg Cemetery, Davisburg, Oakland County, Michigan.[431]

HELEN ELIZABETH GIBSON LACROIX COPE (1889-1992)
(Anna McDonald Gibson, Theodore F. McDonald, William M., William R., Maj. Richard, Col. William,
 William MacDonel)

Helen Elizabeth Gibson, the second child of Dr. Edward Branford and Anna Elizabeth (McDonald) Gibson, was born Nov. 2, 1889, in Detroit, Wayne County, Michigan.[432] She married a Mr. LaCroix, but nothing more is known about him. The marriage may have ended in divorce. When Helen was about 58 years old, she married Edge Taylor Cope III, the son of Jesse Kersey and Lucy (Ingram) Cope, on Nov. 1, 1947, in Detroit.[433]

Edge was born on Dec. 9, 1882, in West Chester, Chester County, Pennsylvania. When he registered for the draft in 1917, he was living in Washtenaw County, Michigan, and working as a district sales agent for Detroit Edison Co. He was of medium build, tall, with brown eyes and black hair.[434]

Edge and Helen took a cruise on the SS *Franconia* of the Cunard White Star Line, arriving in Liverpool, England, on June 22, 1950.[435]

Edge lived to be 91 years old. He passed on May 26, 1974, in Livonia, Wayne County, Michigan.[436] Helen's death has not been verified by any records, but the Fisher-Presnell family tree says she died in Connecticut on Apr. 5, 1992, at the age of 102.[437] She and her brother Theodore must have inherited a longevity gene!

DEBORAH MCDONALD GIBSON (1891-1971)
(Anna McDonald Gibson, Theodore F. McDonald, William M., William R., Maj. Richard, Col. William,
 William MacDonel)

Deborah McDonald Gibson, the third child of Dr. Edward Branford and Anna Elizabeth (McDonald) Gibson, was born in Port Austin, Huron County, Michigan, on Aug.22, 1891.[438] She graduated from the University of Michigan at Ann Arbor with the class of 1916, after which she received her M.A. from Columbia University in New York City.

Deborah became a teacher at Cass Technical High School in Detroit.[439] She never married. On Mar. 17, 1971, in Traverse City, Grand Traverse County, Michigan, she passed away at the age of 79.[440]

FLORENCE E. GIBSON DOWD (1893-1965) AND FAMILY
(Anna McDonald Gibson, Theodore F. McDonald, William M., William R., Maj. Richard, Col. William, William MacDonel)

Florence E. Gibson, the fourth child of Dr. Edward Branford and Anna Elizabeth (McDonald) Gibson, was born in September 1893 in Michigan.[441] She attended the University of Michigan and married Lloyd George Dowd, the son of George P. and Mary L. Dowd, on Nov. 1, 1919, in Ann Arbor, Washtenaw County, Michigan.[442]

Lloyd was born on Apr. 26, 1896, in Angelica, Allegany County, New York. He was working at Packard in Detroit, Michigan, when he registered for the draft in 1917. He was of medium height and build with gray eyes and light brown hair. He served overseas as a private in World War I from May 26, 1918 to May 14, 1919, in Battery C, 307th Field Artillery.[443]

By 1930, Lloyd and Florence had moved to West Almond, Allegany County, New York, and taken up farming. They had six children:
1. Lloyd George Jr. (1921-1988)
2. Edward Gibson (1922-2009, m. Frances Barnes, Elnora Vincent Jennings)
3. Walter Raymond (1929-1997)
4. Gerald (1936-1977)
5. George
6. Mary (m. Unknown Bryant)[444]

Florence passed away in 1965 in Angelica, aged 71.[445] Lloyd died in January 1977, aged 80. His last residence was in Angelica.[446]

LLOYD GEORGE DOWD JR. (1921-1988)
(Florence Gibson Dowd, Anna McDonald Gibson, Theodore F. McDonald, William M., William R., Maj. Richard, Col. William, William MacDonel)

Lloyd George Dowd Jr., the eldest child of Lloyd George and Florence (Gibson) Dowd, was born Feb. 26, 1921, in Ann Arbor, Michigan.[447] On Sept. 7, 1942, at Buffalo, New York, he enlisted for service in the U.S. Army in World War II. He was a machinist who had attended one year of college.[448] He served in the Army until Jan. 2, 1946. Lloyd Jr. died on Nov. 3, 1988, in Marion County, Florida, at the age of 67.[449]

EDWARD GIBSON DOWD (1922-2009) AND FAMILY
(Florence Gibson Dowd, Anna McDonald Gibson, Theodore F. McDonald, William M., William R., Maj. Richard, Col. William, William MacDonel)

Edward Gibson "Eddie" Dowd, the second child of Lloyd George and Florence (Gibson) Dowd, was born Nov. 27, 1922, in West Almond, Allegany County, New York.[450] He married 1) Frances Barnes (1928-1968) and 2) Elnora Vincent Jennings.

Eddie owned and operated his own insurance business. He was also a farmer and school bus driver in his later years for Angelica Central School. For 44 years, he served on the West Almond town board. He was a member of the Belfast United Methodist Church, the Chemung Valley Antique Car Club and the Birdsall Grange.

Eddie was the father of four children:
1. Robert Paul (1956-2002, m. Betty M. Green)
2. Deborah (m. Dan Ford)
3. James (m. Donielle Unknown)
4. William[451]

Eddie died on Aug. 20, 2009, in Angelica, Allegany County, New York, aged 86.[452] He was laid to rest in Until the Dawn Cemetery in Angelica.[453]

ROBERT PAUL DOWD (1956-2002) AND FAMILY
(Edward G. Dowd, Florence Gibson Dowd, Anna McDonald Gibson, Theodore F. McDonald, William M., William R., Maj. Richard, Col. William, William MacDonel)

Robert Paul "Bob" Dowd, the son of Edward Gibson and Frances (Barnes) Dowd, was born July 5, 1956, in Hornell, Steuben County, New York. On Feb. 25, 1979, he married Betty M. Green and had two sons, Robert Paul Jr. and Michael A.

Robert moved to Florida in 1989 and made his home in Brooksville, Hernando County. He was employed as a heavy equipment operator. He died in Brooksville on Dec. 11, 2002, at the age of 46.[454] He is buried in Until the Dawn Cemetery, Angelica, Allegany County, New York.[455]

WALTER RAYMOND DOWD (1929-1997) AND FAMILY
(Florence Gibson Dowd, Anna McDonald Gibson, Theodore F. McDonald, William M., William R., Maj. Richard, Col. William, William MacDonel)

Walter Raymond Dowd, the third child of Lloyd George and Florence (Gibson) Dowd, was born Feb. 22, 1929, in Angelica, Allegany County, New York.[456] He served as a Specialist 5 (SP5) for the U. S. Army in Korea and Vietnam from Sept. 30, 1947 until Dec. 31, 1966.[457]

Walter was a member of Russellville Masonic Lodge No. 17 F&AM, Eastern Star Lodge No. 64, Scottish Rite Mason Valley of Madisonville and Rizpah Shrine Temple.[458]

He had two daughters:
1. Rose (m. Unknown Rogers)
2. Donna (m. Unknown Clark)

Walter died on Dec. 13, 1997, in Lewisburg, Logan County, Kentucky, at the age of 68.[459] He was buried in Russellville Memorial Gardens, Russellville, Logan County, Kentucky.[460]

LT. EDWARD BRANFORD GIBSON JR. (1895-1918)

(Anna McDonald Gibson, Theodore F. McDonald, William M., William R., Maj. Richard, Col. William, William MacDonel)

Edward Branford Gibson Jr., the fifth child of Dr. Edward Branford and Anna Elizabeth (McDonald) Gibson, was born Oct. 20, 1895, in Port Austin, Huron County, Michigan. He graduated in 1917 from the University of Michigan at Ann Arbor and made his home in that city.

On Oct. 2, 1917, Edward enlisted for service in World War I. He was admitted to an Officers' Training School in Aviation and received a commission as a second lieutenant on Mar. 27, 1918.[461] He was assigned as a pilot to the 22nd Aero Squadron of the U.S. Army Flying Corps.

The 22nd Aero Squadron was a fighter group. Their job was to engage and eliminate enemy aircraft from the skies. The perilous encounters of these brave airmen, called "dogfights," are the stuff of legend today. The 22nd or "Shooting Stars," as they were known, also provided escort to bombardment squadrons over enemy territory and sometimes engaged in tactical bombing attacks on enemy forces.[462]

The 22nd was heavily engaged from August 6 to November 11 of 1918 as part of the St. Mihiel and Meuse-Argonne offensives. They conducted 956 sorties and 82 combats in 72 days of flying operations scoring 43 official victories with four of their own men killed, two taken prisoner and six missing in action.[463]

On Nov. 3, 1918, Edward Branford Gibson Jr. boarded his SPAD S.XIII, a French biplane fighter, for the very last time. His flight of six planes had completed their mission of bombing the town of Beaumont[464] and strafing the enemy 25 miles behind the German lines, when they were attacked by eighteen "notorious red-nose and checkerboard" Fokkers.[465] A vicious dogfight ensued with three German aircraft destroyed, but three American lieutenants were listed as missing. Later it was discovered that one of those men, Lt. George Tiffany, was taken prisoner. He was later returned. When he rejoined his comrades, he had plenty of stories to tell about his time in captivity. Another airman, Lt. Howard R. Clapp, was killed in the action. His body was never found.[466]

Lt. Norman M. Hullings was sent to investigate Lt. Gibson's disappearance. Fortunately, he was able to locate the body. He filed the following report:

> At Le Tanne (Dept of Ardennes) I found three American graves marked No. 1, No. 2, and No. 3. Grave No. 1 was marked with a wooden cross which read "1st Lt Aviator, name unknown." A bottle on the grave contained the following note: "Buried Nov 12, 1918. Man taken from aeroplane. No identifying tag left on man. Aeroplane SPAD ID No 200 SURE S 15254. Inside the man's shirt indistinctly marked E.B. Gibs." The note was returned to the bottle. About 1 KM west of Le Tanne on the south side of the railroad I found a crashed plane S. 15254, with squadron number 3, which I identified as the plane Lieutenant Gibson flew on the patrol from which he did not return. It was so badly crashed that I was unable to determine if the controls had been injured in flight. The fuselage and wings contained many bullet holes. Returned to the grave and placed an identifying tag, reading "2d Lieut Edw. B. Gibson, A.S. U.S.A, 22d Aero Squadron" on the wooden cross marking the grave, and left a note in the bottle on the grave saying I had identified the grave to contain Lt Gibson's body.[467]

Lt. Frank R. Tyndall, Edward Gibson's roommate and flight commander, wrote a letter to Edward's mother, Anna McDonald Gibson, informing her of her son's death.

> He was very highly thought of by the men of [the] squadron... It sounds trite and out of place [for] me to offer sympathy, but I feel I must assure you of that which, as his mother, you must feel that he was a man of such ideals, clean in mind and body and that he died the most glorious death that is possible for a man to die: killed in action in the ordinary performance of an extraordinarily hazardous duty. Nothing finer can be said of any man... and in the memory of his comrades of the squadron... he will rank very high among those who made the supreme sacrifice.[468]

On Nov. 11, 1918, the Armistice with Germany was signed ending the fighting in Western Europe – eight days too late for Edward. His remains were eventually relocated to the Meuse-Argonne American Cemetery, 55110 Romagne-sous-Montfaucon, France, Plot G, Row 24, Grave 26.[469]

ANN E. GIBSON (1897-1946)
(Anna McDonald Gibson, Theodore F. McDonald, William M., William R., Maj. Richard, Col. William, William MacDonel)

Ann E. Gibson, the sixth child of Dr. Edward Branford and Anna Elizabeth (McDonald) Gibson, was born Aug. 13, 1897, in Port Austin, Huron County, Michigan. Little is known about her. Apparently, she never married. She died on Apr. 23, 1946, in Farmington, Oakland County, Michigan, at the age of 48, and was buried in Forest Hill Cemetery in Ann Arbor.[470]

DEBORAH A. MCDONALD (1854-1940)
(Theodore F. McDonald, William M., William R., Maj. Richard, Col. William, William MacDonel)

Deborah A. McDonald, the third child of Theodore Frelinghuysen and Elizabeth Ann (Jones) McDonald, was born in Michigan in November 1856.[471] She was living with her father, Theodore F. McDonald, in Ann Arbor in both the 1900 and 1910 censuses. She was probably caring for him in his old age. He died on Jan. 12, 1914.

By 1920, Deborah had gone to live with her sister, Flora Pierce, and her family in St. Petersburg, Pinellas County, Florida. Many census records show her as "Debo," which may have been a nickname. Apparently, Deborah never married and died on Apr. 14, 1940, in Detroit, Wayne County, Michigan, aged 83.[472]

FLORA MCDONALD PIERCE (1859-1927)
(Theodore F. McDonald, William M., William R., Maj. Richard, Col. William, William MacDonel)

Flora McDonald, the third child of Theodore Frelinghuysen and Elizabeth Ann (Jones) McDonald, was born Jan. 1859 in Michigan.[473] She may have been named after Scottish heroine, Flora MacDonald, who helped Bonnie Prince Charlie flee Scotland after the disastrous Battle of Culloden in 1745.

About 1887, Flora married Dr. David Pierce, who was born Feb. 27, 1858, in Elizabeth, Allegheny County, Pennsylvania.[474] Apparently, they had no children. By 1920, they had moved to St. Petersburg, Pinellas County, Florida. Flora reportedly died in Pinellas County in 1927, aged 67.[475]

⟨※⟩

MARGARET A. MCDONALD JENNEY (1823-1858) AND FAMILY
(William M. McDonald, William R., Maj. Richard, Col. William, William MacDonel)

Margaret A. McDonald, the third child of William M. and Joanna (Axford) McDonald, was born in 1823, according to her gravestone, probably in New York.[476] She was probably named after her maternal grandmother, Margaret McDonald Axford. Her middle name could well be "Axford." On Mar. 15, 1843, in Macomb County, Michigan, she married Hiram M. Jenney, who was born in Vermont in 1818.[477]

Margaret McDonald Jenney died young, at age 35, in 1858.[478]

Hiram was a farmer. He and his family lived in Macomb, Macomb County, Michigan, through 1880. After Margaret died, Hiram married again, to a woman named Eliza. She was born in New York about 1822.

Hiram died at the age of 81 on Feb. 11, 1899, in Washington, Macomb County.[479] He and his first wife, Margaret McDonald Jenney, are buried in Clinton Grove Cemetery, Clinton Township, Macomb County, Michigan.[480]

Hiram and Margaret (McDonald) Jenney had five children:
1. Joanna (c. 1845-aft. 1860)[481]
2. Julia (1847-1943, m. Daniel L. Betts)
3. William Walter (1850-1905, m. Anna Trombley, May D.)
4. Leonard DeKalb (1854-aft. 1924, m. Emma Bottomly)
5. Harlan M. (1858-aft. 1930, m. Elva C. Hunt, Cora B. Phillips)

JULIA JENNEY BETTS (1847-1943) AND FAMILY
(Margaret McDonald Jenney, William M. McDonald, William R., Maj. Richard, Col. William,
 William MacDonel)

Julia Jenney, the second child of Hiram M. and Margaret A. (McDonald) Jenney, was born in 1847, in Macomb County, Michigan.[482] She married Daniel L. Betts, the son of Samuel Russell and Charity Betts, on May 12, 1870, in Chesterfield, Macomb County, Michigan.[483]

The name Betts may sound familiar to those who have read *A Revolutionary American Family.* Judge Jacob De Groot, the father-in-law of Col. George McDonald, Esq., owned a slave named Mammy Betts, who was said to have lived to the age of 115 years. It is believed that Jacob freed her before 1840, as the conscience and consciousness of Americans evolved in the 19th century. It would seem unlikely that Daniel L. Betts, husband of Julia Jenney, had any direct link to Mammy Betts, but a little searching on the Internet does reveal that there were Betts families in New Jersey early on.

Daniel L. Betts, the subject of this narrative, was a farmer. He and Julia had four sons:

1. Hiram Mason (1871-1941, m. Alice Parker)
2. Arthur (1874-1917, m. Maycie Van Dyke)
3. Robert Walter (1882-1956, m. Ada Belle Maddox)
4. Eugene Leonard (1883-1966, m. Hattie E. Kreger)

In 1880, the family was living in Prospect, Butler County, Kansas. By 1910, they had moved to Rochester, Thurston County, Washington. Daniel died there on June 15, 1920, at the age of 77.[484]

Julia Jenney Betts died on July 12, 1943, in Centralia, Lewis County, Washington, at the age of 96.[485] She and her husband were buried in Grand Mound Cemetery in Rochester, Washington.[486]

HIRAM MASON BETTS (1871-1941) AND FAMILY
(Julia Jenney Betts, Margaret McDonald Jenney, William M. McDonald, William R., Maj. Richard, Col.
  William, William MacDonel)

Census records show that Hiram Mason Betts was the eldest child of Daniel L. and Julia (Jenney) Betts. He was born Apr. 24, 1871, in Detroit, Wayne County, Michigan.[487]

Hiram completed the eighth grade and made his living as a farmer. In 1940, he was engaged in dairy farming.

Hiram married Alice Parker in 1899. She was born Aug. 22, 1868, in Indiana.[488] She had completed three years of high school. Hiram and Alice had two children: Edith E. (b. abt. 1902) and Rachel (b. 1904).

From 1900-1910, the family was living in Skookcumchuck, Lewis County, Washington. They had moved to Tallman, Linn County, Oregon, by 1930.

Hiram passed away on Jan. 22, 1941, in Lebanon, Linn County, Oregon, at the age of 69.[489] His wife followed a few years later on Aug. 31, 1944. She was 76. Both were buried in Willamette Memorial Park, Albany, Linn County, Oregon.[490]

RACHEL BETTS CONNET (1904-1993) AND FAMILY
(Hiram M. Betts, Julia Jenney Betts, Margaret McDonald Jenney, William M. McDonald, William R.,
  Maj. Richard, Col. William, William MacDonel)

Rachel Betts, the second of two daughters of Hiram Mason and Alice (Parker) Betts, was born on Aug. 4, 1904, in Centralia, Lewis County, Washington.[491] She completed two years of college. About 1924, she married Darwin Bardwell Connet, the son of John and Julia Connet.

Those who have read *A Revolutionary American Family* may recall that it was a man named John Connet who raced to the rescue of Rachel Betts's ancestor, Maj. Richard McDonald, in 1786, only to be brutally murdered by young Samuel McDonald in a fit of rage. Could these Connets somehow be related?

Darwin Bardwell Connet was born Jan. 29, 1900, in Seneca, Nemaha County, Kansas.[492] Tall and slender with blue eyes and brown hair, he attended the Oregon Agricultural College in Corvallis, Benton County, Oregon.[493] The institution was originally founded by Freemasons as Corvallis College and eventually became Oregon State University.[494]

Darwin became a teacher in the public schools in Coalinga, Fresno County, California, in 1930 and 1940. He and Rachel had three children:
1. John Hiram (1925-1996)
2. Robert J. (b. abt. 1930)
3. Paul Richard (b. 1931, m. Dorothy A. Denton)

The first child, John Hiram, was born in Honolulu, Hawaii, in October 1925, so it could be that Darwin and Rachel were living there at the time. On June 8, 1926, passenger records show that Darwin, Rachel and infant John sailed on the SS *Sonoma* from Honolulu to the Port of San Francisco, arriving on June 15.[495]

Darwin died on Oct. 30, 1979, in San Luis Obispo County, California, at age 79. Rachel, his wife, died on Apr. 12, 1993, in Fresno County, California. She was 88.[496]

Of Darwin and Rachel's children, not much is known about Robert J., who was born about 1930. John Hiram Connet, the eldest son, was born Oct. 21, 1925, in Honolulu. He died three years after his mother on Jan. 20, 1996, in San Luis Obispo County, at the age of 70.[497] The youngest son, Paul Richard Connet, was born June 3, 1931, in California.[498] He married Dorothy A. Denton in Orange County, California, on Dec. 21, 1974.[499]

ARTHUR BETTS (c. 1874-1917) AND FAMILY
(Julia Jenney Betts, Margaret McDonald Jenney, William M. McDonald, William R., Maj. Richard, Col. William, William MacDonel)

Census records show that Arthur Betts was the second child of Daniel L. and Julia (Jenney) Betts. His gravestone, which looks very new and was probably a replacement for an older stone, shows he was born in 1871.[500] Records prove that must be an error. Arthur's older brother, Hiram, was born on Apr. 24, 1871. Arthur couldn't have been born the same year. The best estimate for Arthur's true birth date would seem to come from the Kansas State census of Mar. 1, 1875, which says he was 1 year and 2 months old. We can conclude, then, that Arthur was born about January 1874.[501] When his son, Clarence Arthur, registered for the draft in 1918, he noted that his father (Arthur) was born in El Dorado, Butler County, Kansas.

Arthur married Maycie Van Dyke, the daughter of Edwin and Sarah Ann (Taylor) Van Dyke, on Christmas Eve, Dec. 24, 1895. She was born Oct. 9, 1876 in Franklinville, Cattaraugus County, New York.[502]

In 1900, Arthur was living in a boarding house in Skookcumchuck, Lewis County, Washington. He may have been looking for work; his brother Hiram was living in Skookcumchuck at that time. In any case, by 1910, Arthur and his family were living in Rochester, Thurston County, Washington. He was employed as a mail carrier for a rural delivery route.

Arthur died when he was only 43 years old on Apr. 18, 1917, in Centralia, Lewis County, Washington.[503] Maycie died at the age of 96 in Centralia on Jan. 30, 1973.[504] They were buried in Grand Mound Cemetery in Rochester, Thurston County.[505]

Arthur and Maycie (Van Dyke) Betts had nine children:
1. Clarence Arthur (1896-1988, m. Hilda May Brewer)
2. Julia Marion (b. 1897, m. George Thomas Morris)
3. Edwin Larue (1899-1927, m. Helen Powell)
4. Floyd Jasper (1901-1985, m. Maud Mildred Gordon)
5. Ida May (1903-2008, m. Leslie Nelson French)
6. Laura Belle (1905-1993, m. Emerson Twain Wyse, Unknown Ornstein)
7. Gladys Velma (b. 1908, m. Raymond Drake)
8. Leonard Robert (1910-1955, m. Virginia May)
9. Hilda Lucille (1915-1991, m. Robert F. Bowman)[506]

CLARENCE ARTHUR BETTS (1896-1988) AND FAMILY
(Arthur Betts, Julia Jenney Betts, Margaret McDonald Jenney, William M. McDonald, William R., Maj. Richard, Col. William, William MacDonel)

Clarence Arthur Betts, the eldest of nine children of Arthur and Maycie (Van Dyke) Betts, was born on Oct. 1, 1896, in Rochester, Thurston County, Washington.[507] On Nov. 29, 1916, he married Hilda May Brewer (b. Jan. 24, 1897), the daughter of Preston Colfax and Ida Maud (Morgan) Brewer.[508]

Clarence was working as a farmer when he registered for the draft in World War I. He was short in stature with blue eyes and brown hair.[509] When he registered for the World War II draft, he had his own trucking business in Rochester.

Clarence died on Apr. 10, 1988, it Tacoma, Pierce County, Washington, aged 91.[510] He and his wife, Hilda, who died Jan. 1, 1983, at the age of 85, are buried in Grand Mound Cemetery in Rochester.[511]

Clarence and Hilda May (Brewer) Betts had at least seven children including:
1. Ethel Margaret (1917-1939)
2. Dorothy Mae (1920-1938)
3. George Duane (1922-1990, m. Marie Susan Fleshman)
4. Maxine (b. abt. 1925)
5. Gladys M. (b. abt. 1927)
6. Arthur (b. abt. 1930)
7. Gerald (b. abt. 1934)[512]

GEORGE DUANE BETTS (1922-1990) AND FAMILY
(Clarence A. Betts, Julia Jenney Betts, Margaret McDonald Jenney, William M. McDonald, William R.,
 Maj. Richard, Col. William, William MacDonel)

George Duane Betts, the third child of Clarence Arthur and Hilda May (Brewer) Betts, was born on Apr. 5, 1922, in Rochester, Thurston County, Washington. He married Marie Susan Fleshman on June 30, 1940, in Lewis County, Washington.[513] Born Nov. 18, 1922, in Wallowa County, Oregon, Marie was the daughter of George Andrew and Cora Rowena (Williams) Fleshman.[514]

George served as a private in the U.S. Army Air Corps in World War II.[515] He and Marie had four children.[516]

George died at the age of 67 on Feb. 28, 1990, in Centralia, Lewis County, Washington, and was buried in Grand Mound Cemetery in Rochester.[517] According to relatives, Marie died on June 15, 2015, in Rochester.[518]

WILLIAM WALTER JENNEY (1850-1905) AND FAMILY
(Margaret McDonald Jenney, William M. McDonald, William R., Maj. Richard, Col. William,
 William MacDonel)

William Walter Jenney, the third child of Hiram M. and Margaret A. (McDonald) Jenney, was born about March 1850 in Michigan. He was six months old when the 1850 census was taken on Aug. 28, 1850.

William was a farmer. Probably about 1878, he married Anna Trombley (b. 1858), the daughter of Job and Anna Trombley.[519] They made their home in Macomb, Macomb County, Michigan.

William Walter and Anna (Trombley) Jenney had four children:
1. Anna B. (1877-1881)[520]
2. Robert Walter (1879-1956, m. Florence Sipperley Lawrence)
3. James William (1880-1971, m. Zay Sipperley)
4. Harry Lorenzo (1882-1966, m. Della Lomason)

Anna died at the age of 31 on Mar. 29, 1889.[521] Presumably not long after Anna died, William married for a second time to May D. (maiden name unknown).[522] They had two children together:
1. Henry Leroy (1893-1956)
2. Helen E. (1898-aft. 1930)

By 1900, William and his family were living in Bruce, Macomb County, Michigan. He was working as a florist at the time.

William died in Romeo, Macomb County, Michigan, on Apr. 2, 1905, at the age of 55.[523] He was buried in Romeo Cemetery in Romeo. After William's death, May moved to Detroit. She was the proprietor of a grocery store in 1910. She died in 1939 in Romeo at the age of 71, according to relatives.[524]

ROBERT WALTER JENNEY (1879-1956) AND FAMILY

(William W. Jenney, Margaret McDonald Jenney, William M. McDonald, William R., Maj. Richard,
 Col. William, William MacDonel)

Robert Walter Jenney, the second child of William Walter Jenney and his first wife, Anna Trombley, was born Mar. 20, 1879 in Mount Clemens, Macomb County, Michigan.[525] He received an 8th grade education and, when he was about 28 years old, married Florence Ella Sipperley Lawrence, on Dec. 11, 1907. She was the daughter of Erastus H. and Annette Mary (Everett) Sipperley, born on Mar. 26, 1872, in Rochester, Oakland Co., Michigan. The wedding took place in her hometown. Florence had been married previously (in 1895) to R. W. Lawrence.[526] She was a high school graduate.

Of medium build, tall, with light brown hair and dark brown eyes, photographs show Robert was a handsome fellow. In 1918, when he registered for the draft, he was working on his father-in-law's farm.

By 1930, Robert had moved to Corunna, Shiawassee County, Michigan. He was a salesman in a hardware store. By 1940, he was co-owner of the business.

Florence Ella Jenney died on Jan. 5, 1951, in Corunna. She was 78. Robert died on Apr. 6, 1956, at age 77. Both are buried in Mount Avon Cemetery in Rochester, Oakland County, Michigan.[527]

Robert and Florence (Sipperley) Jenney had two children:
1. Audrey Annette (1909-1970)
2. Russell William (1915-1983, m. Harriet Almina Pratt)

Audrey Annette Jenney never married. She graduated from high school and went into the employ of Old Corunna State Bank. She died in Michigan at age 60 and was buried in Mount Avon Cemetery beside her parents.[528]

RUSSELL WILLIAM JENNEY (1915-1983) AND FAMILY

(Robert W. Jenney, William W., Margaret McDonald Jenney, William M. McDonald, William R.,
 Maj. Richard, Col. William, William MacDonel)

Russell William Jenney, the second child of Robert Walter and Florence Ella (Sipperley) Jenney, was born on Aug. 27, 1915, in Rochester, Oakland County, Michigan. He graduated from high school and married Harriet Almina Pratt, the daughter of Jesse Irvin and Mabel Alta (Conn) Pratt.[529]

Russell and Harriet (Pratt) Jenney had two children:
1. Ronald (b. abt. 1939)
2. Donald James (1942-2005, m. Sarah L. Unknown)

By 1940, Russell and his family were living in Bucyrus, Crawford County, Ohio. He was working as a traveling hardware salesman.

Russell died in Bucyrus on May 20, 1983, at the age of 67. His wife, Harriet, passed on Oct. 30, 2008, also in Bucyrus.[530] She was 90. Both were buried in Oakwood Cemetery in Bucyrus.[531]

JAMES WILLIAM JENNEY (1880-1971)
(William W. Jenney, Margaret McDonald Jenney, William M. McDonald, William R., Maj. Richard,
  Col. William, William MacDonel)

James William Jenney, the third child of William Walter Jenney and his first wife, Anna Trombley, was born on July 31, 1880, in Macomb, Macomb County, Michigan.[532] On Sept. 30, 1916, in Rochester, Oakland County, Michigan, he married Zay Sipperley, the daughter of Erastus H. and Annette Mary (Everett) Sipperley.[533] Zay's sister, Florence, married James's brother, Robert, in 1907.

James was of medium build, tall, with gray eyes and light brown hair. He was working as a steamfitter for Ford Motor Co. in Detroit in 1918.[534]

James and Zay were living in Corunna, Shiawassee County, Michigan, in 1930. James was employed as a merchant for a hardware store at that time, probably the same business operated by his brother, Robert.

James died on Jan. 23, 1971, in Lansing, Ingham County, Michigan. He was 90 years old. His wife, Zay, also lived to the age of 90. She died on Apr. 4, 1975 in Corunna.[535] Both were buried in Mount Avon Cemetery, Rochester, Oakland County, Michigan.[536]

HARRY LORENZO JENNEY (1882-1966)
(William W. Jenney, Margaret McDonald Jenney, William M. McDonald, William R., Maj. Richard,
  Col. William, William MacDonel)

Harry Lorenzo Jenney, the fourth child of William Walter Jenney and his first wife, Anna Trombley, was born July 11, 1882, in Mount Clemens, Macomb County, Michigan.[537] He graduated from high school and became a drapery salesman and buyer. When he was about 44 years old, he married a teacher, 38-year-old Della Lomason, on Dec. 4, 1926, in Detroit, Wayne County, Michigan.[538] Born on July 8, 1888, in Rochester, Oakland County, Michigan, Della was the daughter of William J. and Henrietta (Tienken) Lomason,[539]

By 1940, Harry was working for the J. L. Hudson Company, a retail department store in Detroit. Della was working as a music teacher in a community center.[540] Della died on May 10, 1944, in Detroit, at the age of 55. Harry died in October 1966, also in Detroit.[541] He was 84. Both were buried in Mount Avon Cemetery in Rochester.[542]

SGT. HENRY LEROY JENNEY (1893-1956)
(William W. Jenney, Margaret McDonald Jenney, William M. McDonald, William R., Maj. Richard,
  Col. William, William MacDonel)

Henry Leroy Jenney, also shown as Hiram in early records, was the first child of William Walter Jenney and his second wife, May. He was born July 9, 1893, in Romeo, Macomb County, Michigan. Of medium build, tall, with blue eyes and brown hair, he noted on his World War I draft registration in 1917 that he had served for three years as a sergeant in the cavalry of the Michigan National Guard. He was a bookkeeper at Central Savings Bank at that time.[543]

Henry apparently never married and appears to have lived in Detroit, Wayne County, most of his life. He was an accountant for an auto manufacturer in 1930. He was unemployed and unable to work in 1940. When he registered for the draft in 1942, he was working for Checker Cab Co.

Henry died on May 18, 1956.[544] He was 62 years old.

HELEN E. JENNEY CAVANAGH (1898-aft. 1930) AND FAMILY
(William W. Jenney, Margaret McDonald Jenney, William M. McDonald, William R., Maj. Richard,
  Col. William, William MacDonel)

Helen E. Jenney, the second child of William Walter Jenney and his second wife, May, was born in Nov. 1898, perhaps in Bruce, Macomb County, Michigan, as that is where the family was living in the 1900 census. She was a stenographer at the time of her marriage to Ivan Cavanagh, the son of Daniel and Agnes (Stout) Cavanagh, on July 21, 1919, in Detroit, Wayne County, Michigan. Ivan was born Aug. 24, 1898, in Riverside, Missaukee County, Michigan. [545] He was an inspector of adding machines in 1920.

Ivan and Helen (Jenney) Cavanagh had two children:
  1. Bernice (b. abt. 1921, m. Joseph Paul Matweychek)
  2. Harold Alton (1924-2004, m. Patricia C. Unknown)

By 1930, the family was living in Ferndale, Oakland County, Michigan, and Ivan was working as a bus driver. The 1940 census shows Ivan and Harold living in Detroit. Ivan was a machine operator in automobile manufacturing. His wife was listed as Lena, born about 1893, in West Virginia. If accurate, she was probably a second spouse. That's all we know of them.

HAROLD ALTON CAVANAGH (1924-2004) AND FAMILY
(Helen Jenney Cavanagh, William W. Jenney, Margaret McDonald Jenney, William M. McDonald,
  William R., Maj. Richard, Col. William, William MacDonel)

Harold Alton "Harry" Cavanagh, the second child of Ivan and Helen (Jenney) Cavanagh, was born on Feb. 6, 1924, in Detroit, Wayne County, Michigan.[546] He attended Michigan Technological University in Houghton, Michigan. A Navy veteran of World War II, Harold worked as a marketing director and belonged to the Baptist Church. In retirement, he lived in Marion, Ocala County, Florida.[547]

Harold died at the age of 80 on July 9, 2004. He was buried in Oak Grove Cemetery, Coldwater, Branch County, Michigan.[548] He was survived by his wife Patricia, and sons, Brian and David.[549]

LEONARD DEKALB JENNEY (1854-aft. 1924) AND FAMILY
(Margaret McDonald Jenney, William M. McDonald, William R., Maj. Richard, Col. William,
  William MacDonel)

Leonard DeKalb Jenney, the fourth child of Hiram M. and Margaret A. (McDonald) Jenney, was born in April 1854 in Michigan according to the 1900 federal census. He married Emma Bottomly on Nov. 10, 1881, in Armada, Macomb County, Michigan.[550] She was born in Michigan in November 1854.

Leonard and his wife were living in Mount Clemens, Macon County, in 1900. Leonard was in the grocery business at that time. Previously, he had been a farmer. By 1910, they had moved to Greenfield, Wayne County, Michigan and Leonard was selling real estate. By 1924, the family had moved to Royal Oak, Oakland County. Leonard was still engaged in real estate.[551] Thereafter, they disappear from the records.

Leonard and Emma (Bottomly) Jenney had one daughter, Evelyn Jessie.

EVELYN JESSIE JENNEY MORGAN (1888-1969) AND FAMILY
(Leonard D. Jenney, Margaret McDonald Jenney, William M. McDonald, William R., Maj. Richard,
 Col. William, William MacDonel)

Evelyn Jessie Jenney, the only known child of Leonard DeKalb and Emma (Bottomly) Jenney, was born July 1, 1888, in Detroit, Wayne County, Michigan. She attended one year of college and was a teacher of music and drawing. She married Conly MacNeal Morgan, the son of Henry Culver and Mae (Renwick) Morgan, on Feb. 6, 1913, in Nueva Gerona, Isle of Pines, Cuba.[552]

Conly was born Sept. 15, 1890, in Cuba, Allegany County, New York.[553] He and his bride settled in his hometown after the wedding. A tall fellow, of medium build, with blue eyes and brown hair, Conly was a high-school graduate working as a clerk for the Cuba Knife Co. in 1917. By 1920, he was the company's secretary-treasurer. Evelyn Jessie was a church choir director that year.

Conly and Evelyn Jessie (Jenney) Morgan had three daughters:
1. Elizabeth R. (1913-2011, m. Reginald J. Richardson, Thomas C. Hower)
2. Ruth E. (b. abt. 1915)
3. Margaret (b. abt. 1923)

By 1930, the family had moved to Royal Oak, Oakland County, Michigan. Conly embarked on a second career as a clerk in a department store.

Conly died on June 25, 1954, at age 63.[554] His wife, Evelyn Jessie, passed on July 10, 1969, in Orange County, California.[555] Both are buried in Cuba Cemetery, Cuba, Allegany County, New York.[556]

ELIZABETH R. MORGAN RICHARDSON HOWER (1913-2011) AND FAMILY
(Evelyn Jenney Morgan, Leonard D. Jenney, Margaret McDonald Jenney, William M. McDonald, William R.,
 Maj. Richard, Col. William, William MacDonel)

Elizabeth R. "Betty" Morgan, the eldest of three daughters of Conly MacNeal and Evelyn Jessie (Jenney) Morgan, was born in New York on Dec. 11, 1913.[557] She completed two years of college and married Reginald J. Richardson on Aug. 24, 1931, in Pontiac, Oakland County, Michigan.[558] The marriage did not work out. They divorced on Dec. 27, 1932.[559]

Elizabeth married again on May 25, 1935, in Leoni, Jackson County, Michigan, to Thomas C. Hower, the son of Harry and Sara (Chester) Hower.[560] Thomas was born on Apr. 17, 1910, in Pittsburgh, Allegheny County, Pennsylvania.[561] They had a son, Thomas C. Hower Jr., born about 1939.

Thomas Hower Sr. was very well educated, completing 5 years or more of higher education. He was a petroleum engineer for the Shell Oil Company.

The family lived in Ann Arbor for a while and then moved to Wichita County, Texas, by 1940. They were living in Green Valley, Pima County, Arizona, when Thomas died on May 26, 1988, at the age of 78.[562] Elizabeth survived as a widow for many years. She passed on May 1, 2011, at the age of 97. Her last residence was in Spring Branch, Comal County, Texas, [563] Both are buried in Desert Lawn Memorial Park, Calimesa, Riverside County, California.[564]

THOMAS C. HOWER JR. (c. 1939-Living) AND FAMILY
(Elizabeth Morgan Hower, Evelyn Jenney Morgan, Leonard D. Jenney, Margaret McDonald Jenney,
  William M. McDonald, William R., Maj. Richard, Col. William, William MacDonel)

Thomas C. Hower Jr., the son of Thomas and Elizabeth (Morgan) Hower, was born in Kansas about 1939. He graduated from the University of Oklahoma in 1962 with a B.S. in chemical engineering and now works as a project manager for Hudson Engineering Corporation in Houston, Texas. He lived in Humble, Texas, with his wife, Joane, and four children: Melissa, Vickie, Chad and Kent.[565]

HARLAN M. JENNEY (1858-aft. 1930)
(Margaret McDonald Jenney, William M. McDonald, William R., Maj. Richard, Col. William,
  William MacDonel)

Harlan M. Jenney, the youngest of five children of Hiram M. and Margaret A. (McDonald) Jenney, was born about April 1858 in Mount Clemens, Macomb County, Michigan.[566]

Harlan (also spelled Harlen) was a farmer. When he was about 19 years old, he married Elva C. Hunt on June 7, 1887, in Romeo, Macomb County.[567] They had no children. They were living in Lenox, Macomb County, in 1900. By 1910, Harlan was still married, according to the census, but he and Elva were no longer living together. He was working in a lumber yard in Flint, Genesee County, Michigan. They probably divorced a short time later.

On Sept. 11, 1918, Harlan married a second wife, Cora B. Phillips Hoover, the daughter of Solomon and Margaret Jane (Todd) Phillips, in Kalamazoo, Kalamazoo County, Michigan.[568] Cora died a little over a year later on Nov. 12, 1919, at the age of 58.[569]

In 1930, Harlan was living in Portland, Ionia County, Michigan, and making his living as a farmer. He was 71 years old at the time. That is the last we know of him.

BENJAMIN FOWLER MCDONALD (1825-1878) AND FAMILY
(William M. McDonald, William R., Maj. Richard, Col. William, William MacDonel)

Benjamin Fowler McDonald, the fourth child of William M. and Joanna (Axford) McDonald, was born Sept. 12, 1825, in Macomb County, Michigan.[570]

In 1850, Benjamin was farming in Macomb. He married Marie Duncan, the daughter of Daniel and Sybil (Sheldon) Duncan, in 1852 in Oakland County, Michigan. Marie was born Dec. 2, 1835, in Macomb County. They had one child, Charles Sheldon McDonald, born on Oct. 2, 1853. Marie died on his birthday two years later, Oct. 2, 1855, in Rochester, Oakland County.[571] She was only 19 years old. She was laid to rest in Utica Cemetery, Utica, Macomb County, Michigan.[572]

About 1860, Benjamin married a second time to Phoebe Burt, the daughter of Albert and Harriet (Amsbry) Burt.[573] Phoebe was born about 1840 in Michigan.[574] They were living in Avon, Oakland County. Benjamin was farming. On Jan. 15, 1861, a daughter was born, Maria.

Benjamin was still farming in Avon in 1870. According to his son, Charles Sheldon McDonald, Benjamin died on Mar. 30, 1878, in Rochester, Oakland County, aged 52.[575] His gravestone shows he died Mar. 31, 1878, but *Michigan, Deaths and Burials Index* says that he died in Avon Apr. 18, 1878, at age 57 (born about 1821).[576] In any case, he was buried in Mount Avon Cemetery in Rochester.[577]

Benjamin's widow, Phoebe, had to carry on without him. In 1880, she and her daughter, Maria, were living in Avon. Maria was teaching school at the time. A 26-year-old farmer named Cyrenus Parker (b. abt. 1854) was living with them. It's not clear what their relationship was at the time, but Cyrenus (or Cyrene) would become Phoebe's second husband.[578]

Cyrenus was deceased by 1910, at which time Phoebe, widowed, was living with her daughter, Maria Harger, the wife of K. D. Harger. Phoebe apparently continued to live with the Hargers until her death at the age of 92 on Jan. 18, 1832, in Los Angeles County, California.[579] She and her Harger relatives now rest in Hollywood Forever Cemetery, Hollywood, Los Angeles County, California.[580]

CHARLES SHELDON MCDONALD (1853-1936)
(Benjamin F. McDonald, William M., William R., Maj. Richard, Col. William, William MacDonel)

Charles Sheldon McDonald, the only child born to Benjamin Fowler McDonald and his first wife, Marie Duncan, was born Oct. 2, 1853, in Ray, Macomb County, Michigan.[581] He studied law at the University of Michigan at Ann Arbor, graduating with the class of 1875.[582] He was a member of the Psi Upsilon fraternity. He then went to Germany to further his studies at the University of Göttingen. He became an attorney with law offices in the Hammond Building in Detroit.[583]

On July 11, 1900, in Detroit, when he was about 36 years old, Charles married 31-year-old Linda Harris, the daughter of Truman and Melissa (De Groff) Harris.[584] She was born June 5, 1859, in Michigan City, LaPorte County, Indiana.[585]

Charles and Linda must have done some traveling in Britain. They sailed from Liverpool, England, on the SS *Montclare* on Sept. 11, 1925, arriving in the Port of Quebec on Sept. 18,1925.[586]

Charles took great pride in his ancestry. He applied for membership in the Sons of the American Revolution (SAR) tracing his maternal line, Marie Duncan McDonald, through her mother Sybil Sheldon Duncan to Sybil's grandfather, William Whiting, who served as a private in the 8th regiment of the Connecticut Line. His regiment fought at the battles of Germantown and Monmouth.[587] Charles's ancestor, Maj. Richard McDonald, the evidence suggests, also fought at Monmouth.

It is curious that Charles did not trace his McDonald line to Maj. Richard McDonald of Somerset County, New Jersey. Certainly, you would think he would have done so if he knew about it. It seems likely that this important family legacy, sadly, was not handed down to him. This is not at all unusual. So many people do not take the time to discuss family history with their children. Many do not know who their grandparents are, much less their great grandparents or their great great grandparents. They grow up knowing very little about who they are and where they come from.

Charles Sheldon McDonald died in 1936 at the age of 82. He had no children. He was the last male to bear the surname McDonald in the line of Benjamin Fowler McDonald. Linda Harris McDonald, Charles's wife, died in 1949, aged 89. Both were buried in Mount Avon Cemetery, Rochester, Oakland County, Michigan.[588]

MARIA MCDONALD HARGER (1861-1937) AND FAMILY
(Benjamin F. McDonald, William M., William R., Maj. Richard, Col. William, William MacDonel)

Maria McDonald, the only child born to Benjamin Fowler McDonald and his second wife, Phoebe Burt, was born on Jan. 15, 1861, in Rochester, Oakland County, Michigan.[589] She graduated with the University of Michigan's class of 1887.[590] Two years later, on July 17, 1889, in Avon, Oakland County, she married K. D. Harger, the son of Joel P. and Harriet (Wyman) Harger.[591]

K. D. Harger was born on Dec. 8, 1856, in West Bloomfield, Oakland County, Michigan.[592] He was a lawyer, a graduate of the University of Michigan and the Kent College of Law in Chicago, Illinois. As a young man, he taught school in Michigan, Alabama and Iowa, and was employed for a while as the principal of a high school in Elgin, Illinois. In 1898, he and Maria moved to California, first settling in Perris, Riverside County. By 1910, they had moved to the city of Riverside. K. D. was a member of the Riverside bar for twenty years. He served as postmaster for Riverside, worked with titles for the Riverside Abstract Company and helped to organize the Peoples Trust & Savings Bank.[593]

Maria McDonald Harger was a schoolteacher. She and K.D. had two children:
1. Donald K. (1903-1994, m. Nino Brown)
2. Solon Burt (1905-1945, m. Unknown)

The younger son, Burt, would become famous in a most bizarre episode of American history.

K. D. Harger died on New Year's Day, Jan. 1, 1922, at the age of 65. His wife, Maria, passed several years later on Christmas Eve, Dec. 24, 1937. She was 76.[594] Both are buried in Hollywood Forever Cemetery in Hollywood, Los Angeles County, California.[595]

DONALD K. HARGER (1903-1994) AND FAMILY

(Maria McDonald Harger, Benjamin F. McDonald, William M., William R., Maj. Richard, Col. William, William MacDonel)

Donald K. Harger, the eldest son of K. D. and Maria (McDonald) Harger was born in California on Apr. 15, 1903.[596] He graduated with a degree in chemistry from Stanford University, Santa Clara County, California, in 1925.[597] About 1926, he married Nino Brown, born Oct. 31, 1886,[598] who was about 17 years older than he was and very well educated.[599]

Donald K. and Nino had a son, Donald Duncan Harger, born in Riverside, Riverside County, California, in 1928. In 1930, they were living in Hermosa Beach, Los Angeles County. Donald K. was a chemical engineer for an oil company.

By 1940, the family had moved to Inglewood, Los Angeles County, California. Donald K. was a management staff executive for an oil refinery. His brother, Burt, a well-known entertainer, was living with them at the time.

Nino Brown Harger died on May 12, 1947, at the age of 60.[600] Donald K. Harger survived her by almost 50 years. He died on Nov. 13, 1994, at the age of 91. His last residence was Santa Barbara, Santa Barbara County, California.[601]

DONALD DUNCAN HARGER (1928-2014) AND FAMILY

(Donald K. Harger, Maria McDonald Harger, Benjamin F. McDonald, William M., William R., Maj. Richard, Col. William, William MacDonel)

Donald Duncan "Deke" Harger, son of Donald K. and Nino (Brown) Harger, was born Mar. 7, 1928, in Riverside, Riverside County, California.[602] He graduated from Stanford University in 1949 and earned his Master's degree there in 1950.

Deke, as he was known to family and friends, enlisted in the U.S. Navy. He attended Officer Candidate School and became an intelligence officer. He was assigned to service in Kodiak, Alaska. After he concluded his active service, he continued in the Naval Reserve intelligence program retiring as a commander.[603]

On Dec. 21, 1968, Deke married Margaret S. Bruns in San Mateo County, California.[604] They had two children: Christina and Charlie.

Deke made his living as a science teacher. He taught three years of middle school in Ventura, California, and another thirty years at Burlingame High School in Burlingame, San Mateo County, California. Deke specialized in biology and Earth science. He was particularly interested in instilling a love of nature in his students, encouraging them to conserve and protect our natural resources. He took them on field trips to various wilderness areas in California. Deke himself loved to backpack in the mountains. He remembered with fondness how his parents often took him on horse camping trips from year to year.

Upon his retirement, the BHS faculty presented Deke with Daisy the dog, who became one of the loves of his life.

Deke was also a man of faith. He attended St. Paul's Episcopal Church in Burlingame.

> Deke taught Bible classes and conducted a series of seminars that are remembered to this day. He helped with the St. Paul's rummage sale, trained new acolytes, was a frequent cupbearer and lector, and was in the church choir for many years. Deke was a deeply religious man, but did not wear his beliefs on his sleeve. Rather, he showed them by the way he lived: with kindness, care, and generosity.[605]

Deke had many varied interests. He loved gardening, reading, singing, and playing guitar and piano. He volunteered his time to Traveler's Aid at the San Francisco airport and helped transport elderly patients to their doctor appointments.[606]

After a long and fulfilling life, Deke passed away from complications of Parkinson's Disease at the age of 85 on Jan. 21, 2014. His obituary said of him:

> All who knew Deke appreciated his unique sense of humor: droll, clever, and sometimes just plain silly. He will be remembered as a loving, humorous, and considerate man, and will be missed greatly.[607]

He was survived by his wife, Marge, his two children, Christina and Charlie, and his grandchildren Caroline, Charlie and Phoebe.

SOLON BURT HARGER (1905-1945)

(Maria McDonald Harger, Benjamin F. McDonald, William M., William R., Maj. Richard, Col. William, William MacDonel)

Solon Burt Harger, the second son of K. D. and Maria (McDonald) Harger, was destined for a tragic end no one could have foreseen when he was born on Oct. 13, 1905.[608] His unusual name came from his great uncle, Solon Burt, the brother of his grandmother Phoebe Burt McDonald Parker. In fact, grandmother Phoebe lived with the Hargers as he was growing up. She died in 1932 at the age of 92.

As a youth, Burt Harger, as he became known, demonstrated a unique ability for ballet and other forms of dance. He began entering – and winning – dance competitions.

He went to seek his fortune in New York City as a young adult and soon achieved local fame as an adagio dancer in the ballrooms of the Big Apple, partnering first with Helen Howell and then with Charlotte Maye. The adagio involves acrobatic poses and balancing movements. Burt, as the stronger and heavier of the two dancers, would act as the base, maintaining contact with the floor, while his partner, the flier, would assume various balancing positions on his hands, feet, shoulders, knees, thighs, back, etc.

Burt apparently enjoyed his greatest success from the late twenties to the early 1940's. He appeared in "Merry-Go-Round," a musical comedy revue in 1927 and "Just a Minute," a musical in two acts, in 1928.[609]

He must have gone back to the west coast for a time, perhaps to seek out some Hollywood film opportunities. The 1940 census shows he was living with his brother Donald and his family in Inglewood, Los Angeles County, California. Burt was back in New York in 1943 and 1944 performing in "Early to Bed," a musical comedy at the Broadhurst Theatre on Broadway.[610]

On Aug. 19, 1945, Burt was scheduled to appear for a performance at the Biltmore Hotel. He never showed up. His dance partner, Charlotte Maye, notified the authorities that he was missing. The police were baffled until a dismembered, "tanned and well-developed" torso was found floating off Rockaway Point on Aug. 21.[611] An arm and a leg were fished out of the Hudson River. The remains were identified as Burt's.[612]

Soon the headlines flashed across the entire country spreading the news of the "Torso Murder Case." Finally, police were able to solve the crime. They interrogated Harger's roommate, Walter H. Dahl Jr. He admitted that he had killed Burt with a hammer during an argument, but he claimed it was self-defense. Then he set about dismembering the body in the bathtub. He wrapped the various parts in towels and transported them one at a time to the Staten Island and Weehawken ferries, where he surreptitiously dumped the remains overboard.[613]

Charged with murder, Dahl pleaded guilty to manslaughter and was sentenced to 10 to 20 years. He died in prison three years later. Eventually, the full story came to light as investigators of the case revealed further details in writing their memoirs in later years. Dahl and Harger had been more than roommates – they were lovers. On that fateful evening in August 1945, Burt told Dahl that he was engaged to be married to a woman.[614] Dahl flew into a jealous rage and hammered him to death.[615]

The next tenant to live in the vacated Harger-Dahl apartment (43 West 46 St., NYC)[616] was a young playwright named Ken Parker. He was so fascinated by the story that it inspired him to write a play, initially titled *Four Flights Up*, and later renamed *There's Always a Murder*. The play was originally produced and directed by Parker himself. It opened on Jan. 6, 1948, in the Provincetown Playhouse in New York City, and is still occasionally produced by theatre companies today.[617]

Burt Harger's macabre and untimely death apparently occurred early in the morning of Aug. 20, 1945.[618] He now rests with his parents in Hollywood Forever Cemetery in Hollywood, California. Many famous show-biz celebrities are also interred there including Don Adams (1923-2005), Mel Blanc (1908-1989), Cecil B. DeMille (1881-1959), Peter Finch (1912-1977), John Huston (1906-1987), Peter Lorre (1904-1964), Hattie McDaniel (1895-1952), Darrin McGavin (1922-2006); Tyrone Power (1914-1958), Carl Switzer, aka Alfalfa of *Our Gang* (1927-1959) and Rudolph Valentino (1895-1926), just to name a few.

Chapter 4

PHILO FOWLER AND THIRZA (SPENCER) MCDONALD
and Their Descendants

Great Great Grandparents: William and Florance MacDonel
Great Grandparents: Col. William McDonald and Unknown First Wife
Grandparents: Maj. Richard McDonald and Margrietje Schamp
Parents: William R. McDonald and Abigail Fowler

PHILO FOWLER MCDONALD (1800-c. 1854)
+ Thirza Spencer (c. 1804-1846)

1. Harriet McDonald (1827-1872, m. Herbert W. McCrory)
2. William McDonald (1830-1912, m. Eliza D. Kent)
3. John McDonald (1834-1913, m. Ellen C. Kent)
4. Amos McDonald (1838-aft. 1850)
5. Philo McDonald (1841-1863)
6. Newell McDonald (1845-1899)

Philo Fowler McDonald, the seventh child of William R. and Abigail (Fowler) McDonald, was born on Oct. 14, 1800, possibly in Massachusetts.[619] He may have been named after his maternal grandfather.[620]

The blueprint of Philo Fowler McDonald's son, Mayor John McDonald (1834-1913), states that "Philo Fowler McDonald was a pioneer in the dairy business" in Herkimer County, New York.

Family Sketches of Ohio, Herkimer County, NY, says that Philo settled in Gray, Herkimer County, New York, in 1818. He built a sawmill on the north bank of Black Creek, carrying on the traditions of his McDonald ancestors whose McDonalds/Klines sawmill still stands in Bedminster, Somerset County, New Jersey, today.[621]

The 1840 census shows Philo living in the town of Ohio in Herkimer County. Named after the state of Ohio, the town had a population of 1002 in 2010.[622]

There is also evidence that Philo F. McDonald served as an ensign in the 8th Infantry Regiment, 21st Brigade, 13th Division of the New York Militia.[623]

On Jan. 4, 1827, probably in Herkimer County, New York, Philo married Thirza Spencer, the daughter of John and Nancy (Carr) Spencer.[624] Thirza was descended from the immigrant, Michael Spencer, through his son, John Spencer (1638-1684), who settled in East Greenwich, Kent County, Rhode Island.[625] Michael came to America in the early 1630's and settled in Massachusetts.

Sometime before 1841, Philo and Thirza relocated to the state of Ohio.[626] The 1850 federal census shows Philo and his children were living in Russell Township in Geauga County, Ohio. Russell Township had officially formed a few years before in 1827.

> In that same period, settlement was occurring in the southwest corner of Russell along the Chagrin River. Several mills began to flourish here, harnessing the power of the beautiful river. A new village took form around the rushing rapids, and through the 1830s, Chagrin Falls took shape. Great wealth was attained here by proprietors, investors and landowners. In 1840-41, land was officially set aside to form Chagrin Falls township.[627]

No doubt Philo was one of those who took advantage of the burgeoning opportunities in Russell. The 1850 census shows he was a farmer, but given his background, it seems likely he may have been involved in the mill business as well.[628]

Philo's wife, Thirza, died in 1846. She was buried in Grove Hill Cemetery, Chagrin Falls, Cuyahoga County, Ohio.[629] She was only about 42 years old. Not long after, Philo Fowler McDonald himself died – about 1854.[630] He was only about 53 years old. Philo's burial location is unknown.

Philo Fowler and Thirza (Spencer) McDonald had six known children: one daughter, Harriet, and five sons, William, John, Amos, Philo and Newell. Amos disappears from the records after 1850; he probably died young. Philo and Newell died without issue. Only the line of Philo Fowler's son, John, has any known living male descendants who still carry the surname McDonald. In fact, John's line is the only descendant branch of the entire William R. and Abigail (Fowler) branch of the McDonald tree that still has living descendants with the surname McDonald.

HARRIET MCDONALD MCCRORY (1827-1872) AND FAMILY
(Philo F. McDonald, William R., Maj. Richard, Col. William, William MacDonel)

Harriet McDonald, the eldest child of Philo Fowler and Thirza (Spencer) McDonald, was born Nov. 11, 1827, in Herkimer County, New York.[631] She was living with her family in Russell, Geauga County, Ohio, in 1850. After her father, Philo, died about 1854, Harriet and her four brothers, William, John, Philo and Newell headed out west to Wright County, Minnesota. Minnesota had become a territory in 1849. Wright County was established on Feb. 20, 1855. It must have been an exciting time for eager pioneers who were looking to establish themselves there.

Also in 1855, the first sheriff of Wright County was appointed at the first board of commissioners meeting in Monticello. His name was Herbert W. McCrory. He served for three months, then resigned to take the position of county commissioner.[632]

On May 1, 1856, in Clearwater, Wright County, Minnesota, Harriet married the former sheriff, Herbert W. McCrory. It was the first marriage officially recorded with the clerk of court for Wright County. The ceremony was conducted by Justice of the Peace, Samuel Wilder. The witnesses were William McDonald, Harriet's brother, and Frederick M. Cadwell.[633]

Born in New York in May 1824, Herbert was the son of Irish immigrant William G. McCrory and his wife, Esther Ormsbee.[634] By 1857, Harriet's brother, Newell McDonald, was living with the newlywed couple, probably helping them out on their farm.[635]

Herbert and Harriet's only child, Adelaide A. McCrory, was born in 1859 in Wright County, probably in Clearwater. Herbert was farming. Newell McDonald was still living with them.[636]

By 1870, the McCrorys had moved to Fawn Creek, Montgomery County, Kansas. On Mar. 12, 1872, Harriet died at the age of 44. Her husband, Herbert, died less than two years later on Feb. 3, 1874, at the age of 49. Both of these death dates were recorded in the Mayor John McDonald family blueprint, which presumably came from the family bibles.

ADELAIDE A. MCCRORY (1859-1931)
(Harriet McDonald McCrory, Philo F. McDonald, William R., Maj. Richard, Col. William,
 William MacDonel)

Adelaide A. "Addie" McCrory, the only child of Herbert W. and Harriet (McDonald) McCrory, was born Apr. 29, 1859, in Minnesota, probably Wright County.[637] She moved with her parents from Clearwater, Wright County, to Fawn Creek, Montgomery County, Kansas, sometime between 1860 and 1870. Her uncles William and John McDonald also moved to Fawn Creek.

Addie's parents, unfortunately, both died in Kansas leaving Addie an orphan by the time she was 15 years old, so she went to live with her uncle, John McDonald. By 1880, he had moved the family to Travis County, Texas, where he would eventually become mayor of the city of Austin. Addie at that time was a teacher.

In 1900, when she was 41 years old, Addie was still living in John McDonald's house. The McDonalds had moved to Jack County, Texas, by that time. Addie was making a living as an artist painting pictures.

Over the years, Addie must have formed a strong sisterly bond with her cousin, Grace E. McDonald, Mayor John's daughter, who was also an artist. Grace was about 11 years younger.

By 1920, both Grace and Addie had moved to Maricopa County, Arizona, where they made a home together. They were living in Creighton in 1930.

Addie McCrory died on Nov. 18, 1931, in Phoenix, Maricopa County, at the age of 72.[638] She was buried in Greenwood Memory Lawn Cemetery in Phoenix.[639] Her uncle William was also buried there in 1912.

Addie's cousin and friend, Grace McDonald, lived many more years in Maricopa County, passing away in 1960, at the age of 89.

WILLIAM MCDONALD (1830-1912) AND FAMILY
(Philo F. McDonald, William R., Maj. Richard, Col. William, William MacDonel)

William McDonald was a farmer and rancher who moved all over the country during his life, from New York to Ohio to Minnesota to Kansas to Tennessee to Oregon and, finally, to Arizona. The second child and the eldest son of Philo Fowler and Thirza (Spencer) McDonald, William was born Aug. 27, 1830, in Herkimer County, New York.[640] By 1850, the family had moved to Russell, Geauga County, Ohio.

Thirza Spencer McDonald, the mother, died in Ohio in 1846. About 1854, the patriarch of the family, Philo Fowler McDonald, also died. With both of their parents gone, William led his siblings – Harriet, John, Philo and Newell – to Wright County, Minnesota, to start a new life. In 1855, they were living in Big Bend, Wright County, and they remained in Wright County at least until 1857.[641]

On Nov. 27, 1855, probably in Wright County, William married Eliza D. Kent (b. Nov. 23, 1834), the daughter of Abel and Sabina (Thornton) Kent.[642] Two years later, William's younger brother, John, married Eliza's older sister, Ellen C. Kent. In 1856, William and John's sister, Harriet, married Herbert W. McCrory, who had been the first sheriff of Wright County. Newell McDonald, the youngest of the McDonald sons moved in with the McCrorys. The second youngest brother, Philo, was living with William and John and their wives in 1857, but he must have moved back to Ohio at some point where he enlisted for service in the Civil War.

William and Eliza D. (Kent) McDonald had two children:
1. Emma (1856-aft. 1900, m. Michael Edward Summerrow, P. K. Wilcox)
2. William K. (1858-1885)

Sadly, Eliza Kent McDonald died at only 25 years old on Apr. 25, 1860.[643] The family has not been found in the 1860 census, just prior to the Civil War, so their location at that time is unknown. Perhaps they were in Jamaica with William's brother, John, and his family. That might be why they can't be located in a U.S. census.

After the war, in 1870, William and his two children were living with his brother, John, and his family in Parker, Montgomery County, Kansas. He apparently made the move with John to Travis County, Texas, in 1874, for in 1879, William's daughter, Emma, married Michael Edward "Ed" Summerow of Travis County.[644]

The 1880 census shows that William had moved again. He and his son, William K., were farming in Bledsoe County, Tennessee. The Summerows were still in Travis County at that time.

In 1884, Ed Summerow died. Emma McDonald Summerow then married P. K. Wilcox, but by 1900, the marriage must have ended. The 1900 census shows her living with her father, William, this time in North Silverton, Marion County, Oregon.

William apparently made one final move before his time on this Earth expired. He must have been a restless and adventurous soul. He made his last home in Phoenix, Maricopa County, Arizona, probably arriving there about 1906 with his daughter, Emma, and granddaughters, Leila and Electa Summerrow.[645] They must have attended to and comforted him in his old age, along with his two nieces, Addie McCrory and Grace McDonald, who were also living in Phoenix about that time.

William died in Phoenix on Mar. 15, 1912, at the age of 81, and was buried in Greenwood Memory Lawn Cemetery in Phoenix.[646] His death date of 1912 was the latest date recorded on the Mayor John McDonald family genealogical blueprint.[647] Perhaps William's death inspired John to record the family history before it was too late. Thankfully, he did so. John outlived William by a little over a year, probably completing the family blueprint before he died on Sept. 3, 1913.

EMMA MCDONALD SUMMERROW WILCOX (1856-aft. 1900) AND FAMILY

(William McDonald, Philo F., William R., Maj. Richard, Col. William, William MacDonel)

Emma McDonald, the eldest child of William and Eliza D. (Kent) McDonald, was born on Nov. 18, 1856, in Minnesota, presumably Wright County.[648] Her mother died before Emma was 14 years old.

In 1879, Emma married Michael Edward "Ed" Summerrow, probably in Travis County, Texas.[649] Born July 2, 1842, in Arkansas, the son of Michael and Electa (Ruggles) Summerrow, Ed had been previously married and had several sons by his first wife: William Price, Robert E., Sidney and Edward Dallas.[650] So immediately, Emma had her hands full with a house full of boys. They were living in Travis County in 1880.

Ed was a retail grocer. He was appointed postmaster of Manchaca, Travis County, on Aug. 27, 1883.[651] He and Emma had two daughters together:
1. Leila E. (1880-1929)
2. Electa (1882-1960)

Ed died much too soon at the age of 41 on May 23, 1884. He was buried in Live Oak Cemetery in Manchaca, Travis County, Texas.

After Ed died, Emma married P. K. Wilcox. They had a son, Thomas K., born Dec. 20, 1889, but the marriage must have ended quickly in divorce. The 1900 census shows Emma and her children living with her father, William McDonald, in North Silverton, Marion County, Oregon.[652] That is the last record we have for Emma. The family probably moved to Phoenix, Maricopa County, Arizona, about 1906. William died there in 1912, but whether Emma died in Oregon or Arizona we simply don't know.[653]

LEILA E. SUMMERROW (1880-1929)

(Emma McDonald Summerrow, William McDonald, Philo F., William R., Maj. Richard, Col. William, William MacDonel)

Leila E. Summerrow, the eldest child of Michael Edward Summerrow by his second wife, Emma McDonald, was born in Texas on Nov. 18, 1880.[654] In 1920, she was living with her sister, Electa, in Maricopa County, Arizona. No occupation is shown for them in the census record. On Mar. 30, 1929, in Phoenix, at the age of 48, Leila died.[655] She never married.

ELECTA SUMMERROW (1882-1960)

(Emma McDonald Summerrow, William McDonald, Philo F., William R., Maj. Richard, Col. William, William MacDonel)

Electa Summerrow, the second child of Michael Edward Summerrow by his second wife, Emma McDonald, was born on Mar. 18, 1882, in Texas.[656] She was named after her paternal grandmother, Electa Ruggles Summerrow. Electa received a 7th grade education. She and her sister, Leila, were living together in 1920 in Maricopa County, Arizona. Leila died in 1929.

In 1930, when she was 38, Electa was living in Los Olivos, Maricopa County, and working as a public school janitor. By 1940, she was living in Phoenix.

Electa died on Jan. 28, 1960, in Phoenix. She was 77. She was buried in Genung Cemetery, Peeples Valley, Yavapai County, Arizona. Her funeral service was held at Yarnell Presbyterian Church.[657]

THOMAS K. WILCOX (1889-1971)

(Emma McDonald Summerrow Wilcox, William McDonald, Philo F., William R., Maj. Richard, Col. William, William MacDonel)

Thomas K. Wilcox, the only child of Emma McDonald Summerrow and her second husband, P. K. Wilcox,[658] was born in Austin, Travis County, Texas, on Dec. 20, 1889.[659] Not long after his birth, the family moved to North Silverton, Marion County, Oregon. The 1900 census identifies Thomas as "Thomas K. Summerrow" and notes his mother, Emma, was a widow. Thomas's grandfather, William McDonald, was the head of the household at that time. It seems likely that the marriage to P. K. Wilcox was brief and ended in divorce.

Thomas received an 8th grade education. Of medium build, tall, with light blue eyes and dark brown hair, he was working as a clerk for the railroad just before he enlisted for service in World War I at the age of 27, on June 23, 1917.[660] He was sent to Fort Bliss, Texas, as a private in the infantry. On Sept. 17, 1918, Thomas accepted a commission as a 2nd lieutenant and was sent to Camp Pike, Arkansas, as part of the 162nd Depot Brigade. Their responsibility was to train replacements for the American Expeditionary Forces and to receive men sent to camps by local draft boards. Thomas was discharged Jan. 9, 1919.[661]

When he was 33 years old, on Jan. 23, 1923, he was admitted to the U.S. National Home for Disabled Soldiers in Sawtelle, Los Angeles County, California, to be treated for tuberculosis. His nearest relative at that time was his father, listed as P. K. Wilcox of Wenden, Arizona. Thomas was a clerk at that time, unmarried, 6' tall with blue eyes and brown hair. He left the Home on June 26, 1924.[662]

In 1940, Thomas was a lodger in Los Angeles, Los Angeles County, California. The census shows he was married, but no spouse was there with him. He was making his living as a book salesman.

Thomas died on Aug. 20, 1971, aged 81 years.[663] His last residence was Pasadena, Los Angeles County, California, but he was buried in Willamette National Cemetery in Portland, Multnomah County, Oregon.[664]

WILLIAM K. MCDONALD (1858-1885)

(William McDonald, Philo F., William R., Maj. Richard, Col. William, William MacDonel)

William K. McDonald, the second child of William and Eliza D. (Kent) McDonald, was born in Minnesota on June 25, 1858.[665] His middle initial probably stands for "Kent." He was living with his family at Parker, Montgomery County, Kansas in 1870.

By 1880, William and his father were working a farm in Bledsoe County, Tennessee. Between 1880 and 1885, William K. must have relocated to Austin, Travis County, Texas. That's where he died, quite young, only 27 years old, on Oct. 18, 1885.[666] He was buried in Oakland Cemetery, in Austin, Travis County.[667]

MAYOR JOHN MCDONALD (1834-1913) AND FAMILY

(Philo F. McDonald, William R., Maj. Richard, Col. William, William MacDonel)

John McDonald, probably in collaboration with his son, Burt, was the man responsible for creating the McDonald family genealogical blueprint, about 1912-1913, in which significant portions of the McDonald family history have been preserved for posterity. The blueprint provides the ONLY evidence that John's grandfather, William R. McDonald, was the son of Maj. Richard McDonald of Pluckemin, Somerset County, New Jersey. If not for John McDonald's conscientious efforts, this book would not have been possible.

John McDonald was born in Norway, Herkimer County, New York, on Oct. 18, 1834, the third child and second son of Philo Fowler and Thirza (Spencer) McDonald.[668] He moved with his parents to Russell, Geauga County, Ohio, sometime before 1850. He attended the public schools in both New York and Ohio, but "his schooling was limited and rudimentary." Still, John was determined to make something of himself. He decided to become a contractor and builder at the age of 18, and quickly began to develop the necessary skills of a carpenter and machinist.[669]

After his father died about 1854, an approximate date that was recorded in the blueprint, John and four of his siblings – Harriet, William, Philo and Newell – moved to Wright County, Minnesota. There John met the love of his life, Ellen C. Kent, the daughter of Abel and Sabina (Thornton) Kent of Clearwater, Minnesota. On Sept. 10, 1857, he married Ellen in Clearwater, almost two years after his older brother, William, married Ellen's younger sister, Eliza Kent.[670] Ellen C. Kent was born May 20, 1833, in Franklin, Delaware County, New York.[671]

John and Ellen (Kent) McDonald had six children:
1. Burton (1860-aft. 1930, m. Edna Walthersdorf)
2. Charles Kent (1865-1946, m. Eleanor Merriam)
3. Lillie (1869-1869, died in infancy)
4. Grace Ella (1870-1960)
5. John Philo (1872-1945, m. Tennie Ford)
6. Ray (1874-1939, m. Sarah Moore)

Apparently, in the next few years following their marriage, John and Ellen did a lot of traveling. Their first child, Burton, was born in 1860 in Saratoga Springs, Saratoga County, New York.[672] They must have been living there at the time, just before the Civil War, but the family has not been found in the 1860 census.

We do know that John "took no part in the war."[673] He was a Republican politically, so it may be that his sympathies lay with Republican President Abraham Lincoln and the preservation of the Union. In fact, he may even have been out of the country at the time, which would explain why he didn't enlist. Author Lewis E. Daniell wrote in *Types of Successful Men of Texas* that John "spent many years in Jamaica."[674] In fact, in 1865, John and Ellen's second child, Charles Kent, was born in Kingston, Jamaica.[675] Unfortunately, there is no account of what John and his family were doing there. We can be assured, however, that he was acquiring valuable life experience that would shape his later life and work.

On June 25, 1869, Ellen gave birth to her third child, Lillie, but tragically the baby died on Aug. 2, 1869.[676]

By 1870, John and his family had moved to Parker, Montgomery County, Kansas. His fourth child, Grace Ella, was born there in June of that year. Also, living in his house at the time were his brothers William and Newell. William was a widower with two children. His wife, Eliza D. Kent, the younger sister of John's wife, Ellen, had died in 1860. In fact, poor Ellen had three younger sisters – Eliza, Emma and Marion – all of whom died in their early twenties. John McDonald and his youngest brother, Newell, were both listed as carpenters in the census, while William was listed as a farmer.

A fifth child was born, John Philo McDonald, in September 1872 in Emporia, Lyon County, Kansas.[677] Apparently, that is where the family was living that year.

The Kansas years ended in 1874 when John moved once again, initially settling his family in Paris, Lamar County, Texas. That is where his sixth child, Ray McDonald, was born in September 1874.[678] John wasted no time establishing himself as an architect and builder.

> During his residence there he acquired some property, and much reputation as a builder, and was the originator and builder of some residences which, evidencing a high order of talent in their design and construction have been much admired.[679]

In 1875, John moved to Austin in Travis County. He made some bad investments, which didn't pan out, and found himself wallowing in debt. But he was a talented man willing to work hard. He had already gained a reputation as being a fine machinist and a master workman. Before long, he had acquired some lucrative building contracts and real estate investments and amassed a "modest fortune."[680] He was the general contractor for the Old Main building on the University of Texas campus.[681]

In November 1889, John was elected Mayor of Austin. The voters "saw in him a pure man, a public spirited citizen, and a sagacious, go-a-head, pushing businessman, and that was the kind of a man they wanted to handle the destiny of the capital city."

Author Lewis E. Daniell described Mayor John at the age of 56 in 1890:

He is tall and spare built, and from habit stoops some in his gait. He is over six feet in height, and has very dark complexion, doubtless acquired from long residence in a semi-tropic country – he having spent many years in Jamaica; black eyes and hair. His hair is not yet gray, nor his beard; but as black as if the frosts of fifty odd years had not passed over them. He is a man of a retiring disposition; but in company with friends, is of a genial and companionable turn... His election to the Mayoralty was without solicitation on his part, and was altogether on personal grounds; politics had no part in it, for Austin is overwhelmingly Democratic; this fact makes the compliment more brilliant.[682]

The biggest project John McDonald had a hand in while mayor was the construction of the Austin Dam on the Colorado River. It was one of the largest dams in the world at the time it was built. The lake that formed behind it was named "McDonald Lake" for Mayor McDonald who had been one of its biggest proponents.

Unfortunately, the dam was an economic disappointment.

The flow of the Colorado proved to be far more variable than the project's promoters had claimed, and the dam was never able to produce the kind of steady power needed to drive a bank of mills. At times it barely sufficed to power the lights and streetcars.[683]

Mayor John McDonald was very active in his community. Like so many of his McDonald ancestors and relations, he was a member of the Presbyterian Church and a Master Mason. He held the position of Grand King of the Royal Arch Chapter of Texas and was Grand Senior Warden of the Grand Commandery of the State for the Knights Templar.[684] In fact, as early as Nov. 26, 1881, John and his youngest brother, Newell, were involved in establishing a new Chapter of Scottish Rite masonry in Austin. They were Charter Members of Philip C. Tucker Chapter of Knights Rose Croix, No. 1. John was elected Junior Warden.[685]

John certainly possessed the qualities and skills of an effective leader. As mayor, however, he was not your typical, bombastic, ego-driven politician.

Since his election to the office of Mayor he has necessarily been thrown more in public than formerly, and has made some speeches, which while possessing few or none of the charms of oratory, were replete with good practical sense, and sound logic. Not being in any other sense a public man, of course he has no record as a writer, speaker or office holder. But few men have so strong a hold upon the respect, confidence and esteem of the community where their lot is cast as John McDonald has upon the good citizens of his adopted city – Austin.[686]

John served as Mayor of Austin from 1890-1895. He was 61 years old when he left office. By 1900, he had moved to Finis, Jack County, Texas. Doctors had suggested he move to the country for the sake of his wife, who was in poor health. He bought 1,640 acres and built a spacious 5-bedroom, two-story home made out of native quarried stone with a fireplace in the living room and in each bedroom. Living with him were his wife, his adult children, Charles K. and Grace, and his niece, Addie McCrory.[687] The place became known for its splendid parties and dances.[688]

On Apr. 7, 1900, the Austin Dam, which had consumed so much of John's time and energy while in office and must have been his crowning achievement, failed spectacularly with catastrophic results.

> Enormous storms upriver sent a torrent of water cascading eleven feet over the crest of the dam. After the rains had stopped, Austinites came out that bright Saturday morning to see their local version of Niagara. Then at 11:20 am they heard a loud crack—"like a gunshot," several said— and watched in horror as a central section of the dam gave way and slid sixty feet downstream. Water blasted into the powerhouse, wrecking it and killing eight people. Lake McDonald vanished, and though the western end of the dam still stood, the eastern half was destroyed. More than a century later, great chunks of it are still to be found scattered in the riverbed, forming part of the present Red Bud Isles.[689]

The collapse of the dam must have been not only a shock, but a huge disappointment for Mayor John. Today, the dam is no more. McDonald Lake is no more. But the Austin Country Club's Hole No. 5 is named "Loch McDonald," in honor of Mayor John McDonald. The left side of the hole marks the former location of the lake and dam.[690]

Ellen Kent McDonald, John's wife, died in Finis, Jack County a few years later on Mar. 28, 1904.[691] She was 70 years old. In 1907, the McDonald house in Finis was sold to Fred C. Chestnut. It burned down on July 3, 1950.[692]

Probably not long after he sold the house, John moved to a rural area near Phoenix, Maricopa County, Arizona.[693] His brother, William, with whom he must have been very close, died in Phoenix on Mar. 19, 1912. John was the informant on his death certificate.[694]

William's death date of 1912 is the last date recorded on the McDonald family genealogical blueprint. It may be that William's death made John acutely aware of his own mortality and spurred him on to complete the blueprint for the sake of posterity. He probably had his son, Burt the architect, make the actual blueprint. It is probably Burt's handwriting on the document, but the information contained in the blueprint must have come from John himself – from family bibles and oral traditions.

John's blueprint was his dying gift to his descendants. He left this Earth only a year and a half after William on Sept. 3, 1913. He was 78 years old. Both John and his wife, Ellen, now rest peacefully in Finis Cemetery, Bryson, Jack County, Texas.[695]

The entire McDonald extended family owes Mayor John McDonald a debt of gratitude for having the foresight to preserve what was then known and believed about the family history.

BURTON MCDONALD (1860-aft. 1930) AND FAMILY
(Mayor John McDonald, Philo F., William R., Maj. Richard, Col. William, William MacDonel)

Burton "Burt" McDonald, the eldest child of Mayor John and Ellen C. (Kent) McDonald, was born on Aug. 17, 1860, in Saratoga Springs, Saratoga County, New York.[696] He graduated from the University of Michigan in Ann Arbor with the class of 1886, B.S. (M.E.). Burt, as he was better known, was a mechanical engineer and architect in Austin, Travis County, Texas. He designed buildings both for the Texas Insane Asylum and the Deaf, Dumb and Blind Institute for Colored Youth in Austin.[697]

He also designed the Chemical Laboratory building at the University of Texas at Austin, which opened in 1892. It was a two-story brick building in the Victorian style with a high-pitched roof and tall, narrow windows. Burt included brick floors and walls into the design of the building for purposes of fire resistance, knowing full well the volatile nature of the science of chemistry. Unfortunately, it wasn't enough to prevent the building's demise.

> Early in the morning of October 16, 1926, a short circuit in the building's old wiring started a blaze that was accelerated when it reached stored chemicals, resulting in a series of colorful explosions. Firefighters, under the energetic direction of Dr. Harry Lochte, labored valiantly to save what they saw as the department's most prized asset: the library. Flames were held at bay while firemen ventured into the building to remove or cover the books and journals, which were irreplaceable. Some were thrown out of the windows in damp or singed condition, but the bulk of the library was saved... Unfortunately, the rest of the building and its contents were a total loss. Over $150,000 worth of instruments, research notes, and equipment was destroyed, and the Department of Chemistry found itself homeless.[698]

On June 29, 1892,[699] at the age of 31, Burt married 20-year-old opera singer Edna Walthersdorf, the daughter of Albert and Alphonsine (Maillot) Walthersdorf. Edna was born on Oct. 13, 1871, in Louisiana. Her father, Albert, was said to be a Baron of Saxony.[700] Edna had studied with the world famous contralto Madame Ernestine Schumann-Heink, who was a regular performer at the Metropolitan Opera in New York, beginning in 1899 until about 1932.[701]

Burt and Edna had one child, Kenneth Walthersdorf McDonald, born in 1893.

Also in 1893, Burt was secretary of the Lake Navigation Company, which operated the *Ben Hur,* a steamboat which made excursions on Lake McDonald, which was named for his father, Mayor John McDonald.[702]

In 1900, Burt was living in Austin with what must have been a bustling household. Not only were his wife and child there, but also his mother-in-law, Alphonsine Walthersdorf, his sister-in-law, Norelle Walthersdorf, both of whom were music teachers, and two 23-year-old boarders, Sam Russel and Robert Mar, both students.

The year 1900 also saw the completion of the four-story, red-brick Austin High School building, nicknamed "Old Red." Burt had designed the building with James Riely Gordon.[703] It was used as a high school until 1925, when it became the John T. Allan Junior High School. It was destroyed by fire in 1956. A State of Texas Subject Marker now stands on the site today.[704]

Burt and Edna's marriage ended in divorce probably sometime before 1903, by which time Edna had apparently moved to Houston and was working with the Houston Conservatory of Music. Edna, in fact, became the first woman director of the Conservatory.[705]

The 1910 census shows Edna living in Houston and teaching music.[706] She is listed as a widow, even though her husband was still alive. It is not unusual, however, for women who were divorced to call themselves "widowed" on census records. There was a stigma to being divorced at the time. Edna was living with her son, Kenneth, her mother, Alphonsine, her sister, Norelle and her husband, Charles Brooks, and their son, Theddy.[707]

Burt, meanwhile, had moved to Phoenix, Maricopa County, Arizona, by 1910. He was a draughtsman living with another draughtsman, 26-year-old, James M. Barker.[708] It may have been Burt's associate James Riely Gordon, who influenced Burt to move to Phoenix. Gordon was the designer for the Arizona State Capitol building in Phoenix.[709]

On Mar. 15, 1912, Burt's uncle, William McDonald, died in Phoenix. Burt's father, John, had moved to Phoenix by that time and was the informant on William's death certificate.[710] Both Burt and John were no doubt present at William's funeral. He was buried in Greenwood Memory Lawn Cemetery in Phoenix.

Soon after William's death, Burt and his father, John, feeling the pressure of time, must have collaborated to produce the McDonald family history blueprint. Burt probably created the actual document in his architect's office with John supplying the information from family bibles and oral historical traditions.[711]

Burt's father, John, the former Mayor of Austin, Texas, died on Sept. 3, 1913, probably in Phoenix. He was buried with his wife, Ellen Kent (d. 1904), in Finis Cemetery in Jack County, Texas. The blueprint must have been completed before John's death. Otherwise, Burt would have included John's death date on it. It seems likely that once the blueprint was finished, it was sent to Burt's ex-wife, Edna Walthersdorf McDonald, in Houston with the request to pass it on to their son, Kenneth. Kenneth eventually received the blueprint but, sadly, he would be told very little about his father, Burt.

Meanwhile, Burt's architectural opportunities were expanding. In 1915, he went into partnership with James M. Creighton (1856-1946), who is considered one of Arizona's first architects. By 1918, he and Creighton had split and Burt established his own independent business.

Apparently, Burt never remarried. In 1920, he was living at the Phoenix Hotel on the corner of First and Jefferson Streets.[712]

One of the most impressive buildings that Burt worked on while he was in Phoenix was the C. P. Stephens DeSoto Six Motorcars building, which is now on the National Register of Historic Places.[713] Chrysler Motors had hired their company architect, R. P. Morrison, to design the building, but because he wasn't registered in Arizona, he needed to partner with a local architect. That man was Burt McDonald.

Built in 1928 for the DeSoto automobile dealership, the building was occupied as an auto sales showroom and service facility until about 1955 by Stephens Motors and its successor Stephens-Franklin Motors.

The DeSoto automobile came out at the height of the roaring twenties when people had plenty of money to spend. Sales skyrocketed.

> The initial model of 1929 resulted in sales figures of 81,065 units. This set a record for the most sales for any new model of vehicle that stood for over thirty years, until the introduction of the Ford Falcon in 1960.[714]

Burt McDonald was 70 years old when the census was taken in 1930. He was still living in Phoenix as a lodger in a building with many other tenants and working at his own architectural business.[715] This is the last record we have of him. We don't know when or where he died, but it was probably in Phoenix sometime between 1930 and 1940.[716]

SGT. KENNETH WALTHERSDORF MCDONALD (1893-1957) AND FAMILY

(Burton McDonald, Mayor John, Philo F., William R., Maj. Richard, Col. William, William MacDonel)

Kenneth Walthersdorf McDonald, the only child of Burton and Edna (Walthersdorf) McDonald, was born on June 5, 1893, in Austin, Travis County, Texas.[717] His father and mother divorced probably sometime between 1901 and 1903, when Kenneth was only about 8-10 years old.

Even though Kenneth was a bright and curious individual, he didn't receive much of an education. His daughter Diane said, "Daddy was a very intelligent man who was always buried in a book or working... he told me once he never got beyond 6th grade in school because he had to leave school to work."[718] Indeed the 1910 census shows that Kenneth was living with his mother in Houston, Harris County, Texas, and doing clerical work for a newspaper.[719]

In 1917, when he registered for the draft in World War I, Kenneth was 6'4" tall with gray eyes and light hair. He was single at the time and working as a cashier and stenographer for Temple Sanitarium in Bell County, Texas.[720]

At the age of 25, Kenneth joined the Army to do his part for the war effort. He served from Apr. 20, 1918 to Mar. 1, 1919 as a quartermaster sergeant at Camp MacArthur, Waco, McLennan County, Texas.[721] Named after Gen. Arthur MacArthur,[722] the camp provided training for infantry replacements and had an officers' training school. The Thirty-Second or Red Arrow Division was one of the units that trained there and went on to fight in France in 1918.[723]

On Aug. 14, 1925 or 1926, Kenneth married Georgia Isabel Dellinger, the daughter of Albert H. and Cora L. (Abernathy) Dellinger.[724] Isabel, as she was known, was born on Mar. 29, 1905, in Miles, Runnels County, Texas.[725] Her father was a Dallas police detective in 1920 and a police sergeant in 1940.[726]

Not long after he got married, Kenneth inquired of his mother, Edna, "Mother, I'd like to get in touch with my father. Can you tell me how to do that?" Edna responded with a dismissive gesture, "Oh, your father died years ago."[727] Unbeknownst to Kenneth, his father Burt was actually still alive at that time, working as an architect in Phoenix, Arizona.

In 1930, Kenneth and Isabel were living in Dallas, Dallas County, Texas. He was working as an assistant manager for an automobile company.

Both Kenneth and Isabel were musically inclined. He was a bass and she was a contralto. They often sang in the church choir. During the years of the Great Depression in order to earn a little more money, Kenneth was a cantor for a synagogue and sang on the radio on weekends.[728]

In 1938, Kenneth was a credit manager for Montgomery-Duggan, Inc.,[729] and in 1942, he was employed by Norman Young, Inc., in Dallas.[730]

About 1949, the family moved to Los Angeles County, California.[731]

Kenneth died on May 3, 1957, in Kern County, California, at the age of 63. Isabel died in Kern County on Nov. s25, 1990, aged 85.[732] Both were buried in Fort Rosecrans National Cemetery, San Diego, San Diego County, California.[733]

Kenneth Walthersdorf and Georgia Isabel (Dellinger) McDonald had four children:
1. Karen (b. 1932, m. Ivan Schroeder, Thomas Nielsen)
2. Kenneth Wayne (b. 1934, m. Barbara E. Vickroy, Jackie Pietak)
3. Diane (b. 1937, m. Homer "Jim" Shaul)
4. David Gordon (1943-2015, m. Margaret Ankers)

Kenneth Walthersdorf McDonald inherited the precious McDonald family genealogical blueprint that had been handed down from his father, Burt McDonald, and his grandfather, Mayor John McDonald. He, in turn, passed it down to his daughter, Diane McDonald Shaul, who kept it safe for more than 50 years.[734]

KAREN MCDONALD SCHROEDER NIELSEN (1932-Living) AND FAMILY
(Kenneth W. McDonald, Burton, Mayor John, Philo F., William R., Maj. Richard, Col. William, William MacDonel)

Karen McDonald, the eldest of four children of Kenneth Walthersdorf and Georgia Isabel (Dellinger) McDonald, was born Sept. 6, 1932, in Dallas, Dallas County, Texas. A talented artist, she married Ivan Schroeder in 1955 and had two children:
1. Eric Karl (1960-1997)
2. Stephanie Elise (1963-2009, + Alex Franz Debler)

The first marriage ended in divorce. Karen then married Thomas Nielsen who passed away about 2008. She now lives with her two grandchildren, Katrina and Franz Debler, in Huntsville, Walker County, Texas.

KENNETH WAYNE MCDONALD (1934-Living) AND FAMILY
(Kenneth W. McDonald, Burton, Mayor John, Philo F., William R., Maj. Richard, Col. William, William MacDonel)

Kenneth Wayne McDonald, the second child of Kenneth Walthersdorf and Georgia Isabel (Dellinger) McDonald, was born Sept. 22, 1934, in Dallas, Dallas County, Texas.[735] He is a United States Army veteran.[736] He married Barbara Edith Bartechko (b. Mar. 1937), the daughter of Lawrence Van and Edith Pearl (Stevens) Bartechko, on June 20, 1955, in San Diego County, California.[737]

Van Bartechko (1913-1981), Barbara's father, was adopted as a child. His birth name was Vickroy, a descendant of George Washington Vickroy (1822-1912) and his wife, Julia Ann, whose maiden name just so happened to be McDonald.[738] Van was the 11th of 12 children. His mother died in childbirth with the 13th child. The only one of his siblings to be given up for adoption, Van never saw his birth family again. His adoptive parents, the Bartechkos, were immigrants from Hungary.

> The Bartechkos... had one daughter and wanted a son. At school, Van was teased "your parents only paid 5 bucks for you." Mr Bartechko told him "when it comes to having children most people have to take what they get. We chose you because you are special, and we wanted you to be our son."[739]

Indeed Van was a special person. He had to drop out of school during the Great Depression to work in the family business. He served in the U.S. Navy during and after World War II. He was a chief petty officer on the U.S.S. *Hector* (AR-7), a repair ship. After the war, he worked as a groundskeeper in civil service at Miramar Naval Air Station in Miramar, San Diego County, California. While at Miramar, he designed the irrigation system for the golf course, using underground watering to conserve water. He and Edith were at Guantanamo Bay in Cuba when Fidel Castro took power in 1959. Thanks to the G.I. Bill, Van obtained dual masters degrees in botany and psychology and became fluent in six languages – all this while working three jobs and going to night school. He told his grandson, Corey, that he got five hours of sleep a night for twenty years. He was also a great singer, a tenor. According to his daughter, Barbara, no one could sing "Danny Boy" better than Van.[740]

Since finding out her father's birth surname was Vickroy, Barbara has changed her name to Vickroy to be true to her genetic heritage.[741]

Kenneth and Barbara (Vickroy) McDonald have four children:
1. Kenneth Lance (b. Nov. 28, 1956, Heidelberg, Germany. One son: Kenneth Chase Spurgin)
2. Raymond Bart (b. Apr. 23, 1958, La Jolla, CA, m. Christine D. Vinson, Patricia Jean McLean, Linda Susan Lea)
3. Thomas Corey (b. July 20, 1960, La Jolla, CA, m. Lisa Magsulit. One son: Daniel Quinn McDonald)
4. Marva Lorraine (b. May 20, 1965, Vista, CA, m. James Lesley Stewart, Dan Dewoody. Two sons: James Stewart, Kenneth William Stewart)[742]

Kenneth Wayne McDonald now lives in Arizona with his second wife, Jackie Pietak.

RAYMOND BART MCDONALD (1958-Living)
(Kenneth Wayne McDonald, Kenneth W., Burton, Mayor John, Philo F., William R., Maj. Richard, Col. William, William MacDonel)

Raymond Bart McDonald, the second child of Kenneth Wayne and Barbara Edith (Vickroy) McDonald, was born Apr. 23, 1958, in La Jolla, San Diego County, California. Bart and his two brothers, Lance and Corey, all go by their middle names. Bart is a veteran of the United States Air Force.

Bart and Corey contacted the author of this book about the Mayor John McDonald genealogical blueprint, which had been handed down to their family through their grandfather, Kenneth Walthersdorf McDonald and their aunt, Diane McDonald Shaul. Bart spent quite a bit of time figuring out how to produce a digital version of the blueprint for examination, for which this author is very grateful.

Bart and his wife, Linda Susan Lea, live near San Diego.

THOMAS COREY MCDONALD (1960-Living) AND FAMILY
(Kenneth Wayne McDonald, Kenneth W., Burton, Mayor John, Philo F., William R., Maj. Richard,
 Col. William, William MacDonel)

Thomas Corey McDonald, the third child of Kenneth Wayne and Barbara Edith (Vickroy) McDonald, was born on July 20, 1960, in La Jolla, San Diego County, California. On Corey's ninth birthday, Jan. 20, 1969, astronaut Neil Armstrong became the first human being to set foot on the moon. Corey watched it on television. He and his brother, Bart, became avid followers of the Apollo space missions and built models of the various spacecraft.

On Jan. 28, 1986, the day of the tragic Space Shuttle Challenger explosion, Corey married Lisa Marie Magsulit in Lake Tahoe, Nevada. The marriage ended in divorce eight years later. They have one son, Daniel Quinn McDonald.

Corey works as a finish carpenter/door hanger and says he is "one happy man." He is keenly interested in family history and has been for years. He credits his fascination on the subject to his maternal grandmother, Edith Pearl Stevens Vickroy (1916-2011), who used to tell stories about her grandfather who rode with the Pony Express.

Corey and his brother, Bart, made contact with the author of this book to tell him about the McDonald family genealogical blueprint that had been handed down to their aunt, Diane McDonald Shaul. Corey, with his knowledge of family history, was able to help clarify the sequence of events related to the creation of the document. This book would not have been written without the concerted efforts of Corey and Bart.

DANIEL QUINN MCDONALD (1986-Living) AND FAMILY
(Thomas Corey McDonald, Kenneth W., Kenneth W., Burton, Mayor John, Philo F., William R.,
 Maj. Richard, Col. William, William MacDonel)

Daniel Quinn McDonald, the only child of Thomas Corey and Lisa (Magsulit) McDonald, was born on July 25, 1986, in Escondido, San Diego County, California. He started saying numbers when he was only 17 months old. His dad, Corey, taught him to add by doubling numbers when he was three years old: "as in, I have two grandfathers, 4 great grandfathers, 8 great great grandfathers, and so on. I didn't know what came after 999 trillion... He bugged me for a week until I found the answer."[743]

Quinn, as he is known, graduated from the University of California, Berkeley, in 2008, with a B.A. in mathematics. He currently works as an actuary, i.e. someone who tells insurance companies how much they should charge people for insurance based on risks. Quinn's father says of him, "He is a great kid and he buys me lunch."

Daniel Quinn McDonald has the distinction of being the youngest surviving male descendant of William R. and Abigail (Fowler) McDonald who still carries the surname McDonald.

DIANE MCDONALD SHAUL (1937-Living) AND FAMILY

(Kenneth W. McDonald, Burton, Mayor John, Philo F., William R., Maj. Richard, Col. William,
 William MacDonel)

Diane McDonald, the third of four children of Kenneth Walthersdorf and Georgia Isabel (Dellinger) McDonald, was born on Oct. 11, 1937, at Rushing Clinic (now The Gaston Episcopal Hospital) in Dallas, Dallas County, Texas. She married Homer "Jim" Shaul and had two lovely daughters, Elizabeth (1962-1984) and Leslie (1963-1969), whose lives were tragically cut short by cystic fibrosis.

Despite the devastating loss of their children, Diane and Jim are enjoying their lives together. They have been married for 57 years. Diane has a keen interest in genealogy and family history and was the keeper of the McDonald family blueprint for over 50 years.

DAVID GORDON MCDONALD (1943-2015)

(Kenneth W. McDonald, Burton, Mayor John, Philo F., William R., Maj. Richard, Col. William,
 William MacDonel)

David Gordon McDonald, the youngest of four children of Kenneth Walthersdorf and Georgia Isabel (Dellinger) McDonald, was born Oct. 13, 1943, in Dallas, Dallas County, Texas.[744] He was a Vietnam veteran. After the war, he went to work in the Navy as a civilian. He acquired valuable computer skills "in the early days of computer technology... on ships from Guam to Sicily."[745] He settled in Norfolk, Virginia, in 1993.

In his retirement, David really enjoyed gardening, "raising some fine vegetables and fruits and developing his culinary skills as the variety of plants he cultivated increased, so that the term 'Old McDonald Had a Farm' became a reality."[746]

Sadly, David's life was taken away when he was 71 years old. He was stabbed to death on June 2, 2015, at his home in Norfolk. He had admitted a man into his house a few days before. Neighbors said McDonald needed help with some chores around the house and so he took the man in. Officers arrested that man while he was sitting in a car outside the house. He confessed to the crime.[747]

A friend and neighbor, George Powell, told reporters, "He [McDonald] was a good guy. He didn't have a mean bone in his body."[748]

David was much loved by many friends and family members, who were shocked by the news of his death. "He will be sorely missed," Powell said. "There's a hole in my world. I look next-door and see his truck and feel like he had to be there, but he's not."[749]

> "No longer sharing daily telephone chats and e-mails with Dave will be an inestimable loss to sister Diane and brother-in-law, Jim," his obituary noted.[750]

The extended McDonald family was very grateful for the "kind service and dedication" of the Norfolk Police Department throughout the ordeal. David's memorial service was held at Lighthouse Community Church in Norfolk.[751]

David is survived by his sisters, Karen and Diane, his brother, Kenneth and his children, and his beloved ex-wife, Margaret Ankers McDonald, of San Diego, California.[752]

⸺◦⟋⟋⟋◦⸺

CHARLES KENT MCDONALD (1865-1946) AND FAMILY
(Mayor John McDonald, Philo F., William R., Maj. Richard, Col. William, William MacDonel)

Charles Kent McDonald, the second child of Mayor John and Ellen C. (Kent) McDonald, was born on May 3, 1865, in Kingston, Jamaica, West Indies.[753] He moved with his family to Parker, Montgomery County, Kansas, by 1870. A decade later, he was in Travis County, Texas.

In 1900, at the age of 35, Charles was living with his parents in Jack County, Texas, and making his living as a farmer.

About 1908, when he was about 43 years old, he married Eleanor Merriam, the daughter of Lucius and Hester (Estabrook) Merriam. Eleanor was born Aug. 1, 1872, in Vermont.[754]

Charles worked as a civil engineer for the U.S. Government. He had completed two years of college. His wife, Eleanor, had four years of college. She was a teacher in 1930 and 1940 in San Antonio.

Charles died in 1946 at the age of 80. Eleanor died on Apr. 27, 1953, also at the age of 80. Both died in San Antonio and were buried in Sunset Memorial Park there.[755]

Charles Kent and Eleanor (Merriam) McDonald had two daughters: Ruth M. (b. 1912, CA) and Edith A. (b. abt. 1915, AZ). Edith disappears from the records after 1930.

RUTH M. MCDONALD MAGNESS (1912-1973)
(Charles K. McDonald, Mayor John, Philo F., William R., Maj. Richard, Col. William, William MacDonel)

Ruth M. McDonald, the eldest child of Charles Kent and Eleanor (Merriam) McDonald was born in California on Sept. 19, 1912. In 1930, she was living with her parents in San Antonio, Bexar County, Texas, and working as a clerk in a ready-to-wear store.

On Mar. 12, 1971, in Comal County, Texas, at the age of 59, she married taxi cab driver Hollis Haywood Magness. Born on Mar. 3, 1912, in Oklahoma, he was a U.S. Army veteran of World War II.[756] He had been a soldier as early as 1940 when he was stationed with the 15th Field Artillery Regiment at Ft. Sam Houston in San Antonio.[757]

Ruth enjoyed married life for only a couple of years. She died in San Antonio on Apr. 10, 1973, at the age of 60. Hollis died of lung cancer on Mar. 25, 1977, in San Antonio.[758] He was 65.

⸺◦⟋⟋⟋◦⸺

GRACE ELLA MCDONALD (1870-1960) AND FAMILY
(Mayor John McDonald, Philo F., William R., Maj. Richard, Col. William, William MacDonel)

Grace Ella McDonald,[759] the fourth child of Mayor John and Ellen C. (Kent) McDonald, was born June 7, 1870, in Parker, Montgomery County, Kansas.[760] She received an 8th grade education.

In 1890, author Lewis E. Daniell, in writing about the family of Austin Mayor John McDonald, called 20-year-old Grace "a refined cultivated and talented young daughter." He seems to have been quite taken by her.

> This young lady is the possessor of a high order of talent as an artist and it has found expression in a number of landscapes figures and portraits which have been pronounced by competent judges highly creditable and breathing the true artistic genius.[761]

Ten years later, in 1900, Grace and her cousin, Addie McCrory, were living with her parents, John and Ellen (Kent) McDonald, in Finis, Jack County, Texas. Grace was working as an artist and photographer. Addie McCrory was also an artist. She was the daughter of Grace's aunt, Harriet McDonald McCrory. In those days, the elegant McDonald home was the scene of some splendid parties and dances, which Grace and Addie must have thoroughly enjoyed.

Grace has not been found in the 1910 census, but she probably moved with her dad to Phoenix after her mother died and he sold the house. It seems likely that she cared for him in his old age (perhaps assisted by cousin Addie) until he died in 1913.

In any case, the 1920 census shows that Grace and Addie were living together in Maricopa County, Arizona. They must have been very good friends. They were still living together in 1930 in Creighton, Maricopa County. Addie died the next year at the age of 72.

By 1940, Grace was living in Phoenix with Electa Summerrow, the daughter of her cousin, Electa McDonald Summerrow. Electa was the daughter of Mayor John McDonald's brother, William.

Grace disappears from the records after 1940, but some say she died in Maricopa County on Jan 23, 1960, at the age of 89.[762]

JOHN PHILO MCDONALD (1872-1945) AND FAMILY
(Mayor John McDonald, Philo F., William R., Maj. Richard, Col. William, William MacDonel)

John Philo McDonald, the fifth child of Mayor John and Ellen C. (Kent) McDonald, was born Sept. 24, 1872, in Emporia, Lyon County, Kansas.[763] He acquired an 8th grade education. About 1894, he married Tennie Ford, the daughter of Sherwin and Nancy (Walker) Ford. Born on Sept. 17, 1874, in Austin, Travis County, Texas, Tennie had had three years of high school.[764]

Though census records from 1900-1940 show the family living in Austin, John's mailing address was in Orange, Orange County, Texas, when he registered for the draft in 1918, aged 46. Tall and slender with gray eyes and gray hair, he was working as a ship carpenter for the National Ship Building Co.[765]

John was a general contractor working in cement and road building in 1930 and 1940. He died on Dec. 8, 1945, in Austin, at the age of 73. Tennie passed away in Austin on June 27, 1951, at the age of 76. Both are buried in Oakwood Cemetery in Austin.[766]

John Philo and Tennie (Ford) McDonald had three children:
1. Richard Ford Sr. (1896-1955, m. Myrtle Mollie Marshall)
2. John Russell (1898-1906, buried Oakwood Cemetery, Austin)
3. Roy William (1905-1972, m. Gladys Eugenia Castle)

RICHARD FORD MCDONALD SR. (1896-1955) AND FAMILY
(John P. McDonald, Mayor John, Philo F., William R., Maj. Richard, Col. William, William MacDonel)

Richard Ford McDonald, the eldest child of John Philo and Tennie (Ford) McDonald, was born Aug. 28, 1896, in Austin, Travis County, Texas.[767] He was a general contractor. He married Myrtle Mollie Marshall, the daughter of John Henry and Mary Ann (Rawls) Marshall.[768]

On May 27, 1918, Richard enlisted for service in World War I. He was a corporal in the Army's 47th Artillery of the Coast Artillery Corps. He was discharged on Mar. 19, 1919.[769]

When Richard registered for the draft in World War II, he was living in Austin and working for the Tulsa Rig and Reel Manufacturing Co. in Bastrop, Texas.[770]

Richard was the informant on his father John Philo McDonald's death certificate in December 1945. He believed that his grandfather, Mayor John McDonald, was born in Scotland and his grandmother, Ellen Kent McDonald, was born in Ireland.[771] Obviously, he was mistaken. But this is an example of how quickly family history is lost and distorted.

Richard died on Dec. 1, 1955, in Temple, Bell County, Texas, aged 59. He was buried in Oakwood Cemetery in Austin.[772] His wife, Myrtle, passed in Travis County on Apr. 9, 1989, at the age of 93. She was buried in Evergreen Cemetery, Jasper, Jasper County, Texas.[773]

Richard Ford and Myrtle (Marshall) McDonald had two children:
1. Richard Ford Jr. (1920-2014, m. Helen Cook, Betty Spires)
2. Mary Jo (1923-2002, m. Ross M. Correll Jr.)

CAPT. RICHARD FORD MCDONALD JR. (1920-2014) AND FAMILY
(Richard F. McDonald Sr., John P., Mayor John, Philo F., William R., Maj. Richard, Col. William, William MacDonel)

Richard Ford "Dick" McDonald Jr., the eldest child of Richard Ford Sr. and Myrtle (Marshall) McDonald, was born in Austin, Travis County, Texas, on Feb. 16, 1920.[774] Dick was attending the University of Texas when Pearl Harbor was bombed on Dec. 7, 1941, thrusting the United States into World War II. Ten days later, he enlisted in the U.S. Army Air Corps, first going to pilots' school before being transferred to Bombardier School in Midland, Midland County, Texas. After completing his schoolwork, he remained as an instructor there for two years. He was then assigned to a combat unit that was shipped to Italy. In August of 1944, he and his nine-man B-24 Bomber crew were shot down after completing a successful mission at Lake Constance between Switzerland and Germany. Dick was one of only three men to survive. He was seized by the Germans as a Prisoner of War and sent to a camp near Breslau. He spent nine months in captivity.[775] By war's end, Dick had attained the rank of captain.

After the war, in 1950, Dick moved to Aiken, Aiken County, South Carolina, to work as a builder and developer. He was a partner in the firm Combs, McDonald & Parks. He was an avid golfer. In fact, he designed and built the clubhouse at Midland Valley Country Club in Graniteville, South Carolina, where he maintained a lifetime membership. In 1977, he won the Devereux Milburn Tournament at Palmetto Golf Club in Aiken. Dick was also a member of the Aiken Coffee Club.[776]

Dick passed away on Apr. 5, 2014, at the Charlie Norwood VA Medical Center in Augusta, Richmond County, Georgia. He had lived for 94 years. He was married twice – to Helen Cook and Betty Spires. He had two daughters: Sharyn Lynn McDonald and Lee Quinn (m. Fred Cavanaugh).[777]

Dick and his wife, Helen, are buried at Aiken Memorial Gardens, Aiken, Aiken County, South Carolina.[778]

MARY JO MCDONALD CORRELL (1923-2002) AND FAMILY
(Richard F. McDonald Sr., John P., Mayor John, Philo F., William R., Maj. Richard, Col. William, William MacDonel)

Mary Jo McDonald, the second child of Richard Ford Sr. and Myrtle (Marshall) McDonald, was born Dec. 21, 1923, in Nacogdoches, Nacogdoches County, Texas.[779] She graduated from Austin High School and served in the U.S. Navy. In June 1946, she married Ross Mathieu Correll Jr. , the son of Ross M. Sr. and Mae Correll.[780]

Ross Jr. was born in Bedford, Lawrence County, Indiana, on Nov. 18, 1920. His family moved to Austin, Texas, in the 1930's, where he graduated from Austin High School. Ross served as an air traffic controller in the United States Air Force in World War II. He was first stationed in the Marshall Islands and later was assigned to the Air Force Reserve at Bergstrom Air Force Base in Austin, where he trained air traffic controllers.[781]

After their marriage, Mary Jo worked in the accounting and payroll department of the Texas National Guard for 33 years, retiring in 1988. Ross worked as a stone carver with his father and grandfather. They were involved in many interesting projects including the Last Supper on the Tidwell Bible Building at Baylor University in Waco and the Good Shepherd sculpture at the Episcopal Church of the Good Shepherd on Windsor Rd. and Exposition Blvd. in Austin.[782]

Mary Jo and Ross Correll were married for 56 years. She preceded him in death on Dec. 18, 2002, aged 78. Ross passed peacefully at his home in Austin at the age of 91 on Nov. 23, 2011.

Ross and Mary Jo (McDonald) Correll Jr. had three children:
1. Beverly (m. Roger Knowles)
2. Michelle (m. Steve Turnquist)
3. Richard Ross (m. Renee Unknown)[783]

ROY WILLIAM MCDONALD (1905-1972)
(John P. McDonald, Mayor John, Philo F., William R., Maj. Richard, Col. William, William MacDonel)

Roy William McDonald, the third child of John Philo and Tennie (Ford) McDonald, was born on June 20, 1905, in Austin, Travis County, Texas.[784] He graduated in 1927 from the Austin School of Law at the University of Texas.

In November 1930, he married Gladys Eugenia Castle, the daughter of Eugene Franklin and Emma (Mann) Castle. She was born Dec. 29, 1908, in Honey Grove, Fannin County, Texas.[785] In 1940, they were living in Dallas. Roy was teaching law at a college.

Roy was quite successful as an attorney. He was the author of the book *McDonald Texas Civil Practice*. He and Eugenia lived in Washington, D.C. and New York City, travelled the world and played golf.[786]

Roy died in New York City in April 1972, at the age of 66.[787] He was buried in Laurel Land Memorial Park in Dallas. His gravestone shows he was a Mason.[788]

Eugenia returned to Dallas and married Roy J. Weaver in 1979. He died in 1997. Eugenia passed away in Austin on Oct. 27, 2003, at age 94. She was buried at Calvary Hill Cemetery and Mausoleum in Dallas.[789] She had no children.

On Mar. 3, 2004, the Board of Regents of the University of Texas established The Roy W. and Eugenia C. McDonald Endowed Chair of Civil Procedure in honor of Roy and Eugenia.[790]

RAY MCDONALD (1874-1939)
(Mayor John, Philo F., William R., Maj. Richard, Col. William, William MacDonel)

Ray McDonald, the youngest child of Mayor John and Ellen (Kent) McDonald, was born on Sept. 15, 1874, in Paris, Lamar County, Texas.[791] About 1899, he married Sarah "Sadie" Moore, the daughter of Francis M. and Fannie (Freek) Moore. She was born Oct. 18, 1874, in Erie County, Pennsylvania.[792]

Ray was a building and paving contractor. In 1920, they were living in Wichita Falls, Wichita County, Texas, and in 1930, they were living in Dallas.

Ray died on Mar. 15, 1939, in Waco. McLennan County, Texas, at the age of 64. Sarah died on Dec. 3, 1963, in Dallas. She was 89.[793] They had no children.

CORPORAL PHILO MCDONALD (1841-1863)
(Philo F., William R., Maj. Richard, Col. William, William MacDonel)

Philo McDonald, the fifth child of Philo Fowler and Thirza (Spencer) McDonald, was born in Ohio in 1841.[794] After the death of his father, Philo Fowler McDonald, young Philo accompanied his siblings to Wright County, Minnesota. He appears in the census there in 1855.[795] He must have returned to Ohio sometime before the Civil War.

On Dec. 16, 1861, Philo enlisted to fight for the Union as a private in Company D of the 75th Ohio Infantry. On Aug. 30, 1862, he was wounded at Second Bull Run (or Second Manassas), in Prince William County, Virginia.[796] The 75th Ohio lost 113 men that day. Philo survived the ordeal, but fate was set against him.

No doubt Philo was with his regiment on May 2, 1863, at Chancellorsville, Virginia. He may have been a corporal at the time. Military records show he was promoted, but we don't know exactly when.[797] The commander of the regiment was Col. Robert Reily. He sensed that his men would be tested that day. He told them bluntly:

> A great battle is pending in which many lives will be lost. Some of us will not see another sunrise. If there is a man in the ranks who is not ready to die for his country, let him come to me, and I will give him a pass to go to the rear, for I want no half-hearted, unwilling soldiers or cowards in the ranks tonight. We need every man we have to fight the enemy. If a comrade falls, do not stop to take him away or care for him, but fight for the soil on which he falls and save him by victory.[798]

Sure enough, at 5:30 p.m., Confederate Gen. Stonewall Jackson launched an assault upon the Union line. The Ohioans stood their ground and fought valiantly. Finally, their lines were overrun and they were forced to retreat. In a half hour they had lost 150 men including Col. Reily who was mortally wounded.[799]

Philo McDonald survived again, but only two months later, he would find himself in a little town in Pennsylvania called Gettysburg. The new commander, on July 1, 1863, when the regiment arrived on the battlefield at mid-day, was Col. Andrew L. Harris, who would later become the 44th Governor of Ohio. The 75th was part of Brig. Gen. Francis Barlow's division. The regiment took a defensive position on Blocher's Knoll (now known as Barlow's Knoll). They were hammered by an attack from Confederate Gen. Richard S. Ewell. The Ohioans were overwhelmed. Barlow himself was wounded and left for dead. They retreated through the streets of Gettysburg and entrenched themselves on the slopes of Cemetery Hill, battle-weary and badly depleted.

The next evening, July 2, beginning at about 7:45 p.m., the 75th was pounded again by an onslaught of rebels, "The Louisiana Tigers," under the command of Gen. Harry T. Hays.

Lieutenant Oscar D. Ladley of Company G recalled what the 75th endured:

> They came on us about dark, yelling like demons, with fixed bayonets. We opened on them when they were about 500 yards off, but still they came, their officers & colors in advance...

We lay behind a stone wall and received them with our bayonets. I was standing behind the wall when they came over. A Rebel officer made at me with a revolver with his colors by his side. I had no pistol, nothing but my sword. Just as I was getting ready to strike him, one of our boys ran him through the body [and] so saved me.[800]

Before long, chaos ensued, as one Ohioan remembered:

For a time, the opposing forces were much mixed up together, and with the uncertainty of the light, in the dusk of evening it was difficult to distinguish friend from foe.[801]

At long last, the Federals managed to repulse the attack. The 75th Ohio had paid a heavy price. More than half of their men were taken prisoners by the Tigers. Lt. Oscar Ladley summed up the encounter:

We finally drove them back. I never saw such fighting in my life. It was a regular hand to hand fight. Our Brig[ade] had sworn never to turn, so they stood, but it was a dear stand for some of them. I have 6 men left [in Company G]; the Regt. had 60; the Brig. 300 out of 1500.[802]

Sadly, Philo McDonald did not live to see July 3 at Gettysburg, that fateful day when the Union Army repelled Pickett's Charge and turned the tide of the war. Military records show Philo died on July 1. Mayor John McDonald's blueprint says July 2. He was only about 22 years old.

We don't know where Philo was buried. Probably somewhere on that blood-soaked battlefield. If you ever get to chance to visit that sacred American ground, be sure to give a thought to Philo.

NEWELL MCDONALD (1845-1889)
(Philo F., William R., Maj. Richard, Col. William, William MacDonel)

Newell McDonald, the youngest child of Philo Fowler and Thirza (Spencer) McDonald, was born in August 1845 in Ohio.[803] He moved with his siblings to Wright County, Minnesota, after his father's death in 1854. In 1857, he was living with his sister, Harriet McDonald McCrory, and her family. He was probably helping them out on their farm.

On Nov. 22, 1862, at Clearwater in Wright County, Newell enlisted for service in the Civil War as a private in Co. G of the 1st Minnesota Cavalry "Mounted Rangers." The regiment was part of the Union Army, guarding the Minnesota and Dakota Territory from the hostile Sioux Nation. They were involved in the battles of Big Mound, Dead Buffalo Lake, and Stony Lake in July of 1863. Newell was discharged after a year of service on Nov. 28, 1863.[804]

After the war, he went with his brothers, William and John, to Parker, Montgomery County, Kansas. He was working as a carpenter there in 1870. While in Kansas, he was a member of the Pap Thomas Post of the Grand Army of the Republic (G.A.R.) in Great Bend, Barton County, Kansas.[805] The G.A.R. was a fraternal organization of Civil War veterans of the Union Army, Navy and Marines.

Newell was also a Mason. As early as Nov. 26, 1881, Newell and his brother, John, were involved in establishing a new Chapter of Scottish Rite masonry in Austin, Travis County, Texas. They were Charter Members of Philip C. Tucker Chapter of Knights Rose Croix, No. 1. Newell was elected treasurer and his elder brother, John, was elected Junior Warden. After the installation ceremony on Jan. 31, 1882, the Chapter and their guests were treated to a "handsome supper" that had been "prepared for the occasion by Bro. Newell McDonald." [806]

It is clear that by 1881, Newell had moved, along with his brother, John, to Travis, Austin County, Texas. He was working as a mechanic and painter in the 1880's, probably involved in brother John's construction business.[807]

Unfortunately, Newell died rather young, at the age of only 43, in February 1889 in Austin.[808] He never married.

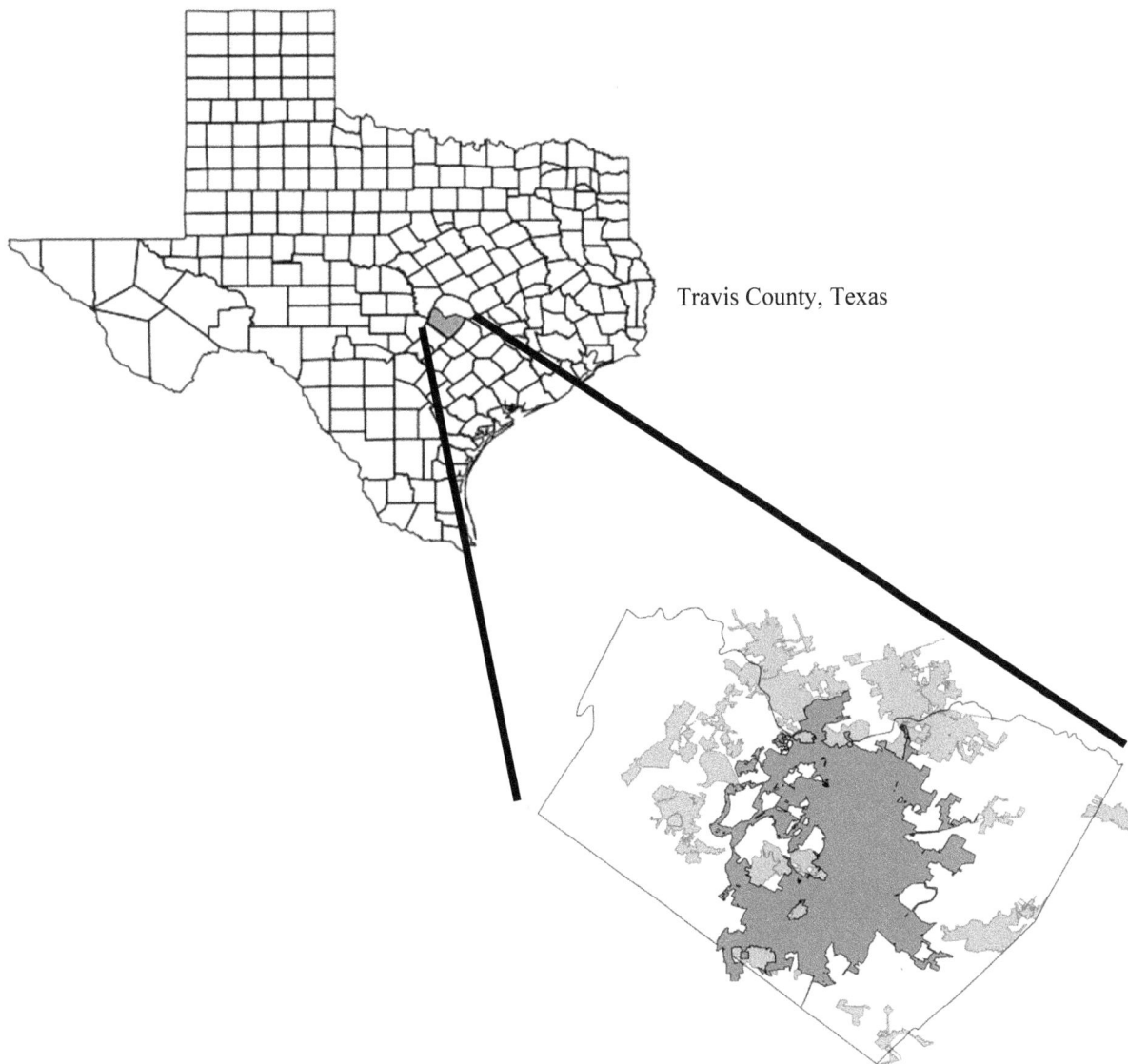

Travis County, Texas

Austin, within Travis County
Both images by 25or6to4, CC BY-SA 3.0

Chapter 5

PROVING THE LINEAGE:
How DNA Confirms the Ancestry of William R. McDonald

As we were researching and writing this book, we realized it would be extremely helpful if a living McDonald descendant of William R. McDonald would have his DNA tested, but there were only a few known male McDonalds of this line still living. We contacted those few and suggested one of them take the test.

Thankfully, after the writing of this book was completed and just prior to submitting it for publication, we received notice that a descendant of William R. McDonald, Thomas Corey McDonald, did indeed have his Y-DNA tested.

The results of his test were received on Nov. 5, 2015. What they tell us has profound significance for all the descendant branches of Maj. Richard McDonald of Somerset County, New Jersey.

Some might be wondering if the test proves that William R. McDonald is indeed the son of Maj. Richard McDonald. After all, the Mayor John McDonald family blueprint is the only document that has been discovered that shows any connection to Maj. Richard whatsoever.

While the research presented in this book clearly demonstrates that the blueprint is accurate and legitimate in many respects, it is really the only piece of evidence we have. The fact that the blueprint dates to about 1912, so many years after the death of William R. McDonald in 1853, is problematic. Because there is an opportunity for human error in every step of the record-keeping process and because it is not unusual for people to completely "make up" stories about their family lineage or jump to conclusions about their ancestry with insufficient evidence, there will always be skeptics, especially among genealogical researchers, who may question whether William R. McDonald is in fact the son of Maj. Richard McDonald.

That's why the DNA test is so crucial.

THE IMPORTANCE OF DNA TESTING

Absolute proof is very hard to come by in genealogy. There is always the possibility that somewhere along the line going back in time, someone who was believed to be the son or daughter of a certain father or mother may not have, in fact, been that parent's legitimate child. That child may have been adopted or born out of wedlock to an unknown partner. We all know about family secrets. The farther you go back in time, the more questionable the genetic relationships from parents to children become, because there simply is no way of knowing for sure.

To overcome this doubt and to establish the highest level of certainty for an ancestral lineage, we need to have a Y-DNA test and compare it with the recorded documentation or "paper trail."

The Y-chromosome is handed down from father to son going all the way back in time, but it is only handed down to males. Maj. Richard McDonald handed down the Y-DNA of his forebears to his sons. They, in turn, handed it down to their sons.

A TALE OF TWO MCDONALDS

Prior to the Y-DNA test of Thomas Corey McDonald, who is a great great grandson of Mayor John McDonald, the author of the blueprint, there was only one descendant of Maj. Richard's who had taken the Y-DNA test. His name is Michael John McDonald. He is a descendant of Maj. Richard through his son, Col. George McDonald, the lawyer.[809]

If the results of Thomas Corey McDonald's Y-DNA test match the test results of Michael John McDonald, then we can be certain that the Mayor John McDonald blueprint is, in fact, legitimate and we can be confident that William R. McDonald is indeed the son of Maj. Richard McDonald of Somerset County, New Jersey.

The big question is – do their results match?

May we have a drum roll please...

YES!!!

The results do indeed match.

This is cause for celebration for the entire extended McDonald family!

We now know with certainty that Michael John McDonald and Thomas Corey McDonald are both descended from a common ancestor. The paper trail tells us that that common ancestor is Maj. Richard McDonald of Somerset County, New Jersey. Maj. Richard McDonald is the 5th great grandfather of both Michael John McDonald and Thomas Corey McDonald. That makes Michael John and Thomas Corey 6th cousins.

Michael John and Thomas Corey each tested for 67 markers. They matched with a genetic distance of 2.[810]

IMPLICATIONS FOR THE ENTIRE MCDONALD CLAN

Thanks to the DNA tests of Michael John and Thomas Corey, we now have a benchmark for identifying other lines of McDonalds who may be descended from Maj. Richard McDonald and his ancestors.

There could be many more lines of American McDonalds, MacDonalds, MacDonnells, McDaniels, etc. who are descended from Maj. Richard McDonald's immigrant Scottish ancestor, who has not yet been positively identified. If we can determine that immigrant's identity through DNA testing and paper trails, we may finally discover where he came from in Scotland.

We strongly urge all male McDonalds (no matter how you spell it) to take a Y-DNA test for at least 67 markers. (Fewer markers, unfortunately, cannot tell us much.) We also recommend taking the test through FamilyTreeDNA,[811] through whom we can compare results to Michael John McDonald and Thomas Corey McDonald. If your results match theirs within a genetic distance of 2 or 3, then we will know your line of McDonalds is also closely related to the McDonalds of Somerset County, New Jersey.

We advise all Y-DNA test takers to join the Clan Donald USA Genetic Genealogy Project (it's free). They can help you to compare and analyze the results, especially when it comes to identifying the ancient forebears in Scotland.

In fact, we urge McDonald males from all over the world to take the Y-DNA test. The more who test, the more all of us will be able to learn about the lineages and the histories of the various branches in the entire MacDonald Clan.

Chapter 6

EXCITING NEW REVELATIONS IN
MCDONALD FAMILY HISTORY

THE SEARCH FOR LOST BRANCHES OF THE MCDONALD FAMILY TREE

Since *A Revolutionary American Family: The McDonalds of Somerset County, New Jersey* was published in 2015, the research on the McDonald family has been ongoing. Two new lines of McDonalds were discovered: the line of William R. McDonald and Abigail Fowler, described in this book, and the line of Richard and Catharine (Lansing) McDonald of Lansingburgh, New York, published separately. William R. and Richard were both sons of Maj. Richard McDonald (1734-1820) of Pluckemin, New Jersey. Their stories and the stories of their descendants shed further light on the extraordinary history of this McDonald family.

There was also a George C. (or G.) MacDonald, an oysterman and painter, born in New Jersey about 1803-1806, married Jane Smith in 1823 in Bergen, Hudson County, New Jersey, and died Nov. 30, 1877, in North Plainfield, Somerset County, New Jersey, who was thought to be the mysterious George, son of Col. George McDonald (1768-1820), the lawyer, who was also a son of Maj. Richard McDonald. A descendant of this George C. MacDonald, one Arthur R. McDonald, took a Y-DNA test. The results showed that he was not from the same McDonald ancestral line as Maj. Richard McDonald. He belonged to a completely different haplogroup (I-P37). It is now speculated that he might have been a descendant of Thomas MacDonald, who settled in Hudson County, New Jersey, about 1776, and has no known relation to the McDonalds of Somerset County, New Jersey.

IS LADY MARY PEMBERTON THE MOTHER OF MAJ. RICHARD MCDONALD?

Now that more people are discovering their McDonald roots, more interesting tales of family history are coming to the fore. The most exciting revelation revolves around a mysterious Lady Mary Pemberton. Could she be the mother of Maj. Richard McDonald, the first wife of Col. William McDonald (d. 1799)?

Despite the extensive research that went into *A Revolutionary American Family,* the first wife of Col. William McDonald was never discovered. Yet Col. William and his McDonald family were in the upper echelons of colonial American society. Col. William was the High Sheriff of Somerset County, appointed by New Jersey Governor William Franklin, the son of Founding Father Benjamin Franklin. Evidence strongly suggests that Col. William was the son of a yeoman William MacDonel and his wife Florance. It has always been a tantalizing mystery as to how Col. William McDonald received an education and rose to such prominence.

Col. William's son, Maj. Richard McDonald, was a man of wealth and status. It is believed he worked directly with Gen. George Washington in the Revolutionary War. Was his unknown mother a woman of high society?

In 2016, Peter Macdonald Blachly a descendant of Mayor Richard McDonald (1803-1894), who was a grandson of Maj. Richard McDonald, sent the following note:

> This morning I happened across a postcard from 1945 addressed to Mrs. William A. Howell (aka Katherine Macdonald Howell, daughter of George E Macdonald), my great grandmother on my maternal grandmother's side. On the back side it has an obituary—apparently from 1923—for Mary Macdonald DeWitt. The obit has one paragraph about Mary, then goes on to praise Mary's great-great grandmother, Lady Mary Pemberton, who "gave up title and wealth for love against her family's wishes to come to America..."—or something to that effect.[812]

Mary MacDonald DeWitt's full name was Mary Antoinette MacDonald. She lived from 1844-1923. She was a great granddaughter of Maj. Richard McDonald. Her great great grandmother would have been Maj. Richard's mother, the first wife of Col. William McDonald. Furthermore, the other great great grandmothers in Mary DeWitt's ancestry have been identified and none of them is a Pemberton.

Mary MacDonald DeWitt's great great grandmothers are:
1. Unknown first wife of Col. William McDonald
2. Kniertje Montfoort Schamp
3. Aeltje Olden DeGroot
4. Sarah Compton Castner
5. Agnes Jones Eastburn
6. Elizabeth Loofbourrow Inglis
7. Unknown White
8. Unknown Kennedy

The Whites and Kennedys shown above are unknown, but their children immigrated from Dublin, Ireland, so it is very unlikely they are the Lady Mary Pemberton in question. Agnes Jones Eastburn also seems unlikely to be Lady Pemberton.

Following Peter Macdonald Blachy's initial inquiry, he kindly sent the entire death notice of Mary MacDonald DeWitt, transcribed below:

> With the entrance into eternal rest of Mary Antoinette Macdonald, wife of the late David Miller deWitt, there passed one of the gentlewomen of the old school. With her tender sympathy for the joys and sorrows of all with whom she came in contact, only those to whom she gave it so unsparingly, can measure the void that is left.
>
> Her wonderful personal beauty was a fitting casket to enshrine the jewel of her soul. When her great, great grandmother, Lady Mary Pemberton, for whom Mrs. deWitt was named, following the dictates of her heart, gave up title and wealth in opposition to her family and came with her husband to America, it was to found a large family, conspicuous for its piety, loyal Americanism

and the unsullied faithfulness of its members to their country's welfare which they were often called to administer.

Devoted and unselfish in all the relations of life, as daughter, wife, mother and friend the sense of Mrs. deWitt's loss will only be deepened by the passing of time. J.H.B.[813]

The mystery of the origins of the family of Col. William McDonald deepen considerably with this new revelation. Was Lady Pemberton, in fact, the mother of Maj. Richard McDonald? We cannot say for sure, but it does seem to be a very good possibility. Did Col. William McDonald and Lady Mary Pemberton come to America as man and wife, she "giving up title and wealth in opposition to her family?" If true, it might explain why Col. William and his McDonald family were of such high social status.

Unfortunately, subsequent research has failed to uncover any further information about Lady Mary Pemberton. It may be possible that she was a granddaughter or other relation of Sir Francis Pemberton (1624-1697), Lord Chief Justice of the King's Bench whose descendants are the Pembertons of Trumpington Hall, high sheriffs of Cambridge. If so, that might help explain why Col. William McDonald became Justice of the Quorum and High Sheriff of Somerset County, New Jersey. He certainly must have had connections to very prominent and influential people. Although it is thought that Col. William was probably born in America, could it be that somehow he went to school in England, perhaps Cambridge? Could it be he met Lady Pemberton there, courted her and brought her to America against the wishes of her family? It's just a theory, nothing more. More evidence is definitely needed to unravel the mystery.

MARGARET COE WAS THE SECOND WIFE OF COL. WILLIAM MCDONALD

Another previously undiscovered document came to our attention regarding the surname of Col. McDonald's second wife, Margaret (1733-1808):

New Jersey, Deaths and Burials Index, 1798-1971

Name:	Margaret McDonald [Margaret Coe]
Birth Date:	abt 1733
Death Date:	2 Aug 1808
Cemetery Name:	Old Presbyterian Graveyard
Death Age:	75 years
Gender:	Female
Father Name:	William Coe
Comments:	Old Presby. Graveyard, Hamilton & East Sts.
FHL Film Number:	543520

We can now state with confidence that Col. William McDonald's second wife was Margaret Coe, the daughter of William Coe.

DNA POINTS TO FERMANAGH, IRELAND, AS THE EARLY HOMELAND OF OUR MCDONALDS

The Clan Colla 425 Null Project referenced in *A Revolutionary American Family*, p. 329, is still studying the DNA of closely related branches of McDonalds (and other surnames), including the McDonalds of Somerset County.

The DNA evidence, at this point, suggests that the ancestors of the McDonalds of Somerset County were in ancient times from the Fermanaugh and Monaghan districts of Ireland. Clan Donald believes this Irish DNA branch left the Fermanagh Valley to join Somerled and his father to fight the Vikings in Morvern, Scotland. Consequently, these Irishmen remained in Scotland and merged with Clan Donald to become clansmen sometime about the year 1100 A.D.

Researcher Shawn Marchinek speculates that our McDonalds may have been part of the Macdonalds of Ardnamurchan, which is located north of Morvern.

> The Macdonalds (or MacIains) of Ardnamurchan were one of the first Clans to become Protestant. Then the Campbells broke their clan and scattered them in the early 1600's. The Ardnamurchans became pirates for a while and ended up settling mostly in Morvern and some into Badenoch. No none Ardnamurchan Macdonalds have been located or tested for DNA. So I have a theory that with so many null 425 Macdonalds/Macdaniels our ancestors could have been Ardnamurchan Macdonalds.[814]

Marchinek also reported in April 2019 that a related DNA branch of McDonalds, who are participating in the study, now believe their ancestor John Sparks McDonald was the grandson of Angus McDonald (b. 1769 on the Isle of Skye; d. 1861, NC), who lies buried in Douglas Cemetery, Laurinburg, Scotland County, North Carolina.[815] Marchinek speculates that the common ancestor which binds many of our related DNA branches together could be the 1st to 3rd great grandfather of Angus McDonald, c. 1500. If so, then it may be that the McDonalds of Somerset County were somehow part of Clan Sleat on the Isle of Skye.

None of this is provable at this time, of course, but we have some good theories to pursue.

Genealogy is an endlessly fascinating enterprise. As time goes by, more revelations will be forthcoming and we will learn even more about this intriguing and astonishing McDonald family of Somerset County, New Jersey.

AFTERWORD

The descendants of William R. and Abigail (Fowler) McDonald have certainly made their mark on American history across locales in every region of the United States. They represent, however, just one branch of the much larger McDonald Family Tree, whose progenitors were Col. William McDonald and Maj. Richard McDonald of Pluckemin, New Jersey. They were there when America was being born and helped to shape its destiny. The circumstances of their lives are worthy of a Hollywood movie, complete with envy, lust, murder – and dinner with George Washington! And it's all true.

In fact, the fascinating story of the McDonald forefathers goes all the way back to 17th century Scotland, a dark period known to history as "The Killing Time," and is told in its entirety in *A Revolutionary American Family: The McDonalds of Somerset County, New Jersey* (Indelible Mark Publishing, May 2015).

Indeed, if the Mayor John McDonald family blueprint had come to light a few months earlier, this present manuscript would have been incorporated into its pages. This descendant line certainly deserves to take its place there among the other descendants of Maj. Richard McDonald.

In 2015, this book was produced as an e-book. Now in 2021, it is a physical, soft cover book that you can hold in your hands, put on your bookshelf, and easily hand down to your descendants. The same goes for another newly discovered branch of the tree, available previously as an e-book, now in soft cover, *The McDonalds of Lansingburgh, Rensselaer County, New York: The Pioneering Family of Richard and Catharine (Lansing) McDonald and their Descendants*. Richard McDonald of Lansingburgh was a younger brother of William R. McDonald.

Genealogy is always in process as new material comes to light. The research on the entire McDonald family will continue. No doubt in the future more will be revealed and some of the mysteries will be explained.

We invite you to become a part of this research and to contribute what you have to share about your branch of the tree.

Also be sure to check out our Facebook page, *The McDonalds of Somerset County, NJ, Descendants*, where you can share the latest news and information about the extended McDonald family and meet and greet some of your distant cousins.

NOTES

CHAPTER 1

[1] The Mayor John McDonald family genealogical blueprint, created about 1912-1913, almost certainly by Mayor John McDonald himself, assisted by his son, Burton McDonald, in Phoenix, Arizona.

[2] Correspondence with Diane McDonald Shaul, Aug 8, 2015.

[3] A Y-DNA test of at least 67 markers by a male McDonald descendant of Mayor John McDonald could firmly establish that William R. McDonald was indeed descended from Maj. Richard McDonald if the results matched or nearly matched the Y-DNA of Michael John McDonald, a descendant of Major Richard McDonald through his son, George, the lawyer. (For more on Y-DNA testing, see L. Overmire's *A Revolutionary American Family).*

[4] There is no known existing marriage document for Richard McDonald and Margrietje Schamp. The only information we have on their marriage comes from Schamp family records that have been passed down over the years. Robert Gordon Clarke in *Early New Netherlands Settlers*, ancestry.com, says the marriage occurred about 1761, but it now seems likely it would have been about 1760. See also Early Settlers of Hunterdon County, The Schamp Family, Hunterdon Historical Newsletter (Hunterdon County Historical Society, NJ, Spring 1975), Vol 11, No 2 and Find A Grave Memorial #82859599.

[5] The Mayor John McDonald family blueprint.

[6] William McDonald's gravestone shows W. M. McDonald; Find A Grave Memorial #128435048.

[7] Laurence Overmire, *A Revolutionary American Family: The McDonalds of Somerset County, New Jersey* (Indelible Mark Publishing, 2015).

[8] The Mayor John McDonald family blueprint.

[9] Ibid.

[10] A. V. D. Honeyman wrote in some detail about the McDonalds in Vol. 5 of the *Somerset County Historical Quarterly,* published in 1916. His was the first in-depth published account of Maj. Richard McDonald's family. Mayor John McDonald, who died in 1913, had no knowledge, then, of the McDonald history as revealed by Honeyman. This lends even more credence to the blueprint's authenticity. The blueprint correctly states that Maj. Richard McDonald lived near Pluckemin – this was unknown to most McDonald descendants in 1913.

[11] The Mayor John McDonald family blueprint.

[12] L. Overmire, *A Revolutionary American Family.*

[13] The Mayor John McDonald family blueprint.

[14] Numerous publications identify Washington's secretaries and staff, but Richard McDonald is never listed among them. See for example Mary S. Beall's *The Military and Private Secretaries of George Washington*, Records of the Columbia Historical Society, Washington, D.C., Vol 1 (1897), 89-118.

[15] For an in-depth discussion of the McDonalds' participation in these activities, see *A Revolutionary American Family: The McDonalds of Somerset County, New Jersey.*

[16] Correspondence with Nathaniel Eaton, 2014, a descendant of Helen Howatt Macdonald Eaton (1905-2000).

[17] The Mayor John McDonald family blueprint.

[18] As noted in *A Revolutionary American Family,* this soldier might have been William "Bill" McDonald, son of Col. William McDonald.

[19] The Mayor John McDonald family blueprint.

[20] Absolute proof is hard to come by in genealogy. The results of a Y-DNA test could establish an even higher degree of confidence.

[21] All of these dates are recorded on the Mayor John McDonald family blueprint.

[22] *Early Connecticut Marriages as Found on Ancient Church Records*, Vol 5, ed. by Frederic William Bailey [Bureau of American Ancestry, New Haven, CT, 1902], 74. Text under Washington, Litchfield Co., CT: "William McDonald of York City State of NY & Abigail Fowler Jan 8 1787."

[23] The McDonald family probably endured public scorn and shaming following the hanging of Samuel McDonald, which could help explain why William R. McDonald moved elsewhere to make his way in the world. His younger brother, Richard, we now know, also moved to New York.

[24] Barbara Lewis, Genealogy.com, Forum posting on Mar 1, 2002. Text: "A family bible shows Abagail McDonald (d. Sept. 13, 1849). Her father was Philo Fowler."
Abigail may have had a brother named Philo also who married Hannah Fanning.

[25] Judith McGhan, *Genealogies of Connecticut Families: From the New England Historical and Genealogical Register* (Genealogical Publishing Co., 1983), Vol 1, 623-625.

[26] *U.S. Census Non-Population Schedules, New York, 1850-1880.*

[27] Find A Grave Memorial #88546923.

[28] The Mayor John McDonald family blueprint.

[29] Abigail was born in New York according to the 1850 federal census for Ohio, Herkimer, NY. The birth date comes from the McDonald family blueprint.

[30] The Mayor John McDonald family blueprint shows Abigail's birth and death dates. The 1850 federal census for Ohio, Herkimer, New York, shows she was born in New York.

[31] The Mayor John McDonald family blueprint.

[32] Ibid.

[33] Ibid.

[34] Ibid.

[35] Ibid.

[36] Find A Grave Memorial #88546946 says Aaron died Sept 13, 1831, at the age of 26 years and one month. Aaron's probate record, however, was dated Mar 27, 1835, which is a good indication that Aaron died in 1834 as the McDonald family blueprint shows (*New York, Wills and Probate Records, 1659-1999*). The Find A Grave entry is probably a transcription error. Although if Aaron died at 26 years and 1 month, then perhaps he died Sept 13, 1834.

[37] *New York, Wills and Probate Records, 1659-1999.*

[38] Find A Grave Memorial #88546946.

[39] Barry O'Connell, *On Our Own Ground: The Complete Writings of William Apess, A Pequot* (University of Massachusetts Press, 1992).

[40] Ibid.

CHAPTER 2

[41] The birth and marriage dates come from the Mayor John McDonald family blueprint. Weston Goodspeed says that Margaret McDonald was a native of New York and of Scotch descent in his *Counties of Whitley and Noble, Indiana.*

[42] *Massachusetts, Town Birth Records, 1620-1850*; *U.S. Find A Grave Index, 1600s-Current.*

[43] Weston A. Goodspeed, *Counties of Whitley and Noble, Indiana* (F.A. Battey & Co., Chicago, IL, 1882), 400.

[44] *Massachusetts, Town and Vital Records, 1620-1988.* The Mayor John McDonald family blueprint says Margaret died June 6, 1834. The year, apparently, was in error. Also see Find A Grave Memorial #125446168.

[45] Find A Grave Memorial #33033365. The death date on the gravestone is difficult to read. It looks like Aug 2.

[46] 1860 federal census, Brimfield, Hampden, MA.

[47] Find A Grave Memorial #33033995.

[48] *Massachusetts, Town and Vital Records, 1620-1988.*

[49] *Cuyahoga County, Ohio, Marriage Records, 1810-1973, Vol 3-4, 292.*

[50] Bliss Family Tree 3/21/2015, Owner: MarciaGarrett66, ancestry.com, accessed July 2015.

[51] Obituary of Charles W. Bliss; Find A Grave Memorial #21633595.

[52] 1860, 1870, 1880 federal census records.

[53] Bliss Family Tree.

[54] *Passport Applications, 1795-1905,* National Archives and Records Administration (NARA), Washington D.C., NARA Series: Roll #189, 01 Nov 1872-31 Jan 1873.

[55] *Cook County, Illinois, Marriage and Death Indexes, 1833-1889.*

[56] *Massachusetts, Town and Vital Records, 1620-1988.*

[57] John Homer Bliss, *Genealogy of the Bliss Family in America, from about the year 1550-1880* (published by the author, Boston, MA), archive.org, accessed Oct 2015. J.H. Bliss says Martha died in "Chisago, Ia.", an apparent error. It seems likely she died in Chicago, Illinois.

[58] *Cook County, Illinois, Birth Certificates Index, 1871-1922.*

[59] Find A Grave Memorial #75225828.

[60] Find A Grave Memorial #95924150.

[61] Massey Family of United States, Owner: unigift, ancestry.com, accessed Oct 2015.

[62] Find A Grave Memorial #75225875.

[63] *Iowa, State Census Collection, 1836-1925.*

[64] *Massachusetts, Marriage Records, 1840-1915.* The record shows Marion born in Chagrin Falls, OH.

[65] Nichols of Springfield, Massachusetts Family Tree, Owner: kroghm, ancestry.com, accessed July 18, 2015.

[66] Ibid.

[67] *California, Death Index, 1940-1997.*

[68] *RootsWeb Marriage Records Index.*

[69] Nichols of Springfield, Massachusetts Family Tree; 1900 federal census, Los Angeles Ward 3, Los Angeles, CA.

[70] "Army Names New Alabama Air Base After Famed Pasadena Scientist Prof. Lowe," *Independent Star-News*, Pasadena, CA, Sept 29, 1957, 98.

[71] Ibid. See also 1900 federal census, Puyallup, Pierce, WA.

[72] *California Birth Index, 1905-1995.*

[73] *Washington, Select Death Certificates, 1907-1960.*

[74] Nichols of Springfield, Massachusetts Family Tree.

[75] *California, Death Index, 1940-1997.*

[76] Nichols of Springfield, Massachusetts Family Tree.

[77] *California, Death Index, 1940-1997.*

[78] Ibid.

[79] Ibid.

[80] "Army Names New Alabama Air Base After Famed Pasadena Scientist Prof. Lowe," 98.

[81] *California, Death Index, 1940-1997.*

[82] *California, Marriage Index, 1960-1985.* She appears as both Armes and Nelson. One is probably her maiden name and the other is probably from a previous marriage, but it is not clear which is which.

[83] *California, Death Index, 1940-1997.*

[84] Ibid. See also *Washington, Passenger and Crew Lists, 1882-1961.*

[85] 1910-1940 federal census records.

[86] *Washington, Passenger and Crew Lists, 1882-1961.*

[87] *California, Death Index, 1940-1997.*

[88] *New York City Births, 1891-1902.*

[89] "Parade Set for Colonel," *The Stanford Daily*, Stanford University, CA, Nov. 20, 1952.

[90] 1920 federal census, Camp Meade, Anne Arundel, MD.

[91] "Wayland Flyer to Take Bride," *Rochester Democrat and Chronicle*, Rochester, NY, July 8, 1947, 18.

[92] "Parade Set for Colonel," *The Stanford Daily*, 1952.

[93] Ibid.

[94] *California, Death Index, 1940-1997.*

[95] *California, Marriage Index, 1960-1985.*

[96] Obituary of Col. Henry L. Barrett, *The Daily Press,* Longview, WA, Oct 10, 1974.

[97] Find A Grave Memorial #23193376.

[98] "Parade Set for Colonel," *The Stanford Daily*, 1952; Obituary of Col. Henry L. Barrett; *California, Death Index, 1940-1997.*

[99] Find A Grave Memorials #48105377, #48373443.

[100] *U.S., Social Security Applications and Claims Index, 1936-2007.*

[101] South Carolina, Clemson University (Agricultural College) Directory of Graduates, 1896-1940.

[102] "Calaveras Frogs to Leap Again," *Kingsport Times News*, Kingsport, TN, Mar 15, 1970.

[103] Geni World Family Tree, MyHeritage, myheritage.com, accessed Oct 2015.

[104] Obituary of Mattie Davis Smith Furtick, *The Times and Democrat*, Orangeburg, SC, Aug 24, 2005.

[105] Find A Grave Memorial #48330437; *U.S., Social Security Death Index, 1935-2014.*

[106] "Wayland Flyer to Take Bride," 18.

[107] *California, Death Index, 1940-1997.*

[108] Obituary of Earl Edward DeMun (source unknown), courtesy of U.S. Veteran's Affairs, Find A Grave Memorial #574047.

[109] *Washington, Passenger and Crew Lists, 1882-1961.*

[110] *U.S., World War II Cadet Nursing Corps Card Files, 1942-1948.*

[111] *California, Marriage Index, 1949-1959.*

[112] My Heritage Tree, Owner: Gabrielle Quoidbach, ancestry.com, accessed July 2015.

[113] *U.S., Social Security Death Index, 1935-2014.*

[114] *World War I Draft Registration Cards* shows he was born Aug 18, 1900, *California, Death Index* shows Aug 19, 1901; *Social Security Death Index* shows Aug 19, 1900.

[115] *California, Marriage Records from Select Counties, 1850-1941.*

[116] *California, Death Index, 1940-1997.*

[117] *California Birth Index, 1905-1995.*

[118] Find A Grave Memorial #149253777.

[119] *California, San Francisco Area Funeral Home Records, 1895-1985.*

[120] *Tennessee State Marriages, 1780-2002.*

[121] *California, Death Index, 1940-1997.* See also Find A Grave Memorial #46679173.

[122] *California, San Francisco Area Funeral Home Records, 1895-1985.*

[123] 1940 federal census, Los Angeles, Los Angeles, CA.

[124] Obituary of Orville J. Bliss, *Inter-Ocean*, Chicago, IL, Apr 13, 1875.

[125] *Passport Applications, 1795-1905.*

[126] Obituary of Orville J. Bliss, *Inter-Ocean*, 1875; see also Genealogy Report: Descendants of Robertus Okeden, genealogy.com, accessed July 2015.

[127] Ibid.

[128] W. A. Goodspeed, *Counties of Whitley and Noble, Indiana*, 400.

[129] Obituary of Fannie Bliss, Noble County Indiana Library, gen.nobleco.lib.in.us, accessed July 2015.

[130] Obituary of Charles W. Bliss, Noble County Indiana Library, gen.nobleco.lib.in.us, accessed July 2015.

[131] W. A. Goodspeed, *Counties of Whitley and Noble, Indiana*, 400.

[132] Ibid. See also the obituary of William Bliss, Noble County Indiana Library, gen.nobleco.lib.in.us.

[133] Obituaries of William and Fannie Bliss, Noble County Indiana Library.

[134] Find A Grave Memorial #21633691.

[135] His gravestone shows he was born 1844 (Find A Grave Memorial #21633624), but *Cook County, Illinois, Deaths Index* says Sept 22, 1847. The latter is probably a transcription error, because the same Index says he died at age 70, which would make the 1847 birth date impossible.

[136] 1870 federal census, Chicago, Cook, IL.

[137] *Cook County, Illinois, Deaths Index, 1878-1922.*

[138] Obituary of Charles W. Bliss, Noble County Indiana Library. See also Find A Grave Memorial #130998553

[139] Obituary of Fannie Bliss, Noble County Indiana Library. See also Find A Grave Memorial #21633615.

[140] Obituary of Emily M. Madison, Noble County Indiana Library, gen.nobleco.lib.in.us, accessed July 2015.

[141] Ibid. See also Find A Grave Memorial #21633629.

[142] Find A Grave Memorial #21633070.

[143] W. A. Goodspeed, *Counties of Whitley and Noble, Indiana*, 400.

[144] 1900 federal census, Orange, Noble, IN; Find A Grave Memorial #21633070.

[145] Find A Grave Memorial #21633070.

[146] Find A Grave Memorial #21633022

[147] *U.S., World War I Draft Registration Cards, 1917-1918.*

[148] Jones-Lourcey Family Tree, Owner: Jaxjonesing, ancestry.com, accessed July 2015. Her gravestone says she was born in 1890 and died in 1978.

[149] 1940 federal census, Orange, Noble, IN.

[150] *U.S., World War I Draft Registration Cards, 1917-1918.*

[151] *U.S., Social Security Death Index, 1935-2014.*

[152] Find A Grave Memorial #21633050.

[153] Nashahn Family Tree 3-25-09 (1), Owner: MarciaGarrett66, ancestry.com, accessed July 2015.

[154] Find A Grave Memorial #21633705.

[155] Obituary of Francis T. McCarty, *The News-Sentinel*, Ft. Wayne, IN, Nov 24, 1990.

[156] Obituaries of Max and Mary E. Adair, Noble County Indiana Library, gen.nobleco.lib.in.us, accessed July 2015.

[157] Ibid.

[158] *U.S., Find A Grave Index, 1600s-Current.*

[159] Find A Grave Memorial #20836796.

[160] Obituaries of Max and Mary E. Adair, Noble County Indiana Library.

[161] Obituary of Douglas R. Garrett, KPC News, Kendalville, IN, kpcnews.com, Feb 28, 2006.

[162] Ibid.

[163] *U.S., Find A Grave Index, 1600s-Current.* His son Henry Elmer's death certificate shows Henry E. was born in Westfield.

[164] Find A Grave Memorial #76878009.

[165] *U.S., Find A Grave Index, 1600s-Current;* Find A Grave Memorial #76877536.

[166] Death Certificate of Edward Austin Moseley, State of Michigan, Registered No. 1048, Aug 31, 1906.

[167] 1900 federal census, Grand Rapids Ward 3, Kent, MI.

[168] *U.S. City Directories, 1821-1989.*

[169] *U.S. School Yearbooks, 1880-2012.* He appears as "Edward Louie Moseley" in the University of Michigan Yearbook, *The Palladium,* 1898.

[170] 1940 federal census, Grand Rapids Ward 10, Kent, MI.

[171] *California, Death Index, 1940-1997*; *U.S. City Directories, 1821-1989.*

[172] *U.S. City Directories, 1821-1989.*

[173] *California, Voter Registrations, 1900-1968.*

[174] *U.S., World War I Draft Registration Cards, 1917-1918.*

[175] 1940 federal census, Oakland, Alameda, CA.

[176] *California, Death Index, 1940-1997.*

[177] *California, Marriage Records from Select Counties, 1850-1941.*

[178] *California Birth Index, 1905-1995.*

[179] *California, Marriage Records from Select Counties, 1850-1941.*

[180] "Nuptials Friday," *Berkeley Daily Gazette*, Berkeley, CA, Jan 18, 1933, 6.

[181] *California, Death Index, 1940-1997.*

[182] *California Birth Index, 1905-1995.*

[183] *U.S. Public Records Index, Volume 1.*

[184] *California, Marriage Records from Select Counties, 1850-1941.*

[185] *California, Death Index, 1940-1997.*

[186] *California, Marriage Records from Select Counties, 1850-1941.* Thelma and Russell were married July 7, 1929, in Alameda Co., CA.

[187] *California Birth Index, 1905-1995.*

[188] *U.S. Public Records Index, Vol 1.* See also radaris.com and reainus.com.

[189] *California Marriage Index, 1960-1985.*

[190] *California, Death Index, 1940-1997.*

[191] *California Birth Index, 1905-1995.*

[192] *U.S. School Yearbooks, 1880-2012.*

[193] *California, Passenger and Crew Lists, 1882-1959.*

[194] *U.S., Social Security Death Index, 1935-2014.*

[195] *U.S., Find A Grave Index, 1600s-Current.* The 1900 federal census, Grand Rapids Ward 3 shows her b. Sept 1854. Her gravestone shows her birth as Sept 8, 1849.

[196] 1870 federal census, Painesville, Lake, OH.

[197] Find A Grave Memorial #115371823.

[198] *Michigan Death Certificates, 1921-1952.*

[199] *Michigan, Marriage Records, 1867-1952.*

[200] Find A Grave Memorial #115372433.

[201] Find A Grave Memorial #115372537.

[202] *New York, Passenger Lists, 1820-1957.*

[203] *U.S. City Directories, 1821-1989.* Helen was living with her parents in the 1900 and 1910 censuses. The 1925 Grand Rapids City Directory shows her as an artist living with her father in 1925.

[204] *New York, Passenger Lists, 1820-1957.*

[205] Find A Grave Memorial #115372055.

[206] Death certificate of Henry Elmer Moseley, Arizona State Board of Health, State File No. 362, Nov 10, 1930.

[207] *U.S., College Student Lists, 1763-1924.*

[208] *Michigan, Marriage Records, 1867-1952.* It is possible that Caroline's middle name is Minerva, not Minena. There could be a transcription error.

[209] Death Certificate of Carolyn Moseley, State of Michigan, Registered No. 3, Feb 28, 1912.

[210] *Michigan, Marriage Records, 1867-1952.*

[211] 1900 federal census, Grand Rapids Ward 3, Kent, MI.

[212] Death certificate of Henry Elmer Moseley.

[213] Find A Grave Memorial #115372187.

[214] The date comes from his gravestone, Find A Grave Memorial #115371560. The *Hinsdale Genealogy* by H. C. Andrews, et. al., says he was b. 1861.

[215] Herbert Cornelius Andrews, Sanford Charles Hinsdale, Alfred L. Holman, *Hinsdale Genealogy: Descendants of Robert Hinsdale of Dedham, Medfield, Hadley and Deerfield* (Lombard, IL, 1906), 368.

[216] Wedding of Charlotte Hinsdale and Alvin Bliss Moseley, *The Chicago Tribune*, Chicago, IL, Nov 2, 1892, 5.

[217] H. C. Andrews, *Hinsdale Genealogy*; *U.S., Social Security Death Index, 1935-2014.*

[218] 1910 federal census, Evanston Ward 2, Cook, IL.

[219] *Illinois, Deaths and Stillbirths Index, 1916-1947.*

[220] Ibid; Find A Grave Memorial #149659940.

[221] *Cook County, Illinois, Marriages Index, 1871-1920.*

[222] *Cook County, Illinois, Birth Certificates Index, 1871-1922.*

[223] Princeton University Catalogue 1912-1913 (Princeton University, Princeton, NJ, 1912), 397.

[224] *U.S., World War I Draft Registration Cards, 1917-1918.*

[225] *U.S., World War II Draft Registration Cards, 1942.*

[226] *U.S., Social Security Applications and Claims Index, 1936-2007.*

[227] *U.S., Social Security Death Index, 1935-2014.*

[228] Reber Family Tree, Owner: ca49reber, ancestry.com, accessed July 2015.

[229] Obituary of Henry E. Cooke Jr., *The Chicago Tribune*, Chicago, IL, Apr 3, 2004.

[230] Ibid.

[231] *U.S., Social Security Death Index, 1935-2014.*

[232] Obituary of Henry E. Cooke Jr., *Daily Herald*, Arlington Heights, IL, May 12, 2004.

[233] *U.S., Social Security Death Index, 1935-2014.*

CHAPTER 3

[234] The birth date comes from the Mayor John McDonald family blueprint. The 1850 federal census, Macomb, Macomb, MI, shows William was born in New York about 1794. The date on his gravestone is nearly impossible to read.

[235] William C. Armstrong, *The Axfords of Oxford, New Jersey: A Genealogy Beginning in 1725* (Shawver Publishing Co., Morrison, IL, 1988).

[236] Find A Grave Memorial #128435048.

[237] The marriage date comes from the Mayor John McDonald family blueprint. The blueprint spells Joanna's name Oxford, a variation at the time. The fact that it is spelled Oxford lends even more credibility to the blueprint's authenticity. *New Jersey Marriages, 1684-1895* confirms the marriage date and places the event in Sussex County, New Jersey. Sussex County is about 30+ miles directly north of Somerville, Somerset County, New Jersey.

[238] W. C. Armstrong, *The Axfords of Oxford, New Jersey*, 20. Margaret McDonald's identity is certainly mysterious. Her parents are unknown. To which McDonald family did she belong? She could even be an unknown daughter of Maj. Richard McDonald of Bedminster. We just don't know.

[239] W. C. Armstrong, *The Axfords of Oxford, New Jersey,* 43.

[240] Richard E. Harpster, *Historical Sites of Warren County* (Warren County Tercentenary Committee and Warren County Board of Chosen Freeholders, New Jersey, 1965) 127. Oxford was about 35 miles northwest from Somerville, Somerset County, New Jersey, the home of William M. McDonald's grandfather, Maj. Richard McDonald, at the time of the wedding.

[241] William M. McDonald appears simply as "William McDonald" in the 1820 census with no middle initial.

[242] Margaret's gravestone shows she was b. 1823 (Find A Grave Memorial #121882829).

[243] Find A Grave Memorial #128435048. She is identified as "Anna" in *The Axfords of Oxford, New Jersey*, 43.

[244] The 1820 federal census indicates Philo had an older brother whose identity is unknown and who probably did not live long.

[245] McIntyre Family in MI, NY, MA Tree, Owner: DeannaHester, ancestry.com, accessed July 2015. The date and place make sense, but we have seen no documentation to verify it.

[246] W. C. Armstrong, *The Axfords of Oxford, New Jersey*, 43.

[247] *Michigan, Marriage Records, 1867-1952.* The marriages of Philo's daughter, Kate, show Philo's wife as Lucinda Smith. Deanna Hester, a descendant of Philo and Lucinda, has a photo of Lucinda Smith on her webpage (see McIntyre Family in MI, NY, MA Tree).

[248] *U.S. General Land Office Records, 1796-1907.*

[249] *Michigan, Deaths and Burials Index, 1867-1995.*

[250] *Michigan, Marriage Records, 1867-1952.*

[251] 1900 federal census, Wells, Tuscola, MI. Shows Frances b. Sept 1861 in Arkansas.

[252] McIntyre Family in MI, NY, MA Tree. The 1900 federal census of Wells, Tuscola, MI, shows Katie was b. Oct 1863, Arkansas.

[253] *Michigan, Births and Christenings Index, 1867-1911; Michigan, Deaths and Burials Index, 1867-1995.*

[254] McIntyre Family in MI, NY, MA Tree.

[255] 1900 federal census, Wells, Tuscola, MI.

[256] *Michigan, Marriage Records, 1867-1952.*

[257] McIntyre Family in MI, NY, MA Tree.

[258] *Michigan, Births and Christenings Index, 1867-1911.*

[259] *U.S., World War I Draft Registration Cards, 1917-1918.*

[260] *California, Death Index, 1940-1997.*

[261] 1930 federal census, San Diego, San Diego, CA. See also *New York, State Census, 1892.*

[262] *California, Death Index, 1940-1997.*

[263] Find A Grave Memorial #124839235.

[264] *U.S., World War II Draft Registration Cards, 1942.* Other documents say he was b. June 13, 1881 or July 13, 1883. His WWII draft registration says he was born Aug. 13, 1883, in Rich Twp. On that document, he signed the statement, "I affirm that I have verified above answers and that they are true." We will take him at his word.

[265] *U.S., Headstone Applications for Military Veterans, 1925-1963.*

[266] Original copy of military record, dated July 12, 1807, St. Paul, MN, signed by Capt. F. C. (illegible), 6th Infantry (now in the possession of Marion's granddaughter, Deanna McIntyre Hester). Full quote of commanding officer: "Service honest & faithful, Intitled [sic] to travel allowance. Served in Philippines from Mch 27, 1905 to Oct 10 1906. Enlisted at New York City, N.Y."

[267] *Michigan, Marriage Records, 1867-1952.*

[268] Ibid.

[269] Find A Grave Memorial #115407736.

[270] Several on the Internet show Marion's middle name as Orville, but he signed his name Orman on the draft registration.

[271] *U.S., World War II Draft Registration Cards, 1942.*

[272] *U.S., Headstone Applications for Military Veterans, 1925-1963.*

[273] Find A Grave Memorial #115407703.

[274] *California, Death Index, 1940-1997*; McIntyre Family in MI, NY, MA Tree.

[275] *U.S., Department of Veterans Affairs BIRLS Death File, 1850-2010.*

[276] Valerie Cudnik, Valerie's Genealogy, valeriecudnik.com, accessed Oct 2015.

[277] Ibid.

[278] Ibid.

[279] *California, Death Index, 1940-1997.*

[280] *U.S., Social Security Death Index, 1935-2014*; *Michigan, Marriage Records, 1867-1952.*

[281] *Michigan, Marriage Records, 1867-1952*; *U.S., Find A Grave Index, 1600s-Current.*

[282] *U.S., Social Security Death Index, 1935-2014.*

[283] "464th Bombardment Group," historyofwar.org, accessed Oct 2015.

[284] Obituary of Robert A. Gerren, *The Gazette*, Colorado Springs, CO, June 7, 2009.

[285] *U.S., Department of Veterans Affairs BIRLS Death File, 1850-2010.*

[286] *U.S., Social Security Death Index, 1935-2014*; Find A Grave Memorial # 7788078. See also Nagle/Cook & McIntyre/Knight & Davis/Baugh Families, Owner: DeborahNagle2011, ancestry.com, accessed July 2015.

[287] Obituary of Robert A. Gerren.

[288] "Richard A. Gerren," Colorado Profiles, profiles.ucdenver.edu, accessed Oct 2015.

[289] "Donna Geren," Aerospace Engineering Sciences, University of Colorado Boulder, colorado.edu, accessed Oct 2015.

[290] Obituary of Loy Earl McIntyre, *The Flint Journal*, Flint, MI, Feb 13, 2000.

[291] McIntyre Family in MI, NY, MA Tree.

[292] Ibid.

[293] Obituary of Loy Earl McIntyre, *The Flint Journal*, Flint, MI, Feb 13, 2000.

[294] Find A Grave Memorial #80599058.

[295] *U.S., World War II Draft Registration Cards, 1942.*

[296] *Genesee County, Michigan, Marriage Index, 1836-1934.*

[297] *U.S., World War I Draft Registration Cards, 1917-1918.*

[298] McIntyre-Dawson Family Tree, Owner: C-Braton, ancestry.com, accessed July 2015.

[299] *Michigan Death Records, 1897-1920.*

[300] McIntyre-Dawson Family Tree.

[301] *Michigan, Marriage Records, 1867-1952.*

[302] *Michigan, Divorce Records, 1897-1952.*

[303] McIntyre-Dawson Family Tree.

[304] Ibid.

[305] *Michigan, Divorce Records, 1897-1952; Michigan, Deaths, 1971-1996.*

[306] *Michigan, Marriage Records, 1867-1952.*

[307] *Michigan, Deaths, 1971-1996*; Find A Grave Memorial #82389148.

[308] *U.S., Social Security Death Index, 1935-2014.*

[309] Find A Grave Memorial #82389200.

[310] *U.S., World War I Draft Registration Cards, 1917-1918; U.S., World War II Draft Registration Cards, 1942.*

[311] *U.S., World War I Draft Registration Cards, 1917-1918.*

[312] U.S., Headstone Applications for Military Veterans, 1925-1963; *U.S., World War II Draft Registration Cards, 1942.*

[313] *Michigan, Marriage Records, 1867-1952.*

[314] *U.S., World War II Draft Registration Cards, 1942.*

[315] *U.S., Headstone Applications for Military Veterans, 1925-1963;* Find A Grave Memorial #149705941.

[316] *California Death Index, 1940-1997.*

[317] The death certificate of Theodore Frelinghuysen McDonald, State of Michigan, Registered No. 20, Jan 13, 1914, shows Theodore's birth date and says he was born in NY. The birth date is also recorded on his gravestone (Find A Grave Memorial #9997074). His son James Henry McDonald's passport application says Theodore was born in Little Falls, NY (*U.S. Passport Applications, 1795-1925*). Samuel W. Beake in a biography for Theodore's son-in-law, Edward B. Gibson, M.D., in *Past and Present of Washtenaw County, Michigan* (1906) says Theodore McDonald was born in Trenton, NJ. It is impossible to know which place was correct, but the Herkimer County location seems likely.

[318] Hon. Theodore Frelinghuysen, *Speeches on the Passage of the Bill for the Removal of the Indians Delivered in the Congress of the United States, April and May, 1930* (Perkins and Marvin, Boston, 1830), 29.

[319] The birth date appears on her gravestone (Find A Grave Memorial #9997073). See also James Gibson Family Tree, Owner: XBeanie68, ancestry.com.

[320] Find A Grave Memorial #9997073. Birth and death dates appear on their gravestones.

[321] *U.S. Passport Applications, 1795-1925.* His birth date and place, as well as his middle name, Henry, are shown on the application.

[322] *Michigan, Marriage Records, 1867-1952.*

[323] Find A Grave Memorial #140085424.

[324] Find A Grave Memorial #140085382.

[325] Find A Grave Memorial #140085424.

[326] *Michigan, Marriage Records, 1867-1952.*

[327] James Gibson Family Tree, Owner: XBeanie68, ancestry.com., accessed July 2015.

[328] Ibid.

[329] Find A Grave Memorial #140085321.

[330] *U.S. Passport Applications, 1795-1925.* See also Gudgel Family Tree, Owner: DeniseLeslieKaiser, ancestry.com, accessed July 2015.

[331] *New York, Passenger Lists, 1820-1957.*

[332] *U.S. Passport Applications, 1795-1925.*

[333] *New York, Passenger Lists, 1820-1957.*

[334] *Puerto Rico, Passenger and Crew Lists, 1901-1962.*

[335] Find A Grave Memorial #140085286.

[336] Gudgel Family Tree, Owner: DeniseLeslieKaiser, ancestry.com, accessed July 2015.

[337] *Michigan, Births and Christenings Index, 1867-1911.*

[338] *Michigan, Marriage Records, 1867-1952*; *U.S., World War II Draft Registration Cards, 1942;* Lancashire Family Tree (1), Owner: pinnacletax, ancestry.com, accessed July 2015.

[339] *U.S., World War I Draft Registration Cards, 1917-1918.*

[340] *U.S., World War II Draft Registration Cards, 1942.*

[341] *Florida Death Index, 1877-1998*; Lancashire Family Tree.

[342] *Ohio, Deaths, 1908-1932, 1938-2007.*

[343] *Ohio, Birth Index, 1908-1964;* Lancashire Family Tree.

[344] Henderson, Reid Family Tree, Owner: haydnymom, ancestry.com, accessed July 2015; 1920 federal census, Crane, Wyandot, OH.

[345] *Ohio, Birth Index, 1908-1964.*

[346] 1940 federal census, Toledo, Lucas, OH.

[347] *Georgia Deaths, 1919-98.*

[348] Ibid.

[349] Henderson, Reid Family Tree.

[350] Bryan Boutwell, "Robert L. DuPont, M.D., to speak at commencement," the University of Texas Medical School at Houston, med.uth.tmc.edu, 2003, accessed July 2015.

[351] Interview with Dr. Robert DuPont, PBS Frontline: Drug Wars, 2000, accessed July 2015.

[352] B. Boutwell, "Robert L. DuPont, M.D., to speak at commencement."

[353] Robert L. DuPont, "Why Marijuana is the Most Dangerous Drug," Blog of Robert L. DuPont, World Federation Against Drugs, Feb 24, 2012, wfad.se, accessed July 2015.

[354] B. Boutwell, "Robert L. DuPont, M.D., to speak at commencement."

[355] R. L. DuPont, "Why Marijuana is the Most Dangerous Drug."

[356] B. Boutwell, "Robert L. DuPont, M.D., to speak at commencement."

[357] Biography of Herbert Lancashire DuPont, Prabook, prabook.org, accessed July 2015.

[358] Biography of Herbert Lancashire DuPont.

[359] Ibid.

[360] Herbert L. DuPont, M.D., Baylor College of Medicine, bcm.edu, accessed July 2015.

[361] Biography of Herbert Lancashire DuPont.

[362] Obituary of Josephine McDonald Kutsche, *The Toledo Blade*, Toledo, OH, Mar 10, 2010.

[363] Ibid. The obit says the boat explosion occurred in 1925, but Lucy wasn't born until Nov 1926, so it probably happened sometime after that.

[364] Ibid.

[365] Obituary of Henry Mattimoe Kutsche, *The Toledo Blade*, Toledo, OH, Apr 2, 1991.

[366] Obituary of Josephine McDonald Kutsche.

[367] Obituary of Elizabeth Lancashire Stuckey, *The Arizona Republic*, Phoenix, AZ, Apr 12, 2009.

[368] Obituary of Elizabeth Lancashire Stuckey.

[369] "Stuckey Insurance: Celebrating 75 Years of Service Excellence," prweb.com, June 17, 2014.

[370] *U.S. City Directories, 1821-1989.*

[371] Obituary of Elizabeth Lancashire Stuckey.

[372] Find A Grave Memorial #34324503.

[373] Mr. Jay C. Stuckey Jr., Attorney, Lawyer.com, accessed July 2015.

[374] *Texas, Marriage Record Index, 1966–2008.*

[375] Stuckey & McRae, Lawyers.com, accessed July 2015.

[376] *U.S., Social Security Death Index, 1935-2014;* Lancashire Family Tree.

[377] *U.S. World War II Army Enlistment Records, 1938-1946.*

[378] "Lawrence H. Lancashire," American Air Museum in Britain, americanairmuseum.com, accessed July 2015.

[379] *World War II Prisoners of War, 1941-1946.* The record, unfortunately, isn't very detailed. It shows L. H. Lancashire was detained by Germany and "returned to Military Control, Liberated or Repatriated."

[380] "Lawrence H. Lancashire," American Air Museum in Britain.

[381] Obituary of Florence Lorraine Tallman Lancashire, *Peninsula Clarion*, Alaska, Apr 18, 2000.

[382] Obituary of Florence Lorraine Tallman Lancashire.

[383] *U.S., Social Security Death Index, 1935-2014;* Lancashire Family Tree.

[384] Obituary of Florence Lorraine Tallman Lancashire.

[385] *U.S., Social Security Death Index, 1935-2014.*

[386] Steele Family Tree, Owner: kimberly11161, ancestry.com, accessed July 2015.

[387] *U.S., Department of Veterans Affairs BIRLS Death File, 1850-2010.*

[388] *U.S. World War II Army Enlistment Records, 1938-1946.*

[389] "Special Week of Prayer to Give Christians Opportunity to Demonstrate Their Unity," *Toledo Blade*, Toledo, OH, Jan 11, 1980.

[390] *U.S., Social Security Death Index, 1935-2014.*

[391] Obituary of George Frederick Alter Jr., *Toledo Blade*, Toledo, OH, Mar 22, 2015.

[392] *Ohio, Deaths, 1908-1932, 1938-2007.*

[393] Obituary of George Frederick Alter Jr.

[394] *Ohio, Deaths, 1908-1932, 1938-2007.*

[395] Obituary of George Frederick Alter Jr.

[396] Obituary of Josephine McDonald Kutsche. The obit says the boat explosion occurred in 1925, but that would be impossible since Lucy was born in Nov. 1926.

[397] *Ohio, Deaths, 1908-1932, 1938-2007.*

[398] *New York, Passenger Lists, 1820-1957.*

[399] *Michigan, Marriage Records, 1867-1952.*

[400] *U.S. Passport Applications, 1795-1925.*

[401] 1940 federal census, Lima, Licking, OH.

[402] The 1930 federal census of Athens, Athens, OH, shows Wilmer was a WWI vet.

[403] *U.S., World War II Draft Registration Cards, 1942.*

[404] *Florida, State Census, 1867-1945.*

[405] *U.S., Social Security Applications and Claims Index, 1936-2007.*

[406] Obituary of Joseph Harris, *The Pasadena Citizen*, yourpasadenanews.com, Mar. 8, 2014.

[407] Find A Grave Memorial #127390446.

[408] *Michigan, Births and Christenings Index, 1867-1911* shows her born 1896, but NY Passenger lists shows her born 1897 (*New York, Passenger Lists, 1820-1957*). The 1897 date makes more sense because her sister, Mary M., reportedly, was born June 22, 1896.

[409] *The Michigan Alumnus* (The Alumni Association of the University of Michigan Publishers), Vol 30, 994.

[410] *U.S., World War II Draft Registration Cards, 1942; Michigan, Marriage Records, 1867-1952.*

[411] *Michigan, Marriage Records, 1867-1952.*

[412] *New York, Passenger Lists, 1820-1957.*

[413] *The Michigan Alumnus*, Vol 35, 17.

[414] *Michigan, Marriage Records, 1867-1952; Texas, Death Certificates, 1903–1982.*

[415] *Texas, Death Certificates, 1903–1982.*

[416] *U.S., World War I Draft Registration Cards, 1917-1918.*

[417] *U.S., World War II Draft Registration Cards, 1942.*

[418] *Texas, Death Certificates, 1903–1982.*

[419] Find A Grave Memorial #149907943.

[420] *U.S., Social Security Death Index, 1935-2014.*

[421] James Gibson Family Tree.

[422] Find A Grave Memorial #112546765.

[423] Samuel Willard Beakes, *Past and Present of Washtenaw County, Michigan: together with biographical sketches of many of its prominent and leading citizens and illustrious dead* (S. J. Clarke Publishing Co., Chicago, 1906), 1845.

[424] Ibid.

[425] *Directory of Deceased American Physicians, 1804-1929.*

[426] Find A Grave Memorial #112545684.

[427] *U.S., World War I Draft Registration Cards, 1917-1918.*

[428] *Michigan, Marriage Records, 1867-1952.*

[429] *U.S., World War II Draft Registration Cards, 1942.*

[430] *California, Death Index, 1940-1997.*

[431] Find A Grave Memorial #16862729.

[432] *U.S., Social Security Applications and Claims Index, 1936-2007.*

[433] *Michigan, Marriage Records, 1867-1952.*

[434] *U.S., World War I Draft Registration Cards, 1917-1918.*

[435] *UK, Incoming Passenger Lists, 1878-1960.*

[436] *Michigan, Deaths, 1971-1996.*

[437] Fisher-Presnell 2015 et al, Owner: easytime, ancestry.com, accessed July 2015.

[438] *Michigan, Births and Christenings Index, 1867-1911.*

[439] *The Michigan Alumnus*, Vol 38, 617.

[440] *Michigan, Deaths, 1971-1996.*

[441] 1900 federal census, Pittsfield, Washtenaw Co., MI.

[442] *Michigan, Marriage Records, 1867-1952; The Michigan Alumnus*, Vol 29, 912.

[443] *New York, Abstracts of World War I Military Service, 1917-1919.*

[444] Dowd Family Tree, Owner: steve86051, ancestry.com, accessed July 2015.

[445] Ibid.

[446] *U.S., Social Security Death Index, 1935-2014.*

[447] *U.S., Department of Veterans Affairs BIRLS Death File, 1850-2010; U.S., Social Security Applications and Claims Index, 1936-2007.*

[448] *U.S. World War II Army Enlistment Records, 1938-1946.*

[449] *U.S., Department of Veterans Affairs BIRLS Death File, 1850-2010; Florida Death Index, 1877-1998.*

[450] Obituary of Edward G. "Eddie" Dowd, *The Evening Tribune*, Hornell, NY, Aug 21, 2009.

[451] Ibid.

[452] Ibid.

[453] Find A Grave Memorial #69356424.

[454] Obituary of Robert P. Dowd Sr., *Patriot and Free Press*, Cuba, NY, Jan 8-14, 2003, 6.

[455] Find A Grave Memorial #7057130.

[456] *U.S., Social Security Applications and Claims Index, 1936-2007.*

[457] *U.S. Veterans Gravesites, ca.1775-2006; U.S., Department of Veterans Affairs BIRLS Death File, 1850-2010.*

[458] Obituary of Walter Raymond Dowd, *Daily News*, Bowling Green, KY, Dec 15, 1997, 5A.

[459] *Kentucky Death Index, 1911-2000.*

[460] Obituary of Walter Raymond Dowd; Find A Grave Memorial #150470899.

[461] *The Michigan Alumnus*, Vol 25, 324.

[462] Dr. Maurer Maurer, *The U.S. Air Service in World War I* (Office of Air Force History, Headquarters USAF, Washington, 1978).

[463] "History of the 22d-24th Aero Squadrons," *Gorrell's History of the American Expeditionary Forces Air Service, 1917–1919* (National Archives, Washington, D.C.), Series E, Vol 9.

[464] Beaumont-en-Verdunois is a commune located in the Meuse department of the Lorraine region of northeastern France, near the border with Belgium. It was completely destroyed during World War I, so much so that they decided not to rebuild it, but to maintain it as a testimony to war, "a village that died for France." (*Wikipedia*, accessed July 2015).

[465] Capt. Arthur Raymond Brooks, *A History of the 22nd Aero Squadron*, as recounted in *Cross & Cockade Journal* (Society of World War I Aero Historians, Summer 1963), Vol 4, No. 2, 109-136. In a letter to Edward's mother, Anna McDonald Gibson, telling her of her son's death, Lt. Frank R. Tyndall noted that the official squadron report for the day by Lt. Norman M. Hullings said that Edward's American flight contained six planes that were attacked by 18 Fokkers. The letter and other items related to Edward's death were in the possession of James G. Gibson on Nov 30, 2014.

[466] Capt. A. R. Brooks, *A History of the 22nd Aero Squadron*, Vol 4, No. 2, 109-136.

[467] Lt. Norman M. Hullings, official report on the death of Lt. Edward B. Gibson. A copy was mailed to Anna McDonald Gibson by Lt. Frank R. Tyndall, now in the possession of James G. Gibson.

[468] The letter and other items related to Edward's death were in the possession of James G. Gibson on Nov 30, 2014.

[469] Edward Branford Gibson KIA 191.pdf, James Gibson Family Tree.

[470] *U.S., Find A Grave Index, 1600s-Current;* Find A Grave Memorial #112545846.

[471] 1900 federal census, Ann Arbor Ward 6, Washtenaw, MI.

[472] James Gibson Family Tree.

[473] 1900 federal census, McKeesport Ward 3, Allegheny, PA.

[474] *U.S. Passport Applications, 1795-1925.*

[475] James Gibson Family Tree.

[476] Find A Grave Memorial #121882829. See also W. C. Armstrong, *The Axfords of Oxford, New Jersey*, 43.

[477] Find A Grave Memorial #121882847.

[478] The 1858 date comes from her gravestone, Find A Grave Memorial #121882829.

[479] *Michigan, Deaths and Burials Index, 1867-1995.*

[480] Find A Grave Memorial #12188247.

[481] Joanna disappears from the records after 1860.

[482] The 1847 birth date comes from her gravestone (Find A Grave Memorial #36909331).

[483] *Michigan, Marriage Records, 1867-1952.*

[484] *Washington, Deaths, 1883-1960.*

[485] Ibid.

[486] Find A Grave Memorial #36909331.

[487] Standard Certificate of Death for Hiram Mason Betts, State of Oregon, Registrar's No. 16, Jan 24, 1941. The informant on the death certificate was Robt. Schroeder of Mill City, Oregon. His relationship to the deceased is unknown. Some of the information he provided is in error. He said Hiram's father was Leroy Betts. Perhaps Leroy was Daniel Betts's middle name. He also said Hiram's mother was Julia Mason, an error. Her maiden name was Jenney.

[488] *California, Death Index, 1940-1997.*

[489] Standard Certificate of Death for Hiram Mason Betts.

[490] Find A Grave Memorial #75580244. Hiram has a lovely grave marker with an engraved image of Mt. Hood.

[491] *California, Death Index, 1940-1997*; *California, Passenger and Crew Lists, 1882-1959.*

[492] Ibid.

[493] *U.S., World War I Draft Registration Cards, 1917-1918.*

[494] Ken Munford, "Fraternal Orders Shaped Corvallis," *Gazette Times*, Corvallis, OR, May 25, 2007.

[495] *California, Passenger and Crew Lists, 1882-1959.*

[496] *California, Death Index, 1940-1997.*

[497] Ibid.

[498] *California Birth Index, 1905-1995.*

[499] *California, Marriage Index, 1960-1985.*

[500] Find A Grave Memorial #15976321.

[501] *Kansas State Census Collection, 1855-1925.* The 1900 federal census of Skookumchuck, Lewis, WA, shows Arthur b. Mar 1874.

[502] Betts2 Family Tree (Betts2_2009-05-08_2013-01-09), Owner: inrtrvle, ancestry.com, accessed July 2015.

[503] *Washington, Deaths, 1883-1960.*

[504] Betts2 Family Tree.

[505] Find A Grave Memorial #15976321.

[506] Betts2 Family Tree.

[507] *Washington, Births, 1883-1935*; *U.S., World War I Draft Registration Cards, 1917-1918.*

[508] *Washington, County Marriages, 1855-2008;* Betts2 Family Tree.

[509] *U.S., World War I Draft Registration Cards, 1917-1918.*

[510] *Washington Death Index, 1940-1996.*

[511] Find A Grave Memorial #41151030.

[512] Betts2 Family Tree. See also 1930 and 1940 federal censuses, Rochester, Thurston, MI.

[513] *Washington, Marriage Records, 1865-2004.*

[514] Betts2 Family Tree; Courtney Family, stancourtney.com, accessed Nov 2015.

[515] Find A Grave Memorial #44146315. He has a military marker showing his military service.

[516] Betts2 Family Tree.

[517] *Washington Death Index, 1940-1996*; Find A Grave Memorial #44146315.

[518] Betts2 Family Tree.

[519] *Michigan, Marriage Records, 1867–1952.* Anna Trombley is identified in the marriage record for her son, Robert. See also Spradling Family Tree.

[520] Spradling Family Tree, Owner: Debra Jenney, ancestry.com, accessed July 2015.

[521] Ibid.

[522] May's birth date is unknown. It varies widely in census records from 1867-1878.

[523] Death Certificate of William W. Jenney, Michigan Department of State, Registered No. 8, Apr 5, 1905.

[524] Spradling Family Tree.

[525] *U.S., World War II Draft Registration Cards, 1942.*

[526] *Michigan, Marriage Records, 1867-1952.*

[527] Find A Grave Memorial #26833259; Spradling Family Tree.

[528] Find A Grave Memorial #26833328.

[529] Spradling Family Tree.

[530] *U.S., Social Security Death Index, 1935-2014*; Spradling Family Tree.

[531] Find A Grave Memorial #113861877.

[532] *U.S., World War I Draft Registration Cards, 1917-1918.*

[533] Spradling Family Tree.

[534] *U.S., World War I Draft Registration Cards, 1917-1918.*

[535] *Michigan, Deaths, 1971-1996.*

[536] Find A Grave Memorial #118759032.

[537] *U.S., World War II Draft Registration Cards, 1942.*

[538] *Michigan, Marriage Records, 1867-1952.*

[539] Find A Grave Memorial #114092733.

[540] *U.S., World War II Draft Registration Cards, 1942;* 1940 federal census, Detroit, Wayne, MI.

[541] *U.S., Social Security Death Index, 1935-2014.*

[542] Find A Grave Memorial #118759783.

[543] *U.S., World War I Draft Registration Cards, 1917-1918.*

[544] *U.S., Social Security Applications and Claims Index, 1936-2007.*

[545] *Michigan, Marriage Records, 1867-1952;* Mapes Stearns Family, Owner: WendyOrafferty, ancestry.com, accessed Aug 2015.

[546] *U.S., Social Security Applications and Claims Index, 1936-2007.*

[547] *U.S., Social Security Death Index, 1935-2014.*

[548] Find A Grave Memorial #105088871.

[549] Obituary of Harold A. Cavanagh, *Ocala Star Banner*, Ocala, FL, Jul 10, 2004.

[550] *Michigan, Marriage Records, 1867-1952.*

[551] *U.S. City Directories, 1821-1989.*

[552] *U.S., Consular Reports of Marriages, 1910-1949*; Call Family Tree, Owner: jcall1100, ancestry.com, accessed July 2015.

[553] *U.S., World War I Draft Registration Cards, 1917-1918.*

[554] *U.S., Social Security Applications and Claims Index, 1936-2007.*

[555] *California, Death Index, 1940-1997.*

[556] Find A Grave Memorial #74319633.

[557] *U.S., Social Security Death Index, 1935-2014.*

[558] *Michigan, Marriage Records, 1867-1952.*

[559] *Michigan, Divorce Records, 1897-1952.*

[560] *Michigan, Marriage Records, 1867-1952.*

[561] *U.S., Social Security Death Index, 1935-2014.*

[562] Ibid.

[563] Ibid.

[564] Find A Grave Memorial #70805459.

[565] Terry Colliver, Bio of Thomas C. Hower Jr., OK ChE (Oklahoma Chemical Engineer), 1975 Fall.

[566] Birth date is from 1900 census. Birth place of Mount Clemens is shown in *Michigan Marriages*.

[567] *Michigan, Marriage Records, 1867-1952.*

[568] Ibid.

[569] *Michigan, Deaths and Burials Index, 1867-1995.*

[570] *U.S., Sons of the American Revolution Membership Applications, 1889-1970.* Benjamin's son, Charles Sheldon McDonald, filled out an application for SAR membership dated May 9, 1924. He notes that Benjamin's birth date was Sept. 12, 1825. This date is confirmed by Benjamin's gravestone, Find A Grave Memorial #66450464. There are many conflicting dates for Benjamin's birth on the Internet.

[571] Charles Sheldon McDonald, 1924, *U.S., Sons of the American Revolution Membership Applications, 1889-1970.*

[572] Find A Grave Memorial #130616835.

[573] Michigan Historical Collections (Michigan Pioneer and Historical Society, Lansing, MI, 1908), Vol 13, 260. Phoebe had a brother, Solon Burt, for whom her grandson, Solon Burt Harger, was named.

[574] *California, Death Index, 1905-1939.*

[575] C. S. McDonald, 1924, *U.S., Sons of the American Revolution Membership Applications, 1889-1970.*

[576] The 1821 birth date for Benjamin Fowler McDonald seems very unlikely given that his brother Theodore F. McDonald was born July 30, 1821.

[577] Find A Grave Memorial #66450464.

[578] Michigan Historical Collections (Michigan Pioneer and Historical Society, Lansing, MI, 1908), Vol 13, 260.

[579] *California, Death Index, 1905-1939.*

[580] Find A Grave Memorial #97580685.

[581] C. S. McDonald, 1924, *U.S., Sons of the American Revolution Membership Applications, 1889-1970.*

[582] *Calendar of the University of Michigan for 1873-4* (University of Michigan, Ann Arbor, 1874), 82. See also *The Michigan Alumnus*, Vol 7, 215.

[583] *The Michigan Alumnus*, Vol 7, 215.

[584] *Michigan, Marriage Records, 1867-1952.*

[585] *U.S., Border Crossings from Canada to U.S., 1895-1956.*

[586] Ibid.

[587] C. S. McDonald, 1924, *U.S., Sons of the American Revolution Membership Applications, 1889-1970.*

[588] Find A Grave Memorial #66450518.

[589] *New York, Passenger Lists, 1820-1957.*

[590] "The Strange Story of the McDonald/Harger Family," Remembering Rochester, rochesteravonhistory.blogspot.com, 28 Jan 2012, accessed July 2015.

[591] *Michigan, Marriage Records, 1867-1952.*

[592] *U.S., Find A Grave Index, 1600s-Current.*

[593] Tony Scott, biography of K. D. Harger, Find A Grave Memorial #54612354. Mr. Scott is the author of *The Stars of Hollywood Forever – A Who's Who of Hollywood's Final Resting Place.*

[594] *U.S., Find A Grave Index, 1600s-Current.*

[595] Find A Grave Memorial #54612354.

[596] *California, Death Index, 1940-1997.*

[597] "Faculty Announces Names of Students to Receive Degrees," *The Stanford Daily* (Stanford University, CA, Apr. 14, 1925), Vol 67, 4.

[598] *California, Death Index, 1940-1997.*

[599] The 1940 federal census, Inglewood, Los Angeles, CA, shows Nino had 4 yrs of college plus at least one year of postgraduate work.

[600] *California, Death Index, 1940-1997.*

[601] *U.S., Social Security Death Index, 1935-2014.*

[602] Obituary of Donald Duncan Harger, *San Francisco Chronicle*, San Francisco, CA, Jan 26-Jan 27, 2014.

[603] Ibid.

[604] *California, Marriage Index, 1960-1985.*

[605] Obituary of Donald Duncan Harger.

[606] Ibid.

[607] Ibid.

[608] *California Birth Index, 1905-1995; U.S., Find A Grave Index, 1600s-Current.*

[609] Internet Broadway Database (IBDB), ibdb.com, accessed Aug 2015.

[610] Ibid. Coincidentally, the author of this book performed at the Broadhurst Theater on Broadway in *Amadeus* in the early 1980's.

[611] "Tossed in Alley – Police Solve Torso Murder," *Brooklyn Eagle,* Brooklyn, NY, Oct 6, 1945, front page. The article noted that the head of the victim had not been found.

[612] "The Strange Story of the McDonald/Harger Family."

[613] Ibid.

[614] The 1940 federal census for Inglewood, Los Angeles, CA, shows Burt was divorced. Apparently, he had been married at some point before.

[615] "The Strange Story of the McDonald/Harger Family."

[616] *The Delphos Daily Herald* (Delphos, OH, Jan 24, 1950, 2) states that the apartment was at 43 W. 46 St.

[617] "Story of the Play," *There's Always a Murder,* by Ken Parker, Samuel French, Inc., 1979. Coincidentally, the author of this book also performed at the Provincetown Playhouse in New York in the hit comedy classic, *Vampire Lesbians of Sodom.*

[618] Find A Grave Memorial #99294161.

CHAPTER 4

[619] The birth date comes from the Mayor John McDonald family blueprint. The 1850 federal census, Russell, Geauga, OH, shows Philo was born in Massachusetts. We cannot be sure if he truly was born in Massachusetts. Census dates and places are notoriously inaccurate.

[620] Barbara Lewis, posting to Genealogy.com, Mar 1, 2002, accessed Aug 2015. A family bible in the possession of Barbara Lewis shows Abagail [sic] McDonald (who died Sept. 14, 1839) was the daughter of Philo Fowler. It certainly would make sense that Abigail's father was named Philo and that several generations thereafter were named for him.

[621] *Family Sketches of Ohio, Herkimer County, NY,* herkimer.nygenweb.net, accessed Aug 2015.

[622] Ohio, New York, *Wikipedia*, accessed Nov 2015.

[623] *New York*, Military *Service Cards, 1816-1979.*

[624] The Mayor John McDonald family blueprint. See also Lewis/Eastlick Family Tree.

[625] Lewis/Eastlick Family Tree, Owner: Leslie Lewis, ancestry.com, accessed Aug 2015.

[626] Philo McDonald Jr. was born in 1841 in Ohio according to the 1850 census.

[627] Ty Pilarczyk, "Geauga History – The Rise of Russell," *Geauga News*, Feb 12, 2013, geauganews.com, accessed Nov 2015.

[628] 1850 federal census, Russell, Geauga, OH. The census record incorrectly spells the surname McDonough.

[629] Find A Grave Memorial #92500397. The 1846 death date appears on her gravestone.

[630] The Mayor John McDonald family blueprint.

[631] Ibid.

[632] Joe Hagerty, "History of the Wright County Sheriff's Office," Presentation to the Annandale History Club, Mar 4, 2013, annandaleonline.com, accessed Aug 2015.

[633] Franklin Curtiss-Wedge, *The History of Wright County, Minnesota* (H.C. Cooper Jr. and Co., Chicago, 1915), Vol 1, 96.

[634] The Mayor John McDonald family blueprint; Dawidowicz Family Tree, Owner: dplus9, ancestry.com, accessed Aug 2015.

[635] *1857 Minnesota, Territorial and State Censuses, 1849-1905.*

[636] The family appears in the 1860 census in Clearwater, Wright County, MN.

[637] The Mayor John McDonald family blueprint.

[638] Lewis/Eastlick Family Tree.

[639] Find A Grave Memorial #140849585.

[640] The Mayor John McDonald family blueprint states that William was born in Herkimer County. The death date shown on the blueprint is confirmed by the death certificate of William McDonald, Arizona Territorial Board of Health, County Registrar's No. 1781, Mar 16, 1912.

[641] *Minnesota, Territorial and State Censuses, 1849-1905.*

[642] The Mayor John McDonald family blueprint.

[643] Ibid.

[644] The marriage date is noted on the Mayor John McDonald family blueprint.

[645] Image of obituary of Electa Summerrow, from an unknown newspaper, courtesy of Leslie Lewis, Lewis/Eastlick Family Tree. Electa's obit mentions that she had lived in Arizona 54 years at the time of her death in 1960. She probably came with her mother, her sister and her grandfather, William McDonald.

[646] Death certificate of William McDonald, Arizona Territorial Board of Health, County Registrar's No. 1781, Mar 16, 1912; Find A Grave Memorial #140656108.

[647] The blueprint was made sometime after William's death in 1912, and almost certainly before Mayor John McDonald's death in 1913.

[648] The Mayor John McDonald family blueprint.

[649] The Summerrow family was from Travis County, so that's probably where the wedding took place.

[650] 1880 federal census, Precinct 6, Travis, TX; Eaton Family Tree, Owner: GreggMatthewEaton, ancestry.com, accessed Aug 2015.

[651] *U.S., Appointments of U. S. Postmasters, 1832-1971.*

[652] The census shows Emma as widowed, but a record for her son, Thomas Wilcox, shows that P. K. Wilcox was alive in 1923 (*U.S. National Homes for Disabled Volunteer Soldiers, 1866-1938*).

[653] Emma's daughter Electa Summerrow's obituary mentions that Electa had lived in Arizona 54 years at the time of her death in 1960, so she probably moved to Arizona about 1906 with her mother, if she was still alive, as well as with her sister, Leila, and her grandfather, William McDonald.

[654] The Mayor John McDonald family blueprint.

[655] Death certificate of Lelia Summerrow, Arizona State Board of Health, State File No. 4121, Mar 30, 1929.

[656] Electa's birth date appears on her gravestone, Find A Grave Memorial #35470776.

[657] Obituary of Electa Summerrow, source unknown, courtesy of Lewis/Eastlick Family Tree.

[658] He is identified as "P. K. Wilcox" in the Mayor John McDonald family blueprint.

[659] *California, Death Index, 1940-1997; U.S., World War II Draft Registration Cards, 1942.*

[660] *U.S., World War I Draft Registration Cards, 1917-1918.*

[661] *U.S. National Homes for Disabled Volunteer Soldiers, 1866-1938.*

[662] Ibid.

[663] *U.S. Veterans Gravesites, ca.1775-2006.*

[664] Find A Grave Memorial #36453121.

[665] The Mayor John McDonald family blueprint. William's correct birth and death dates are recorded on the blueprint, which shows he died in Austin, Texas.

[666] His death date and location are recorded on Mayor John McDonald's blueprint.

[667] Find A Grave Memorial #67751108. William K.'s birth and death dates are shown on his gravestone, which now lies on the ground and is broken in half.

[668] John's birth date appears on the family blueprint and on his gravestone. The place of birth is recorded in Lewis E. Daniell's *Types of Successful Men of Texas*, 563-565.

[669] Lewis E. Daniell, *Types of Successful Men of Texas* (published by the author, Austin, TX, 1890), 563-565.

[670] The Mayor John McDonald family blueprint. Lewis E. Daniell's *Types of Successful Men of Texas* states "His wife to whom he was married in 1857 was Mrs G. C. Kent of Clear Water Minnesota." The "G" in Mrs. G. C. Kent is apparently an error. It should be Mrs. "E." C. Kent.

[671] Ibid.

[672] Ibid.

[673] L. E. Daniell, *Types of Successful Men of Texas*, 563-565.

[674] Ibid.

[675] The Mayor John McDonald family blueprint.

[676] Ibid.

[677] Ibid.

[678] Death certificate of Ray McDonald, Texas Department of Health, No. 14556, Mar 30, 1939.

[679] L. E. Daniell, *Types of Successful Men of Texas*, 563-565.

[680] Ibid.

[681] Wes J. Sheffield, "The Frontier Community of Finis," *The Cyclone,* (West Texas Historical Association, Texas Tech University, Lubbock, TX, Mar 15, 2004), Vol 11, Issue 1, 1.

[682] L. E. Daniell, *Types of Successful Men of Texas*, 563-565.

[683] Bruce Hunt, "The Rise and Fall of the Austin Dam," Not Even Past, notevenpast.org, July 9, 2011, accessed Aug 2015.

[684] L. E. Daniell, *Types of Successful Men of Texas*, 563-565.

[685] Charles Albert Hotchkiss, *History of Scottish Rite Masonry in Texas* (Cornell University Library, 1916), 39-43.

[686] L. E. Daniell, *Types of Successful Men of Texas*, 563-565.

[687] 1900 federal census, Justice Precinct 5, Jack, TX.

[688] W. J. Sheffield, "The Frontier Community of Finis."

[689] B. Hunt, "The Rise and Fall of the Austin Dam."

[690] Hole: 5 – Loch McDonald, Austin Country Club Golf Course, austincountryclub.com, accessed Aug 2015.

[691] The blueprint shows Ellen died Mar 8, 1904 in Finis, TX. The death date, however, is apparently an error. Her gravestone clearly shows she died Mar 28, 1904. This may be another indication that it was Burt who actually wrote the blueprint. It seems unlikely his father, John, would have made that mistake. See Find A Grave Memorial #7806525. Find A Grave shows Ellen's maiden name as Chapman, the daughter of Silas and Nancy (Eddy) Chapman, an apparent error. Ellen Kent appears with Abel and Sabina (Thornton) Kent and her family in the 1850 federal census in Columbia, Meigs, OH; this record shows her as "Hellen." By 1857, the Abel Kent family was living in Stearns Co., MN (*Minnesota, Territorial and State Censuses, 1849-1905*).

[692] W. J. Sheffield, "The Frontier Community of Finis."

[693] John has not been located in the 1910 census, but he was definitely living in a rural area of Phoenix at the time of his brother William's death.

[694] Death certificate of William McDonald. John's address is shown as "R. F. D. Phoenix."

[695] Find A Grave Memorial #7806520. John was buried in Jack County with his wife, Ellen, but he was probably living in Phoenix at the time of his death; no death record has yet been located.

[696] The Mayor John McDonald family blueprint.

[697] *The Technic '94*, Engineering Society of the University of Michigan (Register Publishing Co., 1895), Issue 7, Issue 12.

[698] "Chemical Laboratory, 1892-1926," University of Texas Libraries, lib.utexas.edu, accessed Aug 2015.

[699] The Mayor John McDonald family blueprint.

[700] Correspondence with T. Corey McDonald, July 10, 2015, and Diane McDonald Shaul, Aug 12, 2015. Diane reported that Edna Walthersdorf McDonald said that her father was a Baron of Saxony. The surname Walthersdorf is also spelled "Waltersdorf" or "von Waltersdorf."

[701] Richard W. Amero, *"Madame Schumann-Heink: A Legend in her Time,"* balboaparkhistory.net; Correspondence with Diane McDonald Shaul, Aug 12, 2015.

[702] "The Lake Navigation Company," pamphlet of the Colorado Lake Chautauqua Association, Austin, TX, 1893, texashistory.org, accessed Aug 2015.

[703] John H. Slate, *Lost Austin* (Arcadia Publishing Co., Charleston, SC, 2012), 23. James Reilly Gordon is called James Reilly in this book.

[704] Photograph of Old Red Campus building, at the John T. Allan Campus of Stephen F. Austin High School, The Portal to Texas History, texashistory.unt.edu, accessed Aug 2015.

[705] Correspondence with Diane McDonald Shaul, Aug 12, 2015. Diane inherited a gold bracelet from Edna that said, "Houston Class of 1903."

[706] Edna taught voice and piano and was a choir director, according to her granddaughter, Diane McDonald Shaul.

[707] Yes, the name is spelled "Theddy" in the census, probably a nickname for Theodore.

[708] 1910 federal census, Phoenix Ward 2, Maricopa, AZ. James M. Barker is listed as Burt's son, an apparent error. Barker, a little research reveals, was the son of James M. and Jane S. Barker of Huntington, Indiana.

[709] C. P. Stephens DeSoto Six Motorcars (Stephens DeSoto Building), Phoenix, Maricopa Co., AZ, National Register of Historic Places Registration Form, Dec 19, 2012.

[710] Death certificate of William McDonald. John's address is shown as "R. F. D. Phoenix."

[711] Diane McDonald Shaul reported that her mother, Isabel Dellinger McDonald, told her that the blueprint was made by Burt McDonald.

[712] 1920 federal census, Phoenix, Maricopa, AZ.

[713] C. P. Stephens DeSoto Six Motorcars, National Register of Historic Places, 2012.

[714] Ibid.

[715] 1930 federal census, Phoenix, Maricopa, AZ.

[716] Burt has not been located in the 1940 census. He was probably deceased before then.

[717] The Mayor John McDonald family blueprint; *U.S., World War I Draft Registration Cards, 1917-1918*; *U.S., World War II Draft Registration Cards, 1942*. Kenneth's gravestone shows he was b. June 5, 1892, an apparent error. There may have been a transcription error in military records. See *U.S. Veterans Gravesites, ca.1775-2006*.

[718] Correspondence with Diane McDonald Shaul, Aug 10, 2015.

[719] 1910 federal census, Houston Ward 3, Harris, TX. The census shows Edna as "widowed," even though Burt was still, in fact, alive.

[720] *U.S., World War I Draft Registration Cards, 1917-1918.*

[721] *U.S. National Cemetery Interment Control Forms, 1928-1962..*

[722] Gen. Arthur MacArthur's son, Douglas MacArthur, would become a five-star general in World War II.

[723] "Camp MacArthur," Texas State Historical Association, tshaonline.org, accessed Aug 2015.

[724] Correspondence with Diane McDonald Shaul, Aug 12, 2015. Diane said the marriage took place Aug 14, either in 1925 or 1926.

[725] *U.S., Social Security Applications and Claims Index, 1936-2007; California, Death Index, 1940-1997.*

[726] The 1930 and 1940 federal censuses for Dallas. Albert's granddaughter, Diane McDonald Shaul, reports he was Chief of Police at one time.

[727] Correspondence with Diane McDonald Shaul, Aug 10, 2015.

[728] Correspondence with Diane McDonald Shaul, Aug 17, 2015.

[729] *U.S. City Directories, 1821-1989.*

[730] *U.S., World War II Draft Registration Cards, 1942.*

[731] Correspondence with Raymond Bart McDonald, July 11, 2015.

[732] *California, Death Index, 1940-1997.*

[733] Find A Grave Memorial #3417525.

[734] Correspondence with Thomas Corey McDonald, Aug 5, 2015. Diane McDonald Shaul says the original blueprint is now in the possession of her brother, Kenneth Wayne McDonald.

[735] *Texas Birth Index, 1903-1997.*

[736] Correspondence with Raymond Bart McDonald, July 11, 2015.

[737] *California, Marriage Index, 1949-1959.*

[738] Correspondence with Thomas Corey McDonald, Aug 17, 2015; WikiTree, wikitree.com, accessed Aug 2015. Julia Ann McDonald Vickroy (1825-1910) was from St Clair Twp, Bedford, PA.

[739] Ibid.

[740] Ibid.

[741] Correspondence with Raymond Bart McDonald, July 2015.

[742] The Vickroy Family, genealogy.com, accessed Aug 2015.

[743] Correspondence with Thomas Corey McDonald, Aug 5, 2015.

[744] *Texas Birth Index, 1903-1997.*

[745] Obituary of David Gordon McDonald, *The Virginian Pilot*, Norfolk, VA, June 7, 2015.

[746] Ibid.

[747] "Court documents: Man entered Ocean View bar covered in blood and bleeding saying he stabbed someone," WTKR, Newschannel3, wtkr.com, June 2, 2015, accessed Aug 2015.

[748] "Man charged in Grove Ave. murder in Norfolk," WTKR, Newschannel3, wtkr.com, June 3, 2015, accessed Aug 2015. The assailant was already on probation for grand larceny at the time of the stabbing. He was charged with second-degree murder.

[749] "Court documents," WTKR, 2015.

[750] Obituary of David Gordon McDonald.

[751] Ibid.

[752] Ibid.

[753] *Texas, Death Certificates, 1903–1982.*

[754] Ibid.

[755] Ibid; Find A Grave Memorial #109552053.

[756] *U.S., Department of Veterans Affairs BIRLS Death File, 1850-2010.*

[757] 1940 federal census, San Antonio, Bexar, TX.

[758] *Texas, Death Certificates, 1903–1982.*

[759] Some say her middle name was Ellen, after her mother, but the 1870 census shows "Ella."

[760] The Mayor John McDonald family blueprint. She appears as "Ella G." in the 1870 census.

[761] L. E. Daniell, *Types of Successful Men of Texas*, 563-565.

[762] Dawidowicz Family Tree.

[763] Death certificate of John Philo McDonald, Texas Department of Health, No. 56494, Dec 11, 1945.

[764] Death certificate of Tennie Ford McDonald, Texas Department of Health, State File No. 32240, July 2, 1951.

[765] *U.S., World War I Draft Registration Cards, 1917-1918.*

[766] Find A Grave Memorial #67750972.

[767] Death certificate of Richard F. McDonald, Texas Department of Health, State File No. 58353, Dec 3, 1955.

[768] Find A Grave Memorial #45047654.

[769] *U.S., Headstone Applications for Military Veterans, 1925-1963.*

[770] *U.S., World War II Draft Registration Cards, 1942.*

[771] Death certificate of John Philo McDonald.

[772] Death certificate of Richard F. McDonald.

[773] Find A Grave Memorial #45047654.

[774] *Texas, Birth Certificates, 1903-1932.*

[775] Obituary of Richard Ford "Dick" McDonald Jr., *The North Augusta Star*, Augusta, GA, Apr 7, 2014.

[776] Ibid.

[777] Ibid.

[778] Find A Grave Memorial #127543294.

[779] *Texas, Birth Certificates, 1903-1932.*

[780] Obituary of Mary Jo McDonald Correll (source not identified), Message Boards, boards.ancestry.com, Jan 22, 2003.

[781] Obituary of Ross M. Correll Jr., Austin American-Statesman, Austin, TX, Dec 18, 2011.

[782] Ibid.

[783] Ibid.

[784] *Texas, Birth Certificates, 1903-1932.*

[785] *U.S., Social Security Applications and Claims Index, 1936-2007.*

[786] Obituary of Eugenia Castle McDonald Weaver, *Dallas Morning News*, Dallas, TX, Nov 4, 2003.

[787] *U.S., Social Security Death Index, 1935-2014.*

[788] Find A Grave Memorial #52255056.

[789] Find A Grave Memorial #52254560.

[790] Roy W. and Eugenia C. McDonald Endowed Chair of Civil Procedure, endowments.giving.utexas.edu, Mar 3, 2004.

[791] Death certificate of Ray McDonald, Texas Department of Health, No. 14556, Mar 30, 1939.

[792] *Texas, Death Certificates, 1903–1982.*

[793] Ibid.

[794] The Mayor John McDonald family blueprint shows Philo was born 1841. The 1850 census agrees with that date. Civil War records, however, indicate Philo was born about 1836. See, for example, *Seventy-Fifth Regiment Ohio Volunteer Infantry,* Civil War Index, p. 229, civilwarindex.com.

[795] *Minnesota, Territorial and State Censuses, 1849-1905.*

[796] 75th Ohio Infantry, Company D, Rootsweb, freepages.history.rootsweb.ancestry.com, accessed Aug 2015.

[797] *U.S. Civil War Soldiers, 1861-1865.*

[798] Todd Williams, "May 2, 1863 – A Day That Changed Wyoming," *The Historical Record* (Wyoming Historical Society, Wyoming, OH, May 2013), Vol 33, No. 3, 4.

[799] 75th Ohio Regiment, The Civil War in the East, civilwarintheeast.com, accessed Aug 2015.

[800] Scott L. Mingus Sr., *The Louisiana Tigers in the Gettysburg Campaign, June-July 1863* (Louisiana State University Press, 2009), 158.

[801] Ibid, 166.

[802] Ibid, 185.

[803] The Mayor John McDonald family blueprint.

[804] *Minnesota, Civil War Records, 1861-1865; U.S., Civil War Soldier Records and Profiles, 1861-1865.*

[805] *Kansas, Grand Army of the Republic Post Reports, 1880-1940.* This record dated 1885 shows Newell McDonald born in Ohio.

[806] Charles Albert Hotchkiss, *History of Scottish Rite Masonry in Texas* (Cornell University Library, 1916), 39-43.

[807] *U.S. City Directories, 1821-1989.*

[808] The Mayor John McDonald family blueprint.

CHAPTER 5

[809] Michael John McDonald is descended from Col. George McDonald's son, Dr. Jacob D. G. McDonald. For a thorough discussion of DNA and the results of Michael John McDonald's test see L. Overmire's *A Revolutionary American Family: The McDonalds of Somerset County, New Jersey.*

[810] FamilyTreeDNA shows that the results for 67 markers with a genetic distance of 2 has an 85.25% probability that Michael John McDonald and Thomas Corey McDonald share a common ancestor within 8 generations. The paper trail, however, including the Mayor John McDonald blueprint, tells us exactly who that common ancestor is – Maj. Richard McDonald of Somerset County, NJ.

[811] FamilyTreeDNA, familytreedna.com. Note: we have no connection to FamilyTreeDNA, other than that we have tested DNA through them and can recommend their services. Because our DNA tests are registered through them, we also have access to their DNA results for other people and can compare those results to our McDonalds.

CHAPTER 6

[812] Peter Macdonald Blachly (aka Peter Alexander), correspondence with Laurence Overmire, Nov 17, 2016.

[813] Death notice and tribute to Mary Antoinette deWitt, by J.H.B. from a newspaper clipping (source unknown) included in an envelope dated July 13, 1945, in the files of Peter Macdonald Blachly and transcribed by Laurence Overmire, Nov. 2016. The envelope was addressed to Mrs. William A. Howell (Katharine Macdonald Howell). A notation in pencil noted "This Tribute written by cousin Jaelin or Julia? Hastronato? Bruin?, Kingston, NY."

[814] Correspondence with Shawn Marchinek, Apr. 25, 2019.

[815] Find A Grave Memorial #61515756.

INDEX

About the Author

Laurence Overmire has had a multi-faceted career as an actor, director, poet, author, educator, genealogist and lecturer. He received a B.A. and B.S. from Muskingum University and an M.F.A. from the University of Minnesota. As an actor, he has performed on stage and screen in New York, Hollywood and points in between, most notably in *Amadeus* on Broadway and in the television soaps *All My Children* and *Loving*. He was also executive producer for The Writer's Lab, a non-profit organization in Hollywood to promote quality script writing for the entertainment industry.

Overmire is the author of five books of poetry as well as an inspirational work recently published in a second edition titled, *The One Idea That Saves The World: A Message of Hope in a Time of Crisis*. It has been widely acclaimed for its compassionate, common sense approach to many of the world's most pressing issues.

Overmire has spent much of the last three decades immersed in genealogical and historical research, creating several genealogical reference databases on Rootsweb.com including *The Ancestry of Overmire, Tifft, Richardson, Bradford, Reed*, which has helped hundreds of thousands of people trace their family trees and find their connections to famous historical figures. He also maintains over 2,600 memorials on Find A Grave.

Overmire's thorough investigation of his paternal ancestry culminated in the publication of *One Immigrant's Legacy: The Overmyer Family in America, 1751-2009,* which traces the descendants of Revolutionary War Captain John George Overmire and demonstrates the impact that one immigrant can have on the scope and breadth of American history.

A Revolutionary American Family: The McDonalds of Somerset County, New Jersey is Overmire's second major genealogical study in hardcover book form. It uncovers the fascinating story of some of the very first McDonalds to set foot in America, emigrants from an ancient Celtic tradition who established homes for themselves in the colonial East New Jersey wilderness, joined in the struggle for independence, fought alongside George Washington and helped to shape America's destiny.

William R. McDonald and Abigail Fowler of Herkimer County, New York, and Their Descendants is a supplement to the earlier McDonald book containing the history of this heretofore-lost line of descendants of Maj. Richard McDonald of Somerset County.

Overmire's extensive work on the American Overmyers and the McDonalds of Somerset County has made him the world's leading authority on those ancestral lines of research.

History is the story of us all. Each one of us has a story worth telling. Overmire reminds us that greatness lies not only in those who are celebrated on the monumental stages of the world, but also in the quiet, unseen passing of ordinary human beings, those who live their lives with courage and determination to meet the everyday challenges that ultimately move us all further down the path toward a better community, a stronger nation and a kinder, more responsible world.